# Proceedings
## of
# The South Asia Seminar



IV

1985-86

Department of South Asia Regional Studies
University of Pennsylvania

# Making Things in South Asia: The Role of Artist and Craftsman

Edited by

Michael W. Meister



Philadelphia
Department of South Asia Regional Studies
1988

**Library of Congress Cataloging-in-Publication Data**

Making Things in South Asia: The Role of Artist and Craftsman / edited by Michael W. Meister.
xviii + 216 p. — (Proceedings of the South Asia Seminar; 4 (1985-86))
Includes bibliographies and index.
ISBN 0-936115-03-3 : $10.00
1. Artisans — South Asia — Congresses. 2. Handicraft — South Asia — Congresses. I. Meister, Michael W. II. Series: Proceedings of the South Asia Seminar; 4.
HD2346.S64M35 1988
331.7'94—dc19 88-15350
CIP

Typeset on the ITEK 1400 typesetter of
the Department of South Asia Regional Studies, University of Pennsylvania,
under the supervision of Dr. David A. Utz.

# Table of Contents

# Preface: Making Things in South Asia

Michael W. Meister
University of Pennsylvania

Seventy-five years ago Ananda Coomaraswamy could write with fear and anger of the threat of destruction of crafts traditions in South Asia by industrial civilization (1909.1; 1909.2; 1913); at the same time, he characterized the artisan in terms primarily of textual admonishment. The *śilpin,* he wrote, citing the *śilpaśāstras,* was 'one who wears a sacred thread, a necklace of sacred beads, and a ring of *kusha* grass upon his finger: one delighting in the worship of God, faithful to his wife, avoiding strange women, true to his family, of a pure heart and virtuous, chanting the *vedas,* constant in the performance of ceremonial duties, piously acquiring a knowledge of various sciences — such a one is indeed a Craftsman' (Coomaraswamy 1913: 33-34).

*Śilpin,* however, is a word that neither 'artist' nor 'artisan' fully encompasses: 'the arts and crafts in India partake in the nature of rites whose technical performance had magic power,' Stella Kramrisch wrote. 'The range of the crafts extends over the entire culture and comprises the work of the wheelwright and the sculptor, or potter and perfumer, weaver and architect' (Kramrisch 1983: 60). A number of scholars in the last half century have brought us closer to such makers and to the life and practice of their traditions.

Coomaraswamy, in attempting to define the strengths as well as vulnerabilities of 'hieratic' art in India, warned that 'secular and personal art can only apply to cliques: but a hieratic art unites a whole race in one spiritual feudalism. ... Yet there is one fatal weakness of the later phases of a traditional art: it has no power to resist the corruption from without. It is beautiful by habit rather than intention, so that a single generation under changed conditions is sufficient to destroy it' (Coomaraswamy 1913: 23-24). India today preserves many crafts, however, the resilience of whose practitioners is part of a process of change that increasingly we have come to realize is part of 'tradition' and itself must be the subject of study (Singer 1959).

Kramrisch, in her restatements of the traditional role of the Indian craftsman (Kramrisch 1956, 1959), had already given emphasis to a significant new insight: that the patron was as much a part of the artist's responsibility as art itself. 'Vocation and assignment were reciprocal,' she wrote: 'The work of art, as a vehicle to heaven and its bliss, belongs to the patron. He remunerates the artist so that the merit should not accrue to the artist, but should remain with the patron' (Kramrisch 1983: 51, 56).

She pointedly also corrected the assumption that craft in a traditional society was only hereditary:

> It is generally assumed that the selectiveness of free competition did not exert its pressures on a calling which, because it was considered 'hereditary,' was thought to run in smooth channels that endowed the individual with sharpened senses and a high degree of skill. Skill, however, is acquired and not hereditary, nor is heredity a factor to be reckoned with in the transmission of genius. . . . It was not unusual for a young craftsman who had shown promise and was not a relative at all to be educated in the same manner (Kramrisch 1983: 52).

Together, her points suggest that change may come as much from shifts in the pattern of patronage as in the nature of artistic production and that such shifts need not lessen the role of 'genius' nor destroy the possibility for continued artistic 'delight.'

Both industrial civilization and India's crafts' traditions should be looked at from as broad a methodological perspective as possible this late in the twentieth century. Neither has survived nor declined quite as might have been imagined by the Arts-and-Crafts movement that colored Coomaraswamy's thinking at the turn of the century (Lipsey 1977). Milton Singer, in the preface to his volume on *Traditional India: Structure and Change* (1959: ix), already had reminded us, citing Nirmal Kumar Bose, of 'the fact that a civilization is a process of becoming, as well as a state of being.' India's strengths have lain always in her ability to adjust as well as continue.

Coomaraswamy himself began his career using ethnographic methods to study living crafts traditions in South Asia, carrying out his early work among craftsmen in Kandy, Sri Lanka. From this, however, he produced 'a Monograph on Mediaeval Sinhalese Arts and Crafts, Mainly as Surviving in the Eighteenth Century with an Account of the Structure of Society and the Status of the Craftsman' (Coomaraswamy 1908). His interest was in reconstructing from the practices of living craftsmen the nature of medieval guild practices, not in procedures of survival and change.

The variety and strengths of craftsmanship in South Asia, however, have persisted, now, for well more than a century of industrialization, and scholarly methodologies for approaching the role of artisans in contexts beyond the 'hieratic' — rural, tribal, courtly, even commercial and contemporary — and of defining their strategies of survival and change have broadened.

The challenge and opportunity for contributors to this volume have been to define new directions while summarizing contemporary research. While such a survey can hardly provide even a brief introduction to the many 'local' traditions of India — her 'multiple streams' — yet it can, perhaps, help frame a context for approaching any one of them.

* * *

During the Festival Year of India in the U.S.A., 1985-86, the thirty-eighth Annual Seminar of the Department of South Asia Regional Studies at the University of Pennsylvania brought together twenty-three scholars from a variety of disciplines to explore current thinking surrounding the theme 'Making Things in South Asia: the Role of Artist and Craftsman,' — traditional and contemporary. This volume summarizes that dialogue.

Ashoke Chatterjee of the National Institute of Design, Ahmedabad, begins the volume with his report on efforts to make modern design-management a handmaiden for traditional craft. He reflects on 'the confusion we have brought upon ourselves' through inappropriate categories, is not shy about the pressures of a modern market, nor unrealistic about artisans' openness to change.

As pendant, I have ended the volume with Richard Kurin's lively ethnography on the viability of Indian artists in the environment of two Smithsonian-sponsored Festival-of-India exhibitions, and of his staff's need to learn reciprocally. He states that organizers had attempted to construct conceptual 'contexts appropriate for the presentation of Indian folk arts' without fully anticipating 'the role participating folk artists would play in adapting and recasting those efforts in their own terms, for their own purposes.'

Through such papers, a theme of this volume has become living craftspeople: their present roles, environment, variety, and capacity to survive, and their relationship to past practices and patterns of patronage.

In two essays, Romila Thapar and Ludo Rocher review and help redefine our knowledge of 'makers' in ancient India. Rocher traces the status, training, range, and religious function of *śilpins* from image-cutters to barbers. Thapar places 'making' within its economic and social context and provides an historical framework for changing guild organization, status, and markets.

John Mosteller combines observation of living image-makers with analysis of texts and the measurements of ancient sculpture to establish the nature of the 'constructional devices' used by craftsmen to control and form images. His insistence that making lies with makers, and that knowledge of technique is passed down from hand to hand by mnemonic means, enlarges a discussion of transmission and the nature of innovation, returning it to the realm of autonomous, as well as culturally embedded, acts by individual artists.

A series of papers discusses specific case studies from India's past. Walter Spink explores the rapid development of technique as well as the importance of patronage at Ajanta. Carol Radcliffe Bolon presents evidence to support the presence of 'ego' and artistic individuation among artists known to have signed sculptures in the territory of the Calukyas. Mattiebelle Gittinger demonstrates the selective and self-conscious use of textile patterning by artists seeking to communicate specific meanings. All three have focused attention on new types of evidence and new methods for thinking about evidence.

Milo Beach rethinks the roles played by royal patrons in the Mughal period and reattributes to painters and to painters' workshops both the maintenance of tradition and motive sources for change. Karuna Goswamy recalls the reception given by townsmen to coveys of itinerant Kashmiri scribes and painters in past decades and suggests the important role such trade as well as pilgrimage could have played in the dissemination of works in a single style.

Murray Libersat is a carpenter and architect who has worked closely with a traditional *sthāpati* living in Kerala. His paper paraphrases the philosophy and technical knowledge passed down to him by his master. In the intensity of his conviction, his work exemplifies as much the strength and method of its transmission as the survival of a tradition. (Ludo Rocher has commented that to hear Libersat was like hearing an ancient text come to life. Libersat exemplifies the reality that tradition embodies itself in a lineage of individuals.)

David Ludden provides a paradigm with 'art . . . at one end, where producer, product, and consumer interact intensely as individual entities. Industry expands at the other end, where producer, product, and consumer have no individuality.' Manju Parikh-Baruah extends Ludden's example of textile manufacture in Tamil Nadu also to Gujarat and

Coromandel. Both conclude that many craftsmen in India had become industrialized as early as 1800. Ludden argues that 'by 1900 few craft workers should be imagined as village artisans making products for local patrons' and concludes that 'though [handloom and other petty manufactures after Independence] submitted to the rhetoric of traditional crafts production,' towns in Tamil Nadu, in Christopher Baker's words, were becoming 'workhouses for the rural poor.'

Parikh-Baruah, however, also lays out a historical pattern for new trade, with merchants establishing a variety of relationships with craftsmen as intermediaries for both 'traditional' as well as industrializing goods. From such interaction, both new markets and new modes of creativity were possible. As in previous periods, such new patronage often led to the creation of textiles of high quality, which, whatever their derivation, now seem firmly part of India's artistic heritage.

Brian Spooner gives us a case study of ways by which traditional carpet craftsmen, on the other hand, have had difficulty adjusting to 'the grey area of urban (or international) dependency.' Inclusion in a wider market in itself seems less significant to Spooner than a change in cultural criteria. 'As long as there were chains of intermediaries between the two poles of a culturally distant economic relationship, the relationship worked,' Spooner writes. 'We tend to put . . . failure down to straightforward economic factors, but these factors themselves are due to the cultural inability of producers to 'read' the consumers.'

A further group of papers present case studies of specific contemporary craft traditions. Mithilā painting, which Mary Lanius explores, presents an example of the successful commercialization of a traditional and previously transitory craft. While supporting — even creating — 'artists,' this transformation has re-formed the social relationships of the producers.

Stephen Huyler, in surveying village-India's material culture, sees change in that environment 'as a product of history as well as a necessary ingredient for the future.' He concludes that 'adaptation is fundamental to traditional Indian rural society' while still deploring the 'contrast between rural and new urban aesthetics.'

Stephen Inglis instead deplores a Western tendency to define artisans in India either in terms of Coomaraswamy's 'high orders' following 'absolute' laws or as 'humble, anonymous, and organic' craftsmen, content (in Birdwood's words) with 'little food and less clothing.' 'These views,' he writes, 'fail to take into account the changes in technique, style, use, and meaning that constantly occur or the craftsman's dynamic position within cultural change.'

Inglis uses as a case study a group of potter image-makers near Madurai who seem both to express and create a tradition as they adjust to changing needs: 'For the Vēḷār, image-making is a re-cycling and rejuvenation of materials. Each image includes, in the materials used to make it, the refuse of previous images.' He concludes that 'the process and products of craftsmanship are changing, yet not all recent innovations are counter to the tradition of replacement and cyclical time nor are they necessarily deviations from the deeply rooted social placement of craftmanship;' he ends with an example from Canada to show the depth of a culture's continuities.

Louise Cort, in her essay on 'The Role of the Potter,' first looks for deep structures tying together pots and their cultural use. She lays out four levels of historical records available for the community of potters she has been studying in Orissa: myth, a traditional record called the *Mādalā Pāñji,* British records, and the present community. She worries about the community's survival. Yet she and others make clear the immense richness of what survives and the constant boiling evolution that transforms and recreates tradition in India. Her plea that 'we need more studies of local and regional traditions' as well as 'more regional group studies' suggests what many in this volume feel: that we are not faced with the corpse of a culture, but with its living multiple complexities. To understand the 'modernity of tradition' we must understand much more of its parts and their transformations.

Susan Bean's delicate exploration of levels of reinvention in India's symbolic appropriation of spinning to fit national ends can be one case in point. No part of India's twentieth-century reality could be more potent than Gandhi's nationalism, yet his symbols also have been continually reinvented to suit contemporary use.

Joan Erdman also emphasizes that culture must take new configurations as it meets modern needs. She catalogues 'living' institutions that 'in their multiplicity reflect the paradoxical historical development of values and symbols in art and artworks.' As have many in this volume — and reflecting a methodological position appropriate for this moment — Erdman concludes that while 'it is possible to develop analytical categories . . . it is also important to remember that the indigenous (and autochthonous) paths are many, and while comparison and categorization are possible, they do not represent the ways India's craftsmen and artists perceive their development as a process.'

* * *

Objects and their making offer specific challenges to our analysis. A physical object embodies culture in ways that separate it from its making; the making itself 'objectifies' not so much the maker as his 'tradition' — and the object's use then has a life of its own. This mystery in part explains the magic Kramrisch finds attached to the rites of making in India, yet it equally struck such Western writers as Coleridge and Hawthorne in the nineteenth century — the object's mutable immutability.

If Coomaraswamy feared the destruction that industry could bring to traditional arts, it was perhaps most that commerce makes objects disposable: commodities present a much different material reality. Tool-maker, artist, or pot-maker in India by instinct and tradition have made objects that transcend their material function. Objects are signs; and how — not what — they signify is their mystery. The making and reading of signs is a human activity that can survive shifts in status, patronage, and distribution. 'Makers' in South Asia are 'sign-makers,' and that role, however mutable in form, remains immutable in function.

## Acknowledgments

Three speakers were unable to provide summaries of their presentations. I would like, however, to record their participation and to thank them for their substantial contribution to the Seminar. Ray Owens spoke on 'Commercialization of a Folk Art: Mithilā,' Richard Cohen on 'Making Miniatures: Text and Image,' and Brian Q. Silver on 'Musical Instruments: Craft and Performance.'

Haku Shah had agreed to open the Seminar but ultimately was unable to adjust a schedule tied to the movements of his remarkable exhibition on Indian clay. I thank him, however, for his friendship, valuable discussion, and the end-paper designs by Ganesh. Pupul Jayakar — whose work has opened many doors — was unable finally to close our sessions. We thank her, however, for her broad supervision: the Festival of India in the U.S. was her creation. Ted Tanen, Director of the Indo-

U.S. Sub-Commission, and Patrice Fusillo worked with great efficiency to make Festival events successful. Liaison by Maurice Liebl was also exemplary.

Arrangements in Philadelphia during the Seminar were ably and gracefully carried out by Camella Greenway, Assistant to the Chairman. Typesetting and other responsibilities have been supervised and carried through by David Utz, Editorial Assistant to the South Asia Department. My research assistant, Ajay Sinha, has worked closely with the manuscript and made valuable suggestions; the Index was prepared by Katherine Hacker.

The Chairman of the South Asia Regional Studies Department during both the Seminar and the preparation of these Proceedings has been Rosane Rocher, whose contribution to the continuing primacy of our program I would like to acknowledge here.

## Bibliography

Coomaraswamy, Ananda K. *The Arts and Crafts of India and Ceylon.* Edinburgh, 1913.

__________. *Essays in National Idealism.* Colombo, 1909.

__________. *The Indian Craftsman.* London, 1909.

__________. *Mediaeval Sinhalese Art.* Broad Campden, 1908.

__________. *Coomaraswamy, Selected Papers,* edited by Roger Lipsey. 2 vols. Princeton, 1977.

Kramrisch, Stella. 'Artist, Patron, and Public in India,' *The Far Eastern Quarterly* (May 1956): 335-42. Reprinted in Kramrisch 1983: 51-58.

__________. *Exploring India's Sacred Art, Selected Writings of Stella Kramrisch,* edited by Barbara Stoller Miller. Philadelphia, 1983.

__________. 'Traditions of the Indian Craftsman.' In Singer 1959: 18-24. Reprinted in Kramrisch 1983: 59-66.

Lipsey, Roger. *Coomaraswamy, His Life and Work.* Princeton, 1977.

Singer, Milton, ed. *Traditional India: Structure and Change.* Philadelphia, 1959.

# IV

# Making Things in South Asia

# Challenges of Transition: Design and Craft in India

Ashoke Chatterjee
National Institute of Design, Ahmedabad

Any consideration of Indian crafts and the challenge they face today requires first a serviceable definition of 'craft' as an activity. The term in the Indian context has only a limited relationship with connotations assumed in the West, where skilled handwork is most often a studio or museum-oriented activity, largely apart from the mainstream of mass-produced products and systems of everyday use. From immemorial time the essence of craft in India has been everyday function and service (physical, psychological, and symbolic). This perception, often lost in recent efforts at craft regeneration, forms the essential challenge that Indian crafts face today in their transition from tradition to modernity.

Contemporary attitudes reflect the confusion that we have brought upon ourselves through our efforts to distinguish between craft, art, and design in the Indian context. Like 'craft,' 'design' is another term that creates problems for India when by using it one attempts to distinguish between craft and art on the one hand and 'problem-solving' on the other — a division not conceivable in the development of the inheritance that is the subject of our present concern. India's ancient artists respected no such distinction.

Much of what we celebrate today as Indian art was activity associated with creation of sacred images of gods and godesses, as well as of spaces, environments, and votive objects essential to their celebration. Those engaged in this activity — masons, painters, illustrators, stone and clay workers, wood workers, metalsmiths — were believed to be endowed with a certain state of grace that elevated them to positions of status and security. As these artist-craftsmen created artifacts for everyday use, no separate term was needed to distinguish the plastic arts from craft, or 'craft' from the problem-solving attitude of the modern 'designer.' Art, craft, and design were integrated as one inseparable concept in the minds of both maker and user, unified by the single word 'kalā.'

The Indian craftsman was therefore artist, designer, and technician, working in all three ways to serve his users' needs. He was a source both of inspiration and problem-solving, functioning always within the core of his society. With the advent of colonialism and industrialization, the integral quality of his role, however, began to disintegrate. Efforts at craft regeneration during India's freedom movement and in the years after Independence have not yet been able to draw crafts back into the center of national consciousness.

**Colonial Influences**

The need to rediscover and redefine the status of craft in India was felt first in the nineteenth century with the early impact of the Industrial Revolution. Even earlier, British colonialism had brought with it to India (in its considerable cultural baggage) Emmanuel Kant's distinction between 'Pure Beauty' and 'Purposeful Beauty' as well as the debates of eighteenth-century European aesthetes. The history of a modern design movement in India, however, begins with the establishment of teaching schools of arts and crafts in Calcutta, Bombay, and Madras in the 1850s. These were conceived as schools of industrial art and were influenced considerably by the denunciation of the machine as 'destroyer of the joy of hard work' led by William Morris and the Arts-and-Crafts Movement.

It was difficult for teachers and students in these schools to rationalize and integrate the new machine 'crafts' that had by then begun to make an impact on Indian life. The products of textile mills, printing presses, and India's new factories remained outside their thinking. As hothouses of imported concepts of art and craft, these schools were divorced from that unifying philosophy which had brought art, craft, architecture, design, and manufacture together previously in Indian tradition. A few brave efforts to turn learning toward indigenous inspiration were attacked as stratagems to deny Indians the rewards of western progress. Fortunately, however, during this period the British genius for documentation began to create considerable ethnographic records of traditional skills, tools, workplaces, and objects that remain unsurpassed even today, providing a priceless resource for the contemporary Indian designer.

During the well-known renaissance of Indian thought and nationalism in the late nineteenth and early twentieth centuries, political and social reformers recognised the importance of hand industries as a channel for economic regeneration and cultural confidence in the face of the colonial onslaught. This vision inspired poet Rabindranath Tagore's craft experiments at his university at Santiniketan as well as Mahatma Gandhi's stress on village industry as a foundation for India's struggle towards independence. By the early years of this century, craft had become a catalyst for political thought and action.

The Swadeśi ('Buy Indian') movement attempted to restore the concept of self-sufficient village communities in a landscape eroded by the economics of colonial rule. A simple craft tool, the spinning wheel, became the symbol of national revolt, and handspun cloth the livery of freedom.

The handloom revolution that followed was accompanied by promotion of all village industries and by a national awareness of the need to protect and enhance traditional skills, products, and markets within a new industrial environment. Craft development thus became an integral part of the political psychology of independent India when national planning began following 1947.

**Transition**

The problems of transition which we look at today are those that emerged in the post-independence period. Gandhi had established both an economic and moral awareness of the vast craft sector. The need to preserve attitudes and value systems inherent in Indian tradition within the context of rapid industrialization also was deeply felt in independent India. What Gandhi had made symbolic of an independent, self-reliant people was now heralded as evidence of a glorious past, soon to be revived and restored. Crafts became an indispensable element in the wave of cultural revivalism and euphoria. Integrated into development planning, crafts also were recognised as a potent force for economic progress, a status that immediately distinguishes considerations of craft in India from their place in most other economies. Agencies for craft development were established by the government at the center and in each Indian state. Budgets, production targets, and retailing strategies emerged. Exports became a first priority, thereby divorcing craft from its integral role in community and individual life. This shift from traditional craft's utility to home and temple toward newer markets brought with it a particularly contemporary challenge, that of craft becoming 'kitsch.'

The dimensions of the craft sector in India today demonstrate both its power and importance. Official figures suggest that there are more than three million Indians engaged in certain selected craft industries. In reality, the figure should be very much higher: particularly if artisans (a slightly derogatory term as it is used now in current official jargon) are included. These artisans are the village potters, metalsmiths, masons, carpenters, weavers, shoemakers, etc., who provide objects of use to their own communities in time-honored Indian tradition, and whose survival is threatened today by mass industry. Their functional implements and utensils seldom enter urban emporia, craft boutiques, or the export agencies that today promote crafts as fancy goods without any hint of embarassment.

The major client for organised craft-activity today is in fact the Indian government. The All-India Handicrafts Board (with its official directive to concentrate on crafts having export potential) and the All-India Handlooms Board have the national mandate for craft regeneration and for the welfare of craft communities. Parallel organisations operate within each state. Promotional, retail, and export activities are part of this infrastructure. The focus is on a check-list of products with a strong 'artistic' (the adjective is a loaded one) bias: carved ivory, stone and wood, carpets, art metal, embroidery, papier-maché jewelry.

The gigantic Khadi and Village Industries Board is concerned with homespun cloth and artisan products of several categories. Central as well as state agencies operate chain stores, retailing regional crafts under brand identities. Private entrepreneurs, export houses, and representatives of overseas buyers also are major influences on current design. Social activists in many instances have used crafts to promote economic uplift. Craft councils harness the talents of those eager to do a good turn. Craft bazaars and emporia abound in every major city. And in this hive of activity, quality is often drowned in a sea of imitative trash.

Yet another role for craft has now emerged: craft as a vehicle for diplomacy, demonstrated recently through Festivals of India in Britain, France, the United States, and elsewhere. These great explosions of craft and design activity have underlined the strength and potential of surviving traditions as well as the complexity of the task of merchandising crafts overseas, often for usages and in environments light years away from the psychology of the makers' hands, which India otherwise seeks to treasure.

## Design as a Service

Into this mélange come also today's trained industrial designers, who since the 1960s have been graduating from the National Institute of Design at Ahmedabad, which represents a unique experiment in trying to turn Bauhaus principles to the service of India's economy. The intervention of these new designers is based largely on the philosophy of NID's founding spirit, Charles Eames, who saw crafts as a matchless resource for India's problem-solving experience. Eames recommended that the Indian designer draw on the attitudes, skills, and knowledge available in the indigenous craft tradition, returning these to new relevance in an industrial age in which hand production has to find a place alongside mass manufacture. NID's curriculum has reflected this approach from its inception. Students and teachers at NID study craft problems in order to understand traditional skills as well as the urgent economic concerns of those large communities whose age-old markets are now undergoing enormous and permanent change.

As a problem-solving activity today, designing for crafts inevitably has to be linked to marketing. In NID's early years, designers hesitated to involve themselves too deeply in issues of marketing and sales. A certain lack of respectability seemed attached to such concerns as that of 'survival through profit,' yet experience soon revealed that there was no way designers could assist hereditary craftsmen unless their young profession could firmly establish itself as a link in the marketing chain.

Every problem that NID students and teachers have attempted has demonstrated this crucial interdependence. An early example was provided by a community of weavers in south India, whose traditional skills were suffering under the impact of mill-made competition. Additional constraints were imposed on them by equipment and technology that were dependent on outdoor spaces, which meant that the weavers were idle during the long season of monsoon rain. The problem was one of product diversification in order to reach new markets, the revival of traditional designs in new applications, and that of redesigning tools, implements, workplaces, and production techniques so as to move the process indoors and thus facilitate year-round activity.

Bellmetal craftsmen in Kerala — another example — face dwindling demand for votive objects, now prohibitively expensive. In cooperation with the national Handloom and Handicraft Export Corporation and a distinguished British designer with access to high-quality retail outlets, NID has been exploring a product diversification that could sensitively take traditional forms into new usages through an exclusive export range.

The exploration of the cane, bamboo, and textile crafts of tribal communities in India's northeast by NID has provided a documentation base for efforts to develop products and systems that can be exported from these remote regions to new markets within India — architectural elements, knock-down furniture, tableware — extending the earning potential for isolated village communities and providing a sound alternative to other industries that are threatening the delicate ecology of the region.

As a basis for design intervention, research is of primary importance. The documentation of craft traditions begun by British scholars more than a century ago now needs to be extended on a national scale. The trained designer can be an indispensable element in recording and interpreting the richness of India's craft inheritance. Research as a basis for sensitive design, production, and marketing begins with an understanding of the craft community, its traditional practices, markets, materials, price/cost considerations, tools, and workplaces. Development and diversification efforts can bring the craftsmen and the trained designer together in an intelligent search for new opportunities.

The risks of such intervention can be minimized and advantages maximized if the designer's role is seen primarily as one of restoring or inhancing the traditional craftsmen's own design and problem-solving abilities. Equally important is the designer's ability to move nimbly from one problem-sector to the next to keep pace with need: the scarcity of traditional materials (wood, metal, ivory), for example, on one day, a new finish required by new export markets on the next. He can bring modern expertise to such problems as that of carving on treated surfaces, of developing joinery systems in wood for centrally heated environments, of creating packing systems essential to the transport of fragile products, of systems-design applied to traditional skills, or of designing to meet the fickle tastes and fashions of export markets.

The modern trained designer can provide a channel for information and technology relevant to the craftsman's contemporary needs as well as for intelligent guidance on modern processes that are compatible with the integrity of hand production. The challenge in all of this is for the designer to be involved without usurping the role of the master craftsman. Indeed, it is the master craftsman who needs to be restored as the prime source for design inspiration. It is thus a matter of learning together rather than of passing design instructions down the line of a modern bureaucracy.

In this process, who teaches and who learns? There is a mutuality in this learning that requires not merely sensitivity, but enormous reserves of humility as well. In a culture with an unbroken history of over three thousand years and one in which product forms have achieved such perfection and played such an immensely important role in human development in the past, it takes a real measure of audacity to speak of design as a 'profession' new to India. Eames had himself predicted that the modern Indian designer's greatest contribution might often be an anonymous one: that of the self-confidence that modern design skills and insights might help to restore in those traditional craftsmen whose minds and hands carry an inheritance from centuries of tradition.

Another urgent role for craftsmanship in India is to revive the ancient attitude that once integrated the environment, the mind, and the hand in the making of Indian products. A sense of quality is today a desperately felt need. Sub-standard products — machine-made or hand-crafted — are part of every Indian's misery. Attitudes of pride in product quality, in workmanship, and in finish are attitudes sorely needed. These are attitudes that only a regeneration of pride in craftsmanship can provide, setting standards of quality and achievement essential to dynamic growth.

In all of this, one must relearn from the past. The modern designer can be a factor for building confidence, for pathfinding, for establishing linkages that encourage intelligent solutions for the economic, environmental, and cultural challenges that today surround 800 million Indians.

The designer's role as a contemporary problem-solver has been well illustrated by the case history of Jawaja, to which I refer in my Bibliography, where one group of severely under-privileged and oppressed craftsmen were able to turn their commitment to craft into a potent force for economic self reliance and social dignity by working with trained designers and other specialists in a joint effort specifically for a limited period.

## Bibliography

Design for Craft, project documentation. National Institute of Design, Ahmedabad.

Mathai, Ravi J. 'Learning for Development at Jawaja.' *Project Designs of NID.*

Vyas H. K. 'Design: Art and Craft As A United Concept.' *India International Centre Quarterly,* XI, 4 (1984): 91-94.

# The Social Role of Craftsmen and Artists in Early India

Romila Thapar
Jawaharlal Nehru University, New Delhi

The artist or craftsman may be defined as a person who uses material resources and transforms them into objects — such as the transformation of clay into a pot or stone into sculpture. The object may have a variety of roles in the community. A pot, for example, has a practical function as a container. It can also have a magico-religious role as part of ritual in worship, as in the case of Vedic rituals. When the functional role is well developed, the object acquires an aesthetic form, such as with Northern Black Polished ware or medieval Islamic glazed pottery.

The artisan, the object, and the community are knit together in a relationship that derives from whether the object is produced for the artisan's personal use only or is given in exchange, for sale, or for sale to an intermediary (in the latter two cases becoming a commodity). The identity of the craftsman increases or decreases in importance in accordance with such relationship, becoming less important where the object is largely functional, more important when function is combined with aesthetic appeal. When the object becomes an investment, as today, the artist's identity can be fundamental.

Vedic texts refer to *śilpa* as a skill or art of doing something that can range from making an object to something as intangible as the recitiation of music. *Śilpatva* generally refers to adornment, suggesting that the decorative aspect was important. But the word used for craftsmen was generally based on the craft itself and is associated with the more functional aspect of the craft. The carpenter *(takṣaka)* and the chariot-maker *(rathākāra)* were involved with high-status objects often associated with the *rājās* and the *kṣatriyas.* This may explain why they are sometimes included in the list of twelve *ratnins* or jewels who are associated with the *rājā.* The status of the user of the object was extended in a somewhat ambiguous way to the maker of the object. Yet iron technology, however, which, as the source of weaponry, was significant to the power of the *rājā,* did not raise the status of the ironsmith, who held a consistantly low status in ancient India, even in later periods when iron technology played a more crucial economic role.

The patron of the artisan himself became prominent only in the post-Vedic period. Pāṇini makes a distinction between the *grāmaśilpin* who probably worked on daily wages and the *rājaśilpin* who was maintained by the state and had a higher status. If the punchmarked coinage of the time permitted wages to be paid in money, this would have freed the artisan to move to the city where, in the newly emerging urban centers of the immediately pre-Mauryan period, there would have been a great demand for artisans. The *dharmasūtras* refer to the low status of the artisan, who is there frequently associated with the *śūdra.* The fact of manual labor being regarded low is made evident in the statement that a brahman living by craft was to be treated as a *śūdra,* in spite of *Jātaka* sources that refer to brahman weavers and carpenters. Possibly low status was emphasized because these groups in this period came to be taxed on their work. Within the crafts there was a further hierarchy, in which leatherworkers (perhaps because of rules of pollution) were regarded as lower than others, for example, but it is strange that in this hierarchy bamboo workers also should have been treated as low.

Were statements of these social disabilities and low status of artisans confined to *sūtra* texts? Buddhist texts of the Pāli canon in fact present a somewhat different picture. Theoretically, they argue that no one has status by birth, which should have made the status of the artisan more open. However, even these texts differentiate between high *(ucchakula)* and low *(nicakula)* families; here wealth, however, played a large role in determining status. Presumably an artisan, if wealthy, could be included in the *ucchakula.* (There is a problem of giving precise dates to these texts, although most scholars would accept that they were composed just prior to the Maurya period and some may have overlapped with the Mauryas.) Texts do emphasize the importance of urbanization, which crystallizes the status of the artisan. Specialization of labor encouraged the notion of particular parts of the city being given over to artisan production, where artisans could live as equals or had the illusion of equals, even within a hierarchical society. Urban centers were frequently the stage for heterodox teachers, had a freer social atmosphere, and in them the lower orders were less caught in a hierarchy. These centers reached out to the craft village and to those who supplied raw materials. The use of coined money also tended to free the artisan to some degree from a strict social ranking. The market *(nigama)* in this period was still halfway between a *maṇḍi* and a larger city market, nor had it acquired the impersonality of a full-fledged market system. Haggling in the open market was a form of quality control. In the absence of specific patrons, an object was given value according to its quality. The tendency towards a corporate organization in such a market encouraged the emergence of guilds.

The establishment of guilds *(śreṇi)* becomes a noticeable feature of urban life from the Maurya period onwards. The evolution of artisan guilds can be traced to settlements in proximity to raw materials and to villages of craftsmen where there was a distinct location for each craft. This remained the norm also for the settlement of artisans and craftsmen together in larger urban centers, though it is possible that tanners and smiths were kept to a separate part of the settlement because of the unpleasant nature of their work. The structure of the guild was further emphasized by hereditary occupations, and when endogamous marriage became common it led ultimately to the recognition of a *śreṇi* as a *jāti* sometime in the first millennium A.D. The segregation of artisans also made it easier for the state to enforce rules on them, particularly in matters of taxation. The guild consisted of persons practicing the same or related crafts. It was headed by a *jyeṣṭha* or elder who maintained discipline and controlled contracts. The *śilpins* or artistans were assisted by *karmakaras* and *antevesikas* (apprentices) and, when the work increased, by *dāsabhṛtakas* (slaves and hired labour). The profession was taught through apprenticeship and gradually recruitment was from the children of the families constituting the guild. The guild had its own customary law *(śreṇidharma),* which Manu advised the king to recognize. To this extent the guild was similar to the Roman collegium. The more powerful and wealthy guilds had their own militia *(śreṇibala),* which could be called upon by the king to help in campaigns. The guild safeguarded artisans from fraudulent customers and protected clients from fraudulent craftsmen. Some served as local bankers and eventually guilds of financiers were to emerge as trade became extremely lucrative. The *Arthaśāstra* has an extensive discussion on the comparative usefulness of guilds as against individual artisans. The guild was registered with the city superintendent and could not transfer its residence without permission. Doubtless this was due to its being regarded as a major source of urban taxes. There is some suspicion of guilds in this text, where it is argued that the state should control trade in order to control profits. Megasthenes refers to artisans as one of the seven subdivisions of Indian society and brackets them with retail traders and labourers. Of these, some paid taxes to the state and others were employed by the state and paid a wage. Curiously, Megasthenes makes no reference to monumental buildings other than those at the capital of the Maurya empire at Pāṭaliputra, nor does he refer to the making of images. This is surprising from someone coming from the Greek cities of west Asia where both sculpture and architecture were regarded as a necessary part of the urban scene. The *Arthaśāstra* also mentions the salary of artisans as being between 120 and 200 *paṇas.* It is unclear whether this was per month or per annum. In comparison with this, soldiers and clerks were paid 500 *paṇas* and the foreman of labour 60 *paṇas.* Hired labourers were paid one and a half *paṇa* per month and their families were also fed. It would seem that the salaries of artisans were adequate but not confortable. According to the *Jātaka* literature one *paṇa* was sufficient for purchasing a garland, some perfume, and some alcohol for the young man-about-town. It also mentions that the cost of a slave was 100 *paṇas* and that of gold necklaces, golden dishes, and gold embroidered cloth, 100,000 *paṇas.* It is rather likely that the merchants who traded in these items made the maximum of profit, while hired laborers lived on a pittance, a situation not dissimilar to that pertaining in many other ancient societies.

The turn of the Christian era sees a far more powerful identity developing for guilds, which gradually take on *jāti* status. They are often treated as endogamous units, with recruitment from within the guild and with a religious sectarian association. This was in part the result of a tremendous expansion of trade with west Asia and the eastern Mediterranean and eventually with central Asia and southeast Asia. This increase in trade led to the greater prosperity of artisans and guilds. Donations towards the building of Buddhist monuments in particular now frequently drew on artisan and guild sources. As guilds, those of weavers, masons, goldsmiths, corn dealers, ivory workers, woodworkers, blacksmiths, and cloakmakers made donations which have been recorded at Buddhist monuments. Individual craftsman and their families made a larger number of donations. This reflects an overlapping of the donor and the artisan that is unusual in India. The religious link was symbolized as that between *dāna* (gift giving) and *punya* (merit) emphasized in both Buddhism and Jainism. These votive inscriptions suggest a social mobilization of artisans, individually and collectively, locally and from places at a distance. There also develops an economic nexus between the guild, royalty, and religion and occasional inscriptions refer to members of the royal family investing money with a guild, the interest of which was to be used for either brahmanical or Buddhist ritual.

From the perspective of the role of the artisan, two interesting developments are noticeable in the early first millennium A.D. One was the distinction gradually introduced between the craftsman and the supervisor, a distinction that was to harden in subsequent centuries; secondly, the mention of craftsmen by name, which first occurs in inscriptions from Mathurā referring to Kunika and his two pupils. The introduction of names in association with sculpture, and later with painting and architecture, may represent an attempt to establish the identity of objects regarded as qualitatively superior, or to establish a claim for a particular *guru-śiṣya-paramparā* (a claim that would also act as an advertisement for a particular *paramparā*), or else to acquire merit through participating in the presentation of a gift. It is, however, difficult to ascertain any specific sectarian identification, other than through the iconography of the sculpture, with a particular *paramparā*.

An inscription from the Gupta period commemorating a guild of silk weavers provides some worthwhile indications concerning craftsmen. These guild members migrated with their families from the district of Lāṭa to the urban center of Maṇḍasor where they made donations towards the building of a Sūrya temple. They maintained their identity as a guild even though they took up a variety of professions such as becoming archers, soldiers, astrologers, and *kathākāras*. Clearly the silk trade had declined in western India but they were able to find other gainful professions, which enabled them to earn incomes sufficient that they could donate towards the building of a temple. Their identity had probably been crystalized into that of a *jāti* by then and their status was evidently not low. This example forms a counterpart to the patronage by craftsmen recorded for Buddhist monuments.

There is currently a debate among historians as to whether there might not have been a decline of urban centers in the Ganges valley during the Gupta period which continued until the latter part of the first millennium A.D., after which the Ganges valley saw a renewed growth of towns and urban trade. Such a decline of towns would certainly have led to a decline also in urban craftsmanship in this region. The artist continues to be referred to in this period, of course, but more frequently in the context of courts and royal patrons. The aesthetics involved in sculpture, painting, and dancing appears to be an increasing concern also in this period. At one level, craftsmanship continued to be a *śilpa,* or skill, but at another level there was a growing interest in what constituted its aesthetic appeal. We are told that princes had to be familiar with the *śilpas,* presumably because as patrons they could not demonstrate an ignorance of these. In the plays of Kālidāsa, references to artistic representations are based on actual or imagined persons. It is also from this point on that there is growing interest in texts on the *śilpas.*

In the post-Gupta period specific terms for builders and artists become more common. Thus there are references to the *śilpin* and *rūpakāra* but even more often to the *sūtradhāra* and the *sthapati.* The *sūtradhāra,* literally the holder of the thread, can also be interpreted as the one who knows the *sūtras,* namely, the *śilpaśāstras* — the texts on architecture and the arts. This would imply formal education as a qualification for the *sūtradhāra.* There seems to have been a deepening separation between the skilled and unskilled artisan. *Sūtradhāras* are increasingly mentioned by name, either individually or by family, such as Sri Yugadhāra at Ajanta or the Kokāsa family in the Kalacuri inscriptions. Some are described also as authors of texts. The names of these *sūtradhāras* sound more brahmanical than Buddhist. Occasionally a strange name creeps in suggesting that there were individuals outside the recognized castes who were moving into the profession. Some *sūtradhāras* are said to have financed the building of temples.

This evidence gives rise to a number of questions. Clearly building temples and decorating them with sculpture was a lucrative profession. Did it lead to craftsmen moving from place to place where there was a demand, or were local persons trained by attachment to skilled craftsmen or to guilds? The references to families of craftsmen of two to three generations would suggest that at the level of the *sūtradhāra* and the *sthapati,* at least, the guild system was less of importance and that individuals, not guilds, were employed for the overseeing of major buildings. There appears to have been a further separation, this time between the theorist and the practitioner. Both would be required in a large, complex project. Did innovation come from the theorist or from the practitioner?

The period from the latter part of the first millennium A.D. to the early second millennium witnessed a large increase in the building of temples of various sizes depending on the donor. Their skilled designers were often equally proficient as builders and engravers. The writing of *śilpaśāstras* was regarded as a high status occupation judging by the frequency of brahman or royal authorship. It would be interesting to speculate whether the writing of texts attempted to standardize styles, or if it did not do so consciously it might nevertheless have had this effect. Were there ritual consequences if the standard form was changed? How then was innovation introduced and legitimized?

There appears at this time to have been a decline in community patronage, such as had been associated with the early Buddhist *stūpas,* for which the majority of recorded donations come from craftsmen, guilds, and small scale landowners. This impression may, however, be merely the result of an insufficient study of votive inscriptions from this later period. Buildings, in particular, have so consistently been classified using dynastic labels by historians that popular *mis*conception still holds that Indian craftsmen and designers did not identify what they built by name. There is a need to look much more closely at smaller monuments, at inscriptions and texts, and to classify patrons.

Patronage in the form of temples meant merit, status, and publicity for both the builder and craftsmen. Emphasis on the individual patron led to the patron differentiating between the functional and the aesthetic aspects of the object. The patron had to be trained to make such distinctions (hence, perhaps, the royal authorship of certain *śilpaśāstras*). There emerges a nexus between the patron, the artisan, and the object, with artisan lending prestige to the patron by making a beautiful object, though the patron's recognition of its beauty remained deeply embedded in the aesthetics of the community.

## Bibliography

Acharya, P. K. *Indian Architecture According to Mānasāra Śilpaśāstra.* Oxford, 1927.

Bhandarkar, D. R. 'A List of Inscriptions of Northern India in Brahmi and its Derivative Scripts.' *Epigraphia Indica,* XIX-XII (1919-23), appendices.

Bhattacharya, T. P. *A Study of Vāstuvidyā.* Patna, 1963.

Burgess J. *Report on the Buddhist Cave Temples and Their Inscriptions.* London, 1883.

Coomaraswamy, A. K. *The Indian Craftsman.* London, 1909.

Coomaraswamy, A. K. *The Transformation of Nature into Art.* Cambridge, Mass., 1929.

Cunningham, A. *Bhilsa Topes.* London, 1854.

Dehejia, V. *Early Buddhist Rock Temples.* London, 1972.

Dhavalikar, M. K. 'Sri Yugandhāra — A Master Artist of Ajanta.' *Artibus Asiae* XXXI (1969): 301-308.

_________. 'Sūtradhāra.' *Annals of the Bhandarkar Oriental Institute* LII (1971): 34-45.

*Epigraphia Indica,* V (1898-99); X (1909-10).

Fleet, J. F. *Inscriptions of the Early Gupta Kings* (*Corpus Inscriptionum Indicarum,* III), Calcutta, 1886.

Horner, I. B. (trans.) *Milinda's Questions.* London, 1964.

Jain, P. C. *Labour in Ancient India.* Delhi, 1971.

Kangle, R. P. *The Kauṭilya Arthaśāstra.* Bombay, 1965.

Lüders, H. *Bharhut Inscriptions* (*Corpus Inscriptionum Indicarum,* II). Reprint, Ootacamund, 1962.

Marshall, J. *The Monuments of Sanchi.* 3 Vols. Cambridge, 1939.

Mirashi, V. V. *Inscriptions of the Kalachuri-Chedi Era* (*Corpus Inscriptionum Indicarum,* IV). Ootacamund, 1955.

Ranghacharya, A. *Introduction to Bharata's Nāṭyaśāstra.* Bombay, 1966.

Sircar, D. C. *Indian Epigraphical Glossary.* Delhi, 1966.

Sivaramamurti, C. 'The Artist in Ancient India.' *Journal of Oriental Research* VIII (1934): 31-45, 168-199.

# The Artist in Sanskrit Literature

Ludo Rocher
University of Pennsylvania

## Terminology

One Sanskrit term often translated as 'art' is *śilpa* — the artist being *śilpin*. Both Sanskrit terms are, however, much broader than these English translations. The commentators on Pāṇini's *Aṣṭādhyāyī* — an unexpected but rich source of information on this topic — include among *śilpins* not only the dancer *(nartaka),* but also the dyer or washerman *(rajaka)* and the digger or miner *(khanaka)* (3.1.145). Elsewhere (6.2.76) they illustrate a grammatical rule on *śilpin* with the terms for weaver *(tantuvāya),* tailor *(tunnavāya),* potter *(kumbhakāra),* blacksmith *(ayaskāra),* and so forth. Although in Monier-Williams' English-Sanskrit dictionary *śilpa* and *śilpin* are the first terms for 'art' and 'artist,' respectively, in his Sanskrit-English dictionary *śilpa* is 'any manual art or craft, and handicraft or machanical or fine art,' and *śilpin* is 'an artificer, artisan, craftsman, artist.'

Another Sanskrit term for 'art,' *kalā* (probably of Dravidian origin), covers an even wider semantic field. The *kalās* are normally sixty-four in number. According to Vātsyāyana's *Kāmasūtra* they not only include vocal music *(gīta),* instrumental music *(vādya),* dancing *(nṛtya),* and painting *(ālekhya),* but also carpentry *(takṣaṇa)* and architecture *(vāstuvidyā),* and even such items as cooking, preparing drinks, horticulture, cock-fighting, ram-fighting, quail-fighting, training parrots to speak, hairdressing, games to be played with dice, making dolls and toys, and physical culture. Again, according to Monier-Williams, *kalā* is, among many other things, 'any practical art, any mechanical or fine art.'

Other terms for 'artist/artisan' that will be mentioned later in this paper include *kāru, kāruka,* and *karmakāra.* They are all direct derivatives — the last one even twice — of the verbal root *kṛ* 'to do,' and for all practical purposes mean nothing more than 'doer, maker.'

To be sure, not every type of activity qualified as *śilpa.* While explaining Pāṇini's rules bearing on *śilpins,* the commentators explicitly exclude such individuals as the *kāṇḍalāva* 'branch cutter,' *śaralāva* 'reed cutter,' and so forth. *Śilpa* and *kalā* are, therefore, most appropriately interpreted as skills the acquisition of which requires effort and training.

They apply, however, to a far broader variety of occupations than the Western category of 'art.' This means that whenever Sanskrit texts describe characteristics of the *śilpin,* these are characteristics the 'artist' shares with many others we would not consider to be artists. As Kramrisch writes, 'the distinction often made in the West between artist and craftsman did not affect India' (1983: 51).

## The Artist and the Caste System

Neither *śilpa* nor *kalā* appears in Sanskrit law books as the specific occupation of any of the four basic *varṇas.* Hence Kramrisch's conclusion that 'the artists and craftsmen came from all classes of society' (1983: 53).

There is evidence, nevertheless, that in the tightly organized and highly hierarchical society of classical India the practitioners of each individual *śilpa* were assigned specific places within the composite caste system. There are some references to that effect in the law books. The *Nāradasmṛti* (1.288) refers to a blacksmith 'by caste' *(jātyaiva).* According to the *Manusmṛti* (10.22) actors *(naṭa)* are members of a 'mixed caste,' the offspring of a degraded *(vrātya)* kṣatriya and a kṣatriya woman. Other texts, such as the Purāṇas and the Kośas, repeatedly associate the mixed castes with specific occupations. In addition, there exist, in various parts of India, large numbers of so called 'caste Purāṇas': the *Mallapurāṇa* deals with a caste *(jāti)* of professional wrestlers, a *Kālikāpurāṇa* with a caste of coppersmiths, a *Nāpitapurāṇa* with a caste of barbers, and so forth.

There are also definite indications in the texts that the *śilpas* were mostly hereditary. When the dance teacher *(nāṭyācārya)* Gaṇadāsa comes on stage in Kālidāsa's *Mālavikāgnimitra,* he not only refers to his own craft as a *kulavidyā* or 'family craft,' but also indicates that crafts generally remain within the family: 'Everyone is proud of his own *kulavidyā;* why shouldn't I be proud of mine?' The editor of a seventeenth-century inscription from Udaipur was able to trace the ancestors of two brother-masons *(sūtradhāra)* mentioned in the text back for three centuries, thanks to 'the record preserved by their present descendant' (*Epigraphia Indica* 24 [1937-38]: 56-91). The Buddhist Jātakas refer to a dancer family, a drummer family, and a conch blower family. They relate how the son of an elephant trainer practiced the art of his father, and how the son of an acrobat learned the art of jumping *(laṅghanasippa)* (Fick: 299).

## The Training of the Artist

Even as with the Vedic student, the future *śilpin* had to spend time as an apprentice in the house of a *guru* (here called *ācārya)* and be totally dependent on him. The *Nāradasmṛti,* for example, refers to both kinds of 'students' in the same chapter (ch. 5), the only difference being that the Vedic student is called *śiṣya,* whereas the apprentice is called *antevāsin.* Sanskrit texts generally stress that the apprentice's education shall be twofold. On the one hand, he has to acquire necessary technical training: he has to study the *śāstra* of his craft. On the other hand, he has to master the required technical skills, the *prayoga.* When Brahmā had created the *Nāṭyaśāstra* (see later in this article), he needed someone to put it into practice *(prayoktṛ);* after Indra declined his request that the gods do so, Brahmā turned to Bharata: he and his one hundred sons 'studied the *śāstra* and the *prayoga*' (1.25). Both skills are equally important; one without the other is useless.

The selection of an *ācārya* depended on local circumstances. In small and isolated localities, some crafts were obviously represented by a single individual. The commentators on the *Aṣṭādhyāyī* (6.2.62) speak of *grāmanāpita* ('*the* barber of the village') and *grāmakulāla* ('*the* potter of the village'). We may assume that, in such cases, the apprentice learned the craft from his father.

The situation was different in larger agglomerations, in which there were many individuals practicing the same crafts. The *Nāradasmṛti* addresses this situation:

> If (a young man) wishes to be initiated into the art of his own craft *(svaśilpa),* with the sanction of his relations, he must go and live with a master, the duration of his apprenticeship having been fixed.
> The master shall teach him at his own house and feed him. He must not employ him in work of a different description, and treat him like a son.
> When he has learnt the art of his craft within the (stipulated) period, the apprentice shall reward his master as plentifully as he can, and return home, after having taken leave of him. (5.16, 17, 20, transl. Jolly)

All textual evidence, indeed, points to close professional relations between individuals practicing the same crafts. As early as the *Gautamadharmasūtra* we are told that 'cultivators, traders, herdsmen, moneylenders and artisans *(kāru),* are organized in guilds *(śreṇi)*' (11.21); another law book adds *śilpins* to this list (*Bṛhaspatismṛti* 1.74). These guilds were well structured organizations. Their rules and regulations were recognized as sources of law not only by their internal tribunals, but also by the highest law courts in the land.

**General Reputation of the Artist**

Not all *śilpins* enjoyed a high reputation. The *Aṣṭādhyāyī* (6.2.68) provides a special rule on how to accentuate compounds comprising the word *pāpa* ('sin') followed by the name of a *śilpin.* The commentators illustrate this rule with the terms *pāpanāpita* ('a bad barber') or *pāpakulāla* ('a bad potter').

In more general terms, *śilpins* figure in a passage from the *Pañcatantra* (1.266-68) at the end of a list of individuals who abuse their power to exploit those who are weaker than themselves: 'kings exploit their subjects, merchants, their customers . . .; craftsmen exploit everyone *(sarvalokasya śilpinaḥ).*'

Kauṭilya's *Arthaśāstra* devotes an entire chapter (4. ch. 1) to *kārukarakṣaṇa* ('keeping watch over artisans') as part of its fourth book on *kaṇṭakaśodhana* ('suppression of criminals'). The chapter emphasizes the punishments weavers, washermen, tailors, goldsmiths, physicians, actors, and others will incur if they practice their *śilpas* dishonestly. It concludes with the statement: 'Thus shall the king prevent from oppressing the kingdom these *caurān acaurākhyān, i.e.* those who are thieves without being called so.' More than once, in the same text, actors, dancers, singers, and musicians are listed as possible disguises under which the king shall send out secret agents to spy on the affairs of his enemies.

Not all references to *śilpins* in Sanskrit literature are, however, negative. First, at least three law books (*Baudhāyana* 1.9.1; *Manu* 5.129; *Viṣṇu* 23.48) exhibit the interesting statement: *nityaṃ śuddhaḥ kāruhastaḥ* ('the hand of the craftsman is always pure'). This obviously does not imply that the craftsman's hand is ritually pure *per se,* for the same law books forbid brahmans to accept food from a long list of *śilpins.* It means, though, that as long as the *śilpin* is engaged in his craft, his hand is free of any impurity, irrespective of his position in the social hierarchy.

Second, Sanskrit texts are replete with references to show how close kings, nobility, and well-to-do citizens generally were to the arts and their practitioners. Royalty are often described as experts in the arts in their own right. In a dispute between two dance teachers in the *Mālavikāgnimitra* they submit their professional disagreement to the king as an obviously competent arbitrator. In the sixth act of Kālidāsa's *Śakuntala,* king Duṣyanta is made to paint a picture of his beloved Śakuntalā. There is also a well known Pallava inscription in which king Mahendravarman is described as 'a tiger among painters' (see Kramrisch, 1983: 64).

Even if in descriptions of the aristocracy's active participation in the arts we may have to allow for a certain degree of poetic license, there is no doubt that the rich and powerful were generous patrons. Kālidāsa's *Raghuvaṁsa* (16.38) describes how the king had *śilpins* of all sorts join their skills to make Ayodhyā, which had fallen on bad times, into a totally new city. Bāṇa's *Harṣacarita* (ch. 4) vividly describes the preparations at the time when the king decides to give his daughter in marriage: 'from every country were summoned companies of skilled artists' *(śilpin)*. The *Aṣṭādhyāyī* (6.2.63) deals with words composed of the term *rāja* followed by the name of *śilpin*. The compound *rājanāpita,* built according to this rule, does not indicate the king's barber, *i.e.* the barber who actually shaves the king; the text says that such a compound is meant to express 'praise,' and indicates 'excellent barber,' *i.e.* a barber who is good enough to enjoy the patronage of the king. The king's patronage, therefore, was a symbol of the artist's excellence and success.

**Art and Religion**

From the earliest texts onward, Indian literature recognizes the existence of superhuman, divine craftsmen. In the *Ṛgveda* Tvaṣṭṛ, the most skillful of all craftsmen, fashioned Indra's thunderbolt, he made a drinking cup for the gods, and so forth. Two hymns of the *Ṛgveda* (10.81, 82) are addressed to Viśvakarman, the 'All-Maker,' who, in later Vedic literature, is identified with the creator Prajāpati himself, and, in classical literature, takes over Tvaṣṭṛ's earlier role to become the chief artificer of the gods.

More important, many of the *śilpas* ultimately derive from the gods. Viśvakarman learned the art of painting *(citra)* from Nārāyaṇa, *i.e.* Viṣṇu. Nārāyaṇa was so good at painting that, when Indra sent beautiful ladies to him to disturb his penance, he took a fresh mango leaf and, with its juice, painted a nymph on his thigh. The nymph — Urvaśī — came to life, so beautiful that the other ladies ran away in shame (*Viṣṇudharmottara-purāṇa* 3.35.2-5). In the Mahābhārata (13.135.139), too, Viṣṇu is the creator of the *śilpas,* as well as of all other kinds of knowledge.

Brahmā in particular is connected with the origin of specific *śilpas.* According to Varāhamihira's *Bṛhatsaṁhitā* (53.1), *vāstujñāna* (or *vāstu-vidyā,* 'house building') is derived from Brahmā. Also, the sage Bharata, the composer of the *Bhāratīyanāṭyaśāstra,* which is *the* book on dramaturgy, obtained it from Brahmā who had created it at the request of Indra. Brahmā's role in the composition of the *śāstras* for a number of crafts entails one important consequence. If the four Vedas came out of

Brahmā's mouths, and if the *Nāṭyaśāstra* originated from the same source, it logically followed that the *śāstra* of the *nāṭyaśilpins* was considered to be a fifth Veda, the *Nāṭyaveda.*

According to other sources, the textbooks of some *śilpins,* even though they were not Vedas, were at least Upavedas or 'secondary Vedas.' These include not only the *Āyurveda* (medicine) and *Dhanurveda* (archery), but also the *Gāndharvaveda* which is said to consist of four parts: singing *(gīta),* dancing *(nṛtya),* chanting *(sāman),* and instrumental music *(vāditra) (Mahābhārata* 3.89.13-14). Occasionally, the Upavedas also include the *Sthāpatyaveda* or 'the Veda of architecture.'

The link between *śilpa* and ritual found expression in the idea that the patron of a work of art is a *yajamāna, i.e.* the patron of a sacrifice. This identification implies not only that the production of a work of art is comparable to the performance of a sacrifice *(yajña),* but also that the artist, while at work, fulfills the office of a priest, and that the reward he receives for his work from his patron is a *dakṣiṇā* or 'priest's fee.' According to the *Aitareyabrāhmaṇa* (6.27 = 30.1) human *śilpas* are nothing but imitations of divine *śilpas, i.e.* of a set of *mantras* to be recited in the course of the sacrifice.

## Bibliography

Coomaraswamy, Ananda K. *The Indian Craftsman.* London, 1909.

Fick, Richard. *The Social Organisation in North-East India in Buddha's Time.* Calcutta, 1920 (original German, 1897).

Kramrisch, Stella. 'Artist, Patron, and Public in India' (1956), and 'Traditions of the Indian Craftsman' (1958). Reprinted in *Exploring India's Sacred Art. Selected Writings of Stella Kramrisch,* edited by Barbara S. Miller. Philadelphia, 1983.

__________. 'The Ṛgvedic Myth of the Craftsmen (The Ṛbhus).' *Artibus Asiae,* XXII (1959): 113-120.

# Texts and Craftsmen at Work

John F. Mosteller
University of Pennsylvania

My purpose in this brief essay is to show how evidence drawn from texts and from surviving practice can be correlated to provide a better understanding of how Indian images were made in the past. My focus will be particularly on the technique used to make stone images.

Technique — the methods by which an art object is actually made — has not been a prominent concern of art historians. In the context of Western art, technique has been judged as largely irrelevant to the transformation and analysis of artistic styles (Panofsky 1955: 55-6). The application of western art-historical methods to the study of Indian art has led inevitably to a similar bias against the role of technique in that field. I wish to present evidence, however, which suggests that *how* an Indian image is made has a direct bearing on and relationship to its style. By style I mean here the morphology of images, that is, the particular linear and volumetric articulation of sculptural forms unique to a given image.

There are several surviving traditions of stone sculpture in India. The one I have studied directly survives principally at the site of Mahabalipuram in Tamil Nadu. In 1955, the Tamil Nadu state-government established a training institute in Mahabalipuram headed by a traditional *sthāpati* (architect) who was charged with teaching traditional arts to new generations of young craftsmen. These arts included temple architecture, stone and stucco sculpture, bronze image-making, wood-carving, and painting. I visited this institute in 1978 and again in 1982 to interview artists and to observe their working methods. My principal informant for traditional practice was Sri Ganapati Sthapati, the superintendent of the Institute and the son of its founder. A descendant of a long line of *sthāpatis* in Tamil Nadu, Ganapati traces the lineage of his family back to the architect who built the great Bṛhadeśvara Temple of Tanjore.

In addition to interviewing Ganapati Sthapati, I also observed sculptors at work on various stone images. I saw a range of iconic images being made as well as two dancing figures, one of which was under way while another was just being started. Though of a later style, the quality of this work is very high and compares favorably with the Pallava sculpture so much in evidence at Mahabalipuram.

The tools used by these sculptors include four different kinds of chisels made in a graduated range of sizes. Each type of chisel is used for a specific phase of work. Two of these types, straight-pointed and straight-edged chisels, are used for roughing out the stone block and the figure of the image. Chisels with curved points are used for modelling the limbs of the image by undercutting the stone. The final type is that of blunted chisels with serrated surfaces. These are used to finish the surface of the image. The sculptural tradition at Mahabalipuram uses granite and, as a result, the chisels have to be resharpened very frequently. Carving proceeds from removing large and then progressively smaller pieces of stone until, at the end of the process, finishing work is accomplished by pulverizing the granite surface into dust.

The procedure for carving an image begins by drawing it on the surface of the stone block. This drawing is always executed in relation to a constructional device that consists of a vertical line intersected by horizontal lines at specific points. Different types of devices are used for different images. However, they always consist of the same elements, *i.e.,* of vertical and horizontal lines and points. These devices guide both the compositions and proportions of the images.

It would be wrong, however, to think that the function of these devices is only as a guide to the drawing of an image. In fact, they function as mnemonic devices that structure the young artist's memorization of visual forms. Ganapati Sthapati related to me that his father taught him how to carve forms through learning how to draw them. Whether it was an ornamental motif, temple elevation, or an image, Ganapati learned how to create that form through memorizing its drawing. In the case of images, he learned to draw the form of a deity in relation to such devices, repeating them over and over, until he had mastered the original drawing done by his father. In this way he memorizes the 'line' of his father, the way it curved, and the forms it created, in relation to the pre-established framework of the constructional device. According to Ganapati, the drawn line is the essence of an artist's style. Thus, as Ganapati learned the visual vocabulary of his father he also absorbed his father's style.

Seeing the pivotal role that drawing plays in the carving of sculpture in this tradition makes one re-think the emphasis usually placed upon the articulation of volumes in Indian sculpture. In practice, volumes are literally 'drawn' into existence. Because artists destroy the initial drawing of the image on the block's surface, as they work they must constantly re-draw the image. This constant process of re-drawing of forms guides the realization of these forms. In this particular tradition, the lines are first drawn in charcoal and then reinforced with a pigment made from red earth. This red line remains intact until the stone that supports it is actually chipped away. The types of lines used vary: single drawn lines are used to locate, re-position, and refine features; hatching lines are used to indicate surfaces that need to be further reduced; finally, whole areas are covered with pigment or coconut oil, which is then removed by moving a flat serated chisel quickly over the surface. The shaping of the limbs and features of the image is accomplished by repeatedly removing these lines.

This process of drawing and re-drawing the figure is accompanied by various stages of carving. The first is the roughing out of the image by cutting straight back into the stone along the outline of the figure. This relieved mass is then modelled by removing smaller areas of stone using the process of re-drawing detailed above.

The connection between the working techniques of these South Indian sculptors and the morphology or style of their images is centered in the use of constructional devices to memorize and transmit the forms of their images. A similar relationship between technique and morphology can be hypothesized for ancient Indian artists on the basis of a careful reading of early Sanskrit texts, which clearly imply the use of similar types of constructional devices.

The textual passages I have studied prescribe the proportional systems to be used for images. The early texts containing such passages include the *Bṛhatsaṃhitā, Viṣṇudharmottara, Citralakṣaṇa* of Nagnajit, *Pratimālakṣaṇam,* the *Agni-* and *Matsyapurāṇas.* The *Bṛhatsaṃhitā* can be reliably assigned to the first quarter of the sixth century A.D. (Kern, 1865: 20). The passages in the other texts, though the texts themselves have been assigned a wide range of dates, can largely be associated with the *Bṛhatsaṃhitā* because of the close similarity of their contents.

These iconometric passages distinguish two groups of measurements: those of height, which define the vertical system of proportion, and all others. The height measurements are prescribed as a conventional series that clearly implies a similar drawing of a vertical line punctuated by points that in turn imply intersecting horizontals. This drawn line corresponds with the type of constructive systems still used in South India. Dominated by an axis (*brahma* or *madhyasūtra*), this segmented line ultimately represents an abstraction of the human anatomy as defined by its constituent parts. According to the *Bṛhatsaṃhitā* these are called: forehead *(lalāṭa),* nose *(nāsa),* mouth/chin *(mukha/cibuka),* neck *(grīva),* neck to heart *(hṛdaya),* heart to navel *(nābhi),* navel to genital *(meḍhra),* thigh *(uru),* knee *(jānu),* calf *(jaṅghā),* and foot *(pāda)*

(Kern 1865: 313-15). These anatomical terms and the measurements prescribed for them do not refer to the corresponding features of an image. Rather, these refer only to the abstract segments created by the subdivision of the constructive device and to the relative distance between the points that define each segment.

The ancient use of such constructional devices has been demonstrated on the basis of a proportional analysis of a large sample of early Indian sculptures ranging in date from the second century B.C. to *ca.* A.D. 500 (Mosteller 1986). The sites represented by this sample are concentrated in the Gangetic plain. In addition to confirming the use of constructional devices and identifying a series of proportional systems used, this study has also isolated principal variations in the application of the constructive device. I would like briefly to describe these variations here and indicate how they effect the form of images.

The first variation is the way in which the boundaries of the device and proportional system are related to the height of the image. Indian systems of proportion are defined by their modular height and this modular height establishes the boundaries of the constructive device. However, the artist had to relate these boundaries to the form of his image, and my study indicates that while artists always equated the lower boundary with the bottom of the feet, they were free to equate the upper boundary with a variety of features. The relationships documented by my study include: (1) the top of the headdress, (2) the top of the head, and (3) the hairline.

The second variation has to do with what can be called the proportional sequence of the image. The textual prescriptions imply that the torso from neckline to genital *(meḍhra)* should always be three modules long. Different texts agree on this, but they disagree on the proportions assigned the zone of the figure above the neckline and the lower zone of the legs. My study confirms that the constructional device used by early sculptors did, indeed, have a tripartite structure: the torso had always a fixed length of three modules and the upper and lower zones were subject to proportional variation. Thus, two images, each with a torso of three modules, could have different proportions for the upper and lower zones. For example, the internal ratios for the three zones of an image, proportioned using the nine-module system, can vary from an integer sequence of 2:3:4 to fractional sequences such as 1.5 : 3 : 4.5 or 1.75 : 3 : 4.25.

The third variation relates to the proportional subdivision of the upper zone. This centers on the proportional length assigned to the face. Early texts are unanimous in prescribing that face length (from

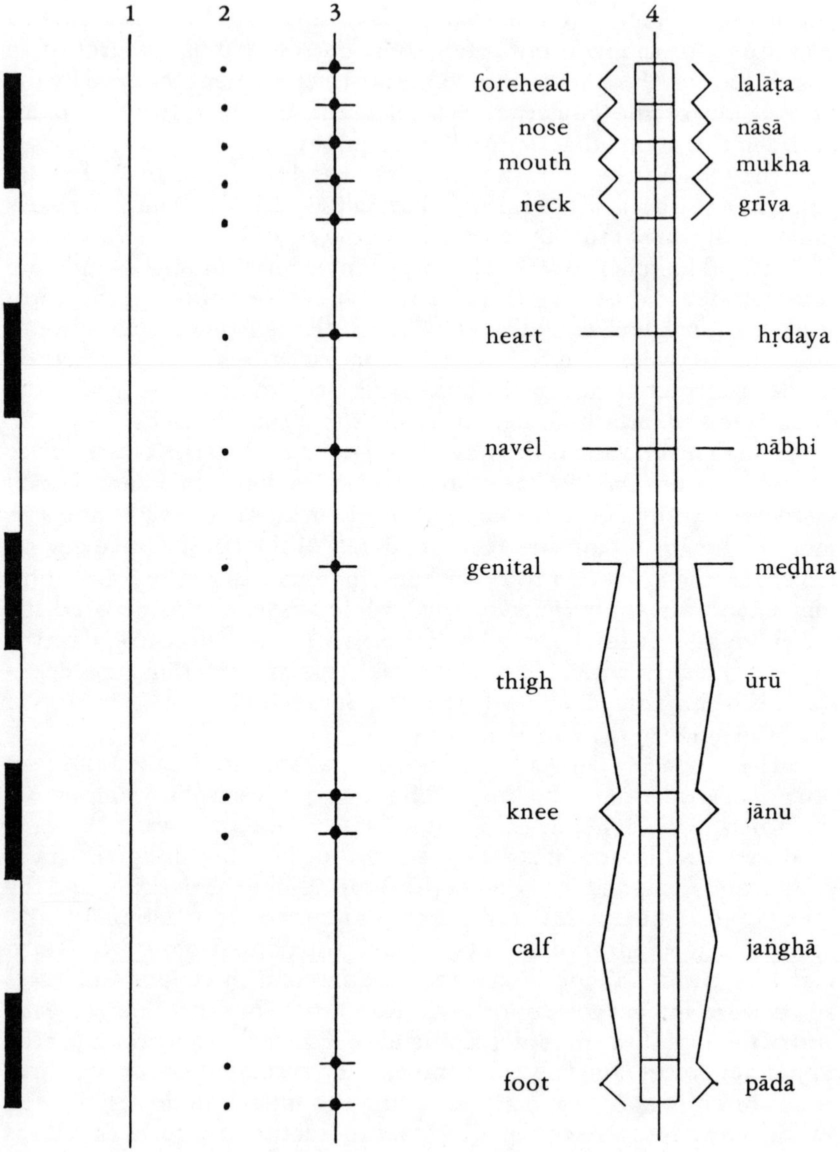


Fig. A.
Diagram of Constructional System.

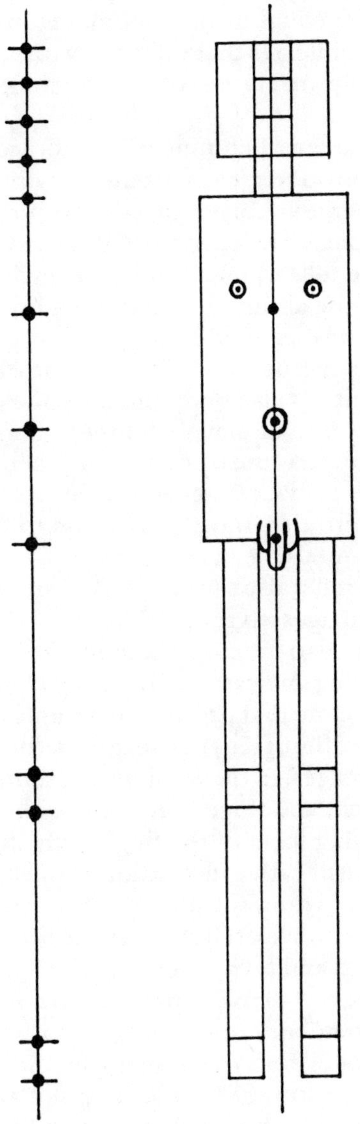

Fig. B.
Comparison of a figure and Contructional System.

hairline to chin) be equal to the module. However, my proportional analysis of images indicates that this is only one of the options available to early Indian sculptors. Other options include fractions such as 1.67 and 1.25 modules.

The possible range of combinations of these different options, in terms of the five proportional systems documented by my sample of images, leads to a large variety of specific proportional solutions for the images I have studied. The existence of these various solutions at the same site and time tells us many things. Principal among these is that Indian artists had the ability to manipulate the proportions and compositions of their images at will.

Just as this constructional device controlled the vertical composition of the figure, it also undoubtedly controlled the outline of the image. As we have seen at Mahabalipuram, the outlines of images are executed in relation to a constructive device. Similarly, we must assume that the use of such a device in ancient sculpture means that the outlines of these images were also drawn in relation to the vertical axis and its intersecting horizontals.

Beyond this, I must also say that it is possible, on the basis of a study of the profiles of images, to suggest that the relieved volumes of these early images were tied to the constructional device through a memorized procedure of drawing and carving. Looking at images while measuring them has convinced me that profiles are unique to specific styles. Thus, for example, the profile of Kuṣāṇa images can be distinguished from the profile of Gupta images. In the former case, there is a clear alignment of the breast, stomach, and thigh. Particularly distinctive of the Kuṣāṇa profile is the swelling form of the thighs, which usually terminate in a concave (and hence negative) definition of the knee. In contrast to this, the Gupta profile moves away from a strict alignment of breast, stomach, and thigh towards a convex relief where the breast moves into a slightly protruding stomach and then receeds back to the thigh. There is also a blending of volumes, as visible in profile as from the front, which differs from the Kuṣāṇa tendency to retain an almost geometric definition to the parts of the body, both from the front and in profile.

The study of sculptural profiles and the analysis of vertical proportions establishes that the drawing and execution of images in ancient times was governed by processes that seem very similar to those we have seen at Mahabalipuram. The use of constructive devices for transmitting the forms of Indian images from one artist to another establishes a nexus between an artist's technique and his style. The ability to reconstruct this nexus, *i.e.*, the constructional device, through the analysis of measurements, has important implications for how we analyze artistic styles in the Indian context.

Comparisons of images and the analysis of their respective styles have traditionally relied on articulating a disparate series of observations about the specific form that selected surface features assume and the presence or absence of various attributes. These diverse observations can now be coordinated with a precise technical analysis of the morphology of images in relation to the constructive devices used to create them. The actual technique of image-making employed by early Indian artists itself provides us with a precise and technical means for understanding the forms of their images.

Though compositional rules and conventions obviously become more diversified for later Indian sculpture, the practice of using such constructional devices to assist artists to memorize forms clearly continued. How else can we explain the ability of the Indian artist to create the myriad decorative and figural forms that cover the exteriors of Indian temples? The endless repetition of like forms over so many monuments — spread over enormous regions of the subcontinent — is itself clear evidence for the use of such an approach to sculpture.

## Bibliography

*I. Critical Editions and Translations*

Apte, Hari Narayan, ed. *Agnipurāṇa* (Anandasrama Sanskrit Series 41). Poona, 1900.

__________. *Matsyapurāṇa* (Anandasrama Sanskrit Series 54). Poona, 1907.

Goswamy, B. N. and A. L. Dahmen-Dallapiccola, trans. *An Early Document of Indian Art, The Citralakṣaṇa of Nagnajit.* New Delhi, 1976.

Kern, H., ed. *The Bṛhat Saṁhitā of Varāhamihira* (Biblioteca Indica, The Asiatic Society of Bengal, nos. 51, 54, 59, 63, 68, 72, and 73). Calcutta, 1865.

Kern, H., trans. 'The Bṛhat Saṁhitā or Complete System of Natural Astrology, of Varāha-mihira.' *The Journal of the Royal Asiatic Society of Great Britain and Ireland* new series, 4 (1870): 430-79; 5 (1871): 45-90, 231-88; 6 (1873): 36-91, 279-388; 7 (1875): 81-134.

Kramrisch, Stella, trans. *The Vishṇudharmottara (Part III), A Treatise on Indian Painting and Image-Making.* Calcutta, 1928.

Majumdar, B. C., S. C. Vasu, H. H. Wilson, Wilford Bentley, and others, trans. *The Matsya Purāṇam* (The Sacred Books of the Aryans, vol. 1). Delhi, 1972.

Ruelius, Hans, ed. *Sāriputra und Ālekhyalakṣaṇa Zwei Texte zur Proportionslehre in der Indischen und Ceylonesischen Kunst.* Göttingen, 1974.

Shah, Priyabala, ed. *Viṣṇudharmottara-Purāṇa Third Khaṇḍa.* Vol. I (Gaekwad's Oriental Series 130). Baroda, 1958. Vol. II (Gaekwad's Oriental Series 137). Baroda, 1961.

Shastri, M. N. Dutt, trans. *Agni Purāṇam A Prose English Translation.* Vol. I (The Chowkhamba Sanskrit Studies LIV). Varanasi, 1967.

*II. Secondary Works*

Banerjea, Jitendra Nath. *The Development of Hindu Iconography.* Calcutta 1941; Revised and enlarged, 1956.

Hadaway, W. S. 'Some Hindu 'Śilpa' Shāstras In Their Relation To South Indian Sculpture.' *Ostasiatische Zeitschrift* 3 (1914-15): 34-50.

Jones, Clifford Reis. 'Dhūlicitra: Historical Perspectives on Art and Ritual.' In *Kalādarśana, American Studies in the Art of India,* edited by Joanna G. Williams, 69-75. New Delhi, 1981.

Mosteller, John Foster. 'Proportionality in Early Indian Sculpture: A Study Based upon the Analysis of 110 Standing Male Images of Ca. Second Century B.C. to 500 A.D. from the Gangetic Plain.' Ph.D. Dissertation, University of Pennsylvania, Philadelphia, 1986.

Panofsky, Erwin. 'The History of the Theory of Human Proportions as a Reflection of the History of Styles.' *Meaning in the Visual Arts, Papers in and on Art History,* 55-107. New York, 1955.

Rao, Gopinatha. *Elements of Hindu Iconography.* Madras, 1914-16.

__________. 'Tālamāna or Iconometry.' *Memoirs of the Archaeological Survey of India,* no. 3, 32-115. Calcutta, 1920.

Ruelius, Hans. 'Some Notes on Buddhist Iconometrical Texts.' *The Journal of the Bihar Research Society* LIV (1968): 168-175.

Vatsyayan, Kapila. *The Square and the Circle of the Indian Arts.* Atlantic Highlands, New Jersey, 1983.

# Making Ajanta

Walter M. Spink
University of Michigan, Ann Arbor

Shortly after A.D. 460 a group of wealthy and powerful devotees decided to honor the Buddha and evidence their own piety by inaugurating a new phase of excavation at the ancient Hīnayāna Buddhist site near Ajanta (Ajaṇṭā), in Maharashtra, where the deep, dead-ended gorge of the Waghora River forms a retreat of great beauty. Their aim was to develop the old site by adding at least two new *caitya* halls along with a larger number of *vihāras* to serve as residences for the growing community of monks who would take up residence there.

The original sponsors included the chief minister of the great Vākāṭaka empire, the wealthy feudatory who ruled in the Ajanta region (Ṛṣīka) itself, and a highly prestigious monk 'who was attached . . . in friendship through many succesive births'[1] to the minister of the adjacent province of Aśmaka. It seems reasonable to assume that many of the architects and craftsmen whom they hired would have moved to Ajanta from the flourishing cities where the patrons lived. These workmen must have been highly trained, having learned their trade constructing such complex structural buildings as those depicted over and over again in Ajanta's own mural paintings. It is clear that the new Mahāyāna halls of worship and residence at the site, 'adorned with windows, doors, beautiful picture-galleries, ledges, statues, . . . [and] ornamented with beautiful pillars and stairs, [and resembling] the palaces of the lord of gods'[2] were built in emulation of familiar structures in the thriving cities of Hariṣeṇa's empire. The new 'monuments in the mountain' which, cut deep into the living rock, were intended to endure 'as long as the sun dispels the darkness by its rays,'[3] use essentially the

[1] Quoted from the dedicatory inscription of Cave 26, verses 9-13. G. Yazdani, *Ajanta,* IV (text), London, 1955, pp. 114-18.

[2] Quoted from the dedicatory inscription of Cave 16, verses 24, 27. See V. V. Mirashi, *Inscriptions of the Vākāṭakas (Corpus Inscriptionum Indicarum, V),* Ootacamund, 1963, pp. 103-11.

[3] Quoted from the dedicatory inscription of Cave 17, verse 29. Mirashi, pp. 120-29.

same architectural and decorative vocabulary and reflect the same optimistic esthetic as the ornate wooden buildings that serve as their models. However, the wooden prototypes, once among the crowning splendours of this 'Golden Age,' have long since crumbled into dust. We know them today only because they figure so prominently in the miraculously preserved illustrated history which still lies open for all to read in Ajanta's deep ravine.

Although most of the artists and artisans must already have been skilled craftsmen when they came to Ajanta, we know that they had little experience working in stone, for there are few stone sculptures and remains of stone buildings dating to this period from any of the Vākāṭaka domains.[4] Thus, the startling magnitude of their new assignment must have stunned them. They would have to scale Ajanta's steep scarps with hammers and chisels in hand and cut the palatial structures they were wont to build from more tractable materials out of living rock. None of them had ever been asked to do such a thing before. Their excavations would become the first of any significant size or complexity made since the rock-cut halls of Hīnayāna Buddhism at least 300 years before.

So how *would* a craftsman start? Daunted at first by such a task, the earliest excavators clearly approached their work with considerable diffidence. The earliest doorway, window, and pillar forms — those cut during the first two or three years of Mahāyāna activity at the site — are notably uncomplicated in their shaping. The exuberant scrolls, garlands, and strands of beads and gems so characteristic of the period are generally painted in this phase rather than rendered with the chisel. The layouts of these earliest halls are invariably simple (in fact, simplified); they forego the added refinements and architectural gracenotes that adorn slightly later excavations. We can immediately see the difference if we compare the plan of a typical early undertaking (as that of King Upendragupta's Cave 17, Fig. A, by and large cut out by A.D. 469) with that of a typical late one (Cave 21, Fig. B, still not quite complete in A.D. 477). The 'doubling' and the 'pillaring' of cells in Cave 21 is a characteristically later feature, but even more telling is the precision of its planning, measuring, and cutting. Even by referring to the plans alone one can see

[4] The only free-standing stone sculpture from another site which seems sufficiently close in style to Ajanta images to warrent a (tentative) dating in Hariṣeṇa's reign is the corpulent Śaivite figure found at Mansar, now in the National Museum, New Delhi. P. Chandra, The Sculpture of India, Washington D.C., 1985, Fig. 40.

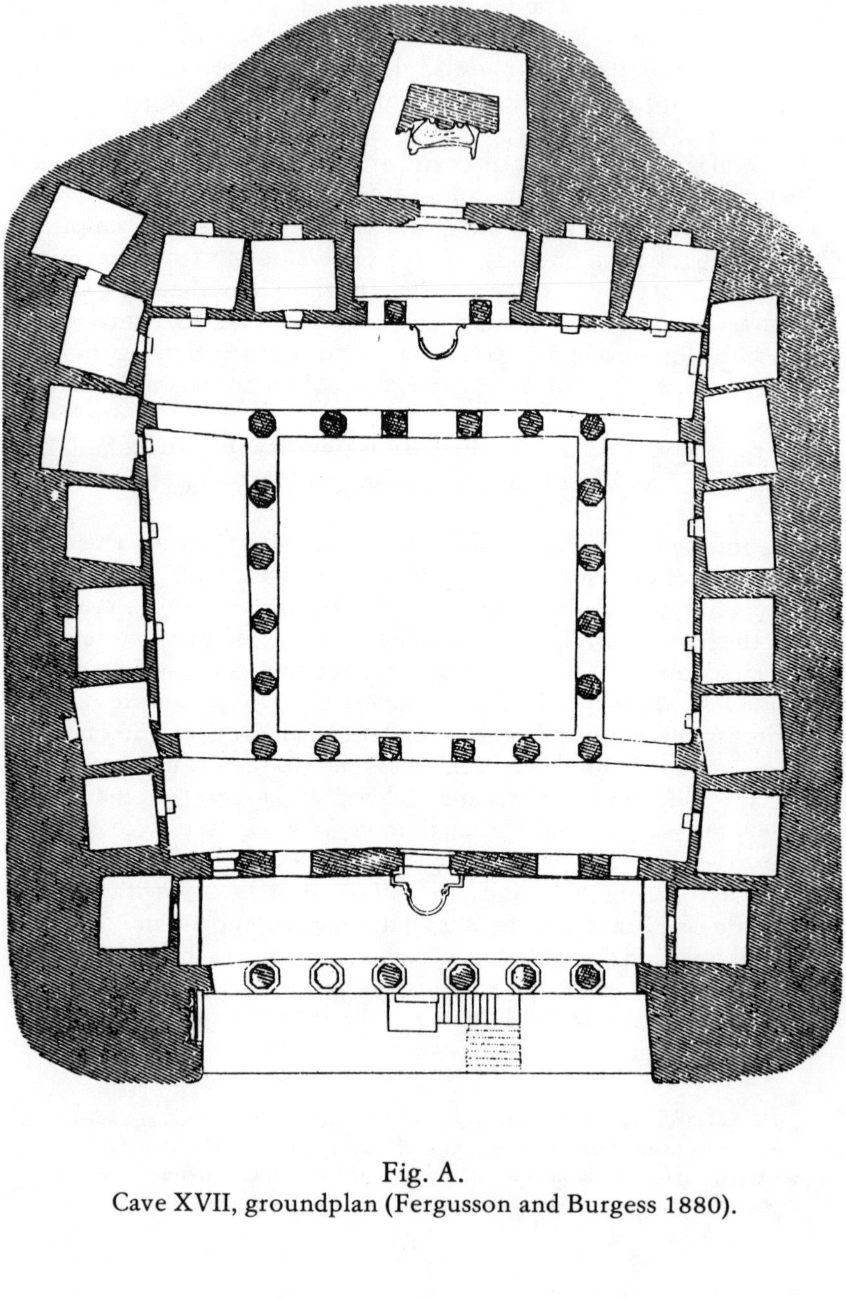

Fig. A.
Cave XVII, groundplan (Fergusson and Burgess 1880).

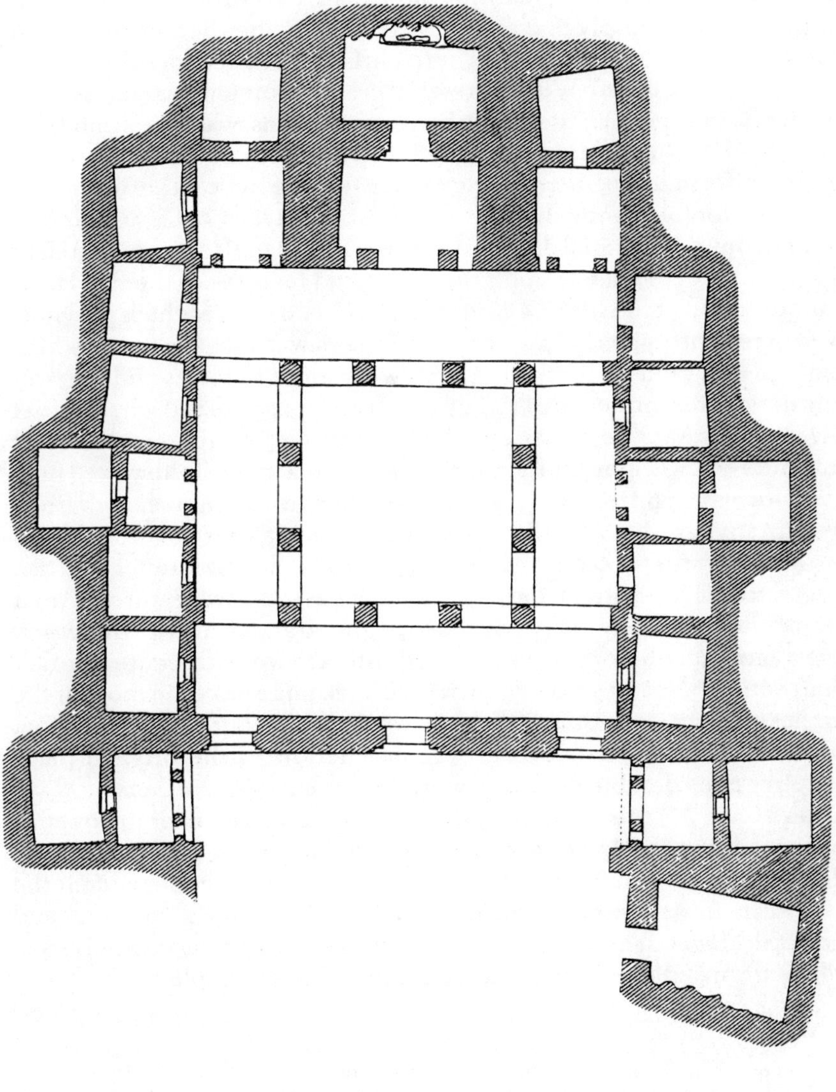

Fig. B.
Cave XXI, groundplan (Burgess 1883).

that the later of the two caves is much more confidently and accurately engineered. This is not because the designers and artisans were different or more talented. In fact, many of the same artists probably worked on both caves. It is simply that as each year went by they became more and more skillful in cutting 'palaces' into cliffs, with little more than string *('sūtra')* to guide them.[5] What Burgess's fine old groundplans and sections suggest is indeed true: in slightly later excavations, walls are straighter, floors and ceilings more level, pillar shapes more consistent, and cells more uniform in size than in the earlier fifth-century excavations.

The notable simplicity of the earliest Mahāyāna caves at Ajanta is due not only to an initial diffidence, however; it can also be attributed to a conscious dependence upon the forms and features of the five Hīnayāna caves cut at the site *ca.* 400 years before. Those severe halls provided welcome prototypes for the earliest of the new Mahāyāna caves, which emerge as a kind of compromise between the old forms and a newer aesthetic. This influence of the earlier cave-types explains why the first Mahāyāna *vihāras* at the site are so surprisingly simple, with astylar interiors and without Buddha shrines at the rear: they follow the Hīnayāna format, typified by Cave 12 at Ajanta and common elsewhere as well. In any case, by A.D. 466 — less than five years after new work began — the excavators at Ajanta had 'caught up with their own times' and had begun to include both shrines and peristyles as standard features in their *vihāra* interiors. They had, in fact, also begun to add shrines to the *vihāras* cut a few years before to bring them into accord with contemporary convention.[6] Needless to say, such revisions, undertaken in most of the earliest Mahāyāna *vihāras* while they were still in course of excavation, obscure their original format. Reconstruction of the original plans requires considerable detective work in some cases; in others (as Cave 11 and Cave 27) the original is fairly easy to perceive under the overlay of late additions. My concern here, of course, is not with such an 'in depth' analysis. Instead, what I wish to emphasize is how dependent the architects initially were on readily available Hīnayāna prototypes and how this dependence was reinforced by the caution of inexperience, which disposed them toward keeping their forms simple.

[5] For the inscription of a *sūtradhāra* ('one who holds threads') in Cave 16, see M. K. Dhavalikar, 'Sri Yugadhara: A Master-artist of Ajanta,' *Artibus Asiae,* XXXI (1969): 301-08.

[6] Spink, 'Ajanta's Chronology: Politics and Patronage,' *Kalādarśana,* ed. Joanna G. Williams, New Delhi, 1981, pp. 109-26.

One of the first things that the new workers at Ajanta would have learned is that the site's scarps are by no means as solid as they seem. Laid down eon after eon by successive volcanic flows, they are full of flaws, which run horizontally every few feet between basaltic layers or appear as vertical or crazily cracked fissures, where steam escaped or cooling processes corrupted the integrity of the forming rock. Again, as a result, the stone-carvers must have felt constraints which recommended simplicity. By contrast, when they or their fellow-workers came to *paint* the caves, once their carved surfaces had been smoothed and plastered, they could approach their task as if they were painting a palace or temple back in the capital. The painting procedures used in a monolithic cave were essentially no different from those used in a structural building. This would seem why, when the Ajanta artists turned to the task of painting caves, they clearly could approach their work with the same confidence in the earliest caves as in the later ones.

We find essentially no stylistic development in the paintings at Ajanta, nor is this surprising, if, as I contend, the paintings were all executed in about a decade and a half. I do not mean to suggest that there are not striking differences in the various paintings in the caves or even among those in a single cave, but this was because the painters came from many different regions and divergent family traditions and included artists who were both young and old, clumsy and accomplished, radical and conservative. Ajanta accomodated them all. As painters, all they needed to do was to apply the brush to the prepared surface in old familiar ways. Ajanta's *painters,* obviously familiar with their themes, had surely gained their experience in other places, by decorating structural halls that are now long vanished — many of which Ajanta's patrons had probably also sponsored, as, in the language of their inscriptions, they 'adorned the earth with *stūpas* and *vihāras.*'[7]

It was not lack of experience, then, in creating fashionable structures that was responsible for the 'tentative' and often explicitly retardatory character of the inaugural Mahāyāna excavations at Ajanta. It was a problem caused by the rock-cut medium itself or, rather, by the craftsmen's unfamiliarity with it. If we do not take such matters into account, we can too easily fall into the error of supposing that the generally severe excavations, begun when the site's Mahāyāna phase commenced, must be separated by decades, generations, or even cen-

[7] See Cave 17 inscription, note 3 above.

turies from highly elaborated caves that actually were designed only a few years later.

Excavated forms at Ajanta, of course, *do* 'develop,' and at times in ways that might seem to require centuries, judging from what we find in other cultures (and even sometimes elsewhere in India) where artistic forms are known to move from restrained and hesitant early types to complex later ones. It had traditionally been assumed that Ajanta's latest excavations should be dated as much as 200 years after Cave 16 and 17, which are dateable by inscriptions to the fifth century, and that Ajanta's first Mahāyāna excavations might date well before that.[8]

When it becomes evident that Ajanta's Mahāyāna phase lasted only a few years rather than a few centuries, its 'development' can usefully serve to caution us against making too hasty judgements about stylistic change anywhere. Ajanta demonstrates how quickly forms can develop. Perhaps even more significantly, it proves how wide a variety of 'styles' can be created even in the course of a single year at one site, under certain particular conditions.[9] If we take A.D. 477, for instance, we can find a remarkably wide range of painting styles being used simultaneously at Ajanta in Cave 1, despite the fact that the artists were all following a single and carefully ordered program of work. If we include the painting being done during that same year in Cave 2 and a few other caves, the diversity of styles had traditionally been spread over two or more centuries.

If we turn to stone Buddha images executed between A.D. 477 and 480,[10] when over 90% of the hundreds of stone images at the site were carved, we find a similar range of 'styles.' Here too we have an obviously diverse group of forms, which few scholars, using intuition and experience alone, would assign to such a brief period. The temptation to date them over a relatively long span of time could be sustained, not only by a consideration of their formal characteristics but also by the fact that there are so many clear and consistent changes in iconographic

[8] J. Burgess and J. Fergusson, *Cave Temples of India,* London, 1880, considered both Cave 11 and Cave 8 to be Hīnayāna caves. Later writers have often made similar errors.

[9] See Spink, 'Ajanta's Paintings: A Checklist for Their Dating,' *Dimensions of Indian Art,* New Delhi, 1986, pp. 457-68.

[10] The reader should allow a small margin of error of perhaps a year or two for these dates, since they are necessarily approximations.

features within the group.[11] Any scholar's familiarity with patterns of iconographic evolution in Buddha images of known date elsewhere might cause him to believe that such changes should occupy a number of decades at the very least.

How then can we explain the remarkable and unwonted speed of consistent change at Ajanta, which involves not only Buddha imagery but also the development of pillars, pilasters, doorways, windows, cell types, and cave layouts, along with purely functional features such as the fittings used to hang doors and window shutters? After their diffident start, the artists and artisans at Ajanta not only 'caught up with the times' with remarkable speed but vigorously continued to evolve, to the degree that Mahāyāna developments at Ajanta must soon have become the leading edge for that period's aesthetic. Intense pressures, both internal and external, must have pushed the site's artists from the start. As they learned more about both the problems and potentialities of the rock-cut medium they increasingly were able both to shape and surface their carved elements in ways to fit the taste of the day, as of course their rich and courtly patrons had intended when they 'expended abundant wealth' upon such 'measureless' monuments that could 'not even be imagined by little-souled men.'[12] It is probably no coincidence that the four excavations of the pious and generous local king, Upendragupta of Ṛṣīka, are the first at the site lavish enough to conform to such contemporary expectations, nor is it surprising that his 'perfumed hall' (the *caitya* Cave 19), which was conceived as the focal center of worship at the site, did this most successfully of all. Its impact upon the later development of the site is manifest, for its innovatively ornate pillars, panels, and friezes provided models upon which carvers in other caves soon began to play obvious variations.

Throughout Ajanta's arching gorge, where, within a mere decade, space suddenly must have been at a premium, everyone kept a watchful eye on what everybody else was doing. Not only were other patrons eager to emulate or even to attempt to outdo first the benefactions of the local king, then of the imperial minister, and finally of the Vākāṭaka

11 During the 'Period of Disruption' in *ca.* A.D. 479 and 480, when original patrons were no longer controlling developments at the site, dozens of new donors sponsored the carving and painting of hundreds of votive Buddhas, many of them small in scale, sometimes forming part of large repetitive groups.

12 See Cave 17 inscription, verse 25, note 3 above.

overlord himself; it is also evident that the artists were constantly influencing and also competing with each other. How else can we explain the fact that, on the one hand, distinctly related decorative and structural motifs are used in so many of the different caves, and, on the other, that these are almost always varied, each motif seeming to be a conscious elaboration of what had gone before. Thus, the amount of foliation upon pilasters grows, literally, year by year; figural groups carved on pillar capitals, in medallions, and on doorways, become more complex;[13] and simple floral panels painted on the earliest ceilings become elaborated by an increasing number of animal, zoomorphic, and human creatures in later caves.

Even more remarkable, considering how conservative and how resistant to change iconography can be, is that Buddha imagery evolved so quickly and consistently at Ajanta. This must certainly have been due, in part, to a constant influx of new ideas as members of the Buddhist community elsewhere made their way to the site along nearby trade routes; it also bears witness, however, once again to the intense creative energies fostered at Ajanta, which both approved and sponsored change. The sense of positive urgency allied with a world-affirming delight that informed the site in its heyday is reflected in the dedicatory inscription of Cave 26, the second new *caitya* hall at the site. 'Why should not,' the donor asks, 'a monument be raised by those possessing wealth, desirous of mundane happiness as also of liberation? . . . A man continues to enjoy himself in paradise as long as his memory is green in the world. One should [therefore] set up a memorial on the mountains that will endure for as long as the moon and the sun continue.'[14]

With innovations so obviously sought and welcomed, change itself early became a convention at Ajanta. As fashion appeared and developed, the modes of the past characteristically were felt no longer worthy of repetition. Everyone opted for some variation of simple octagonal pillars, for example, obviously dependent upon Hīnayāna prototypes, up until about A.D. 465; a much more modern-looking 16-sided type, often with rounded sections, however, became the architect's almost invariable choice in the following year or so. This variant, too, went out of fashion, however, as square-based pillars, with a distinctively new

[13] For such motival changes, see my *Ajanta to Ellora,* Bombay, 1967. I have, however, now shortened the time-span given therein.

[14] See Cave 26 inscription, verse 7-8, note 1 above.

type of capital and with gradually elaborating shaft-designs, took over. Doorways, windows, pilasters, and even plans also underwent remarkably swift and complex evolution, as if, once a new structural refinement or mode of decoration was established, there was no going back, save where revisions to modernize the forms of the past were feasible.

This same insistent progressiveness, for example, is strikingly evident in so simple a thing as the way that cell doorways were treated to facilitate the hanging of doors. No less than eight distinctly different types of fittings (or readjustments of previous fittings) were developed over the course of a single decade and a half, each a considerable practical improvement on the one used earlier. When a new method for hanging cell doors came into use, the previous one was never used again. One might suspect that 'the world will always buy a better mousetrap,' though it may want its Buddha images to be cast always in a familiar mold.

The remarkable consistency with which Ajanta's doorfittings — being purely functional features — change almost year by year makes them a particularly useful tool as an aid in determining the place of each cave and its various parts within the site's overall development. Sometimes cell doorways were blocked out before they were supplied with fittings. Sometimes they were supplied with fittings before the doors were hung. Sometimes the original fittings broke and had to be replaced with a new type. Sometimes, although already completed, fittings were revised in order to make them more up-to-date.[15] Sometimes cell doorways were not completed because work on a cave was abandoned. Sometimes they were not plastered or painted because time ran out.

Wherever we look at Ajanta, during Hariṣeṇa's time, we see a truely remarkable, and quite unusual, pressure for artists to move forward, never back. Constant change, stimulated by the continual influx of new artists and monks as well as other travellers to the site, seems always to have been expected. Seeing the consistent patterns within Ajanta's development, in fact, one might have to conclude that development at the site as constantly being 'juried' by a court of taste and authority. Such a body of involved arbiters might have been composed of the artists themselves and the resident monks under whose watchful eyes they would have worked; to a lesser degree, the pilgrims and merchants who, like the patrons of the caves, supported the site with their funds,

15 For an example, see Fig. 8 in my 'Ajanta's Chronology: Politics and Patronage,' note 6 above.

would have participated. No one could rest on his laurels; old forms and procedures, routinely repeated, would not suffice. New ideas, instead of being resisted by 'the establishment,' as we have commonly taken to be the case in traditional cultures, at this particular establishment were honored by it.

Ajanta was obviously a special and highly creative case; its seemingly unique, constantly emergent energies demand an explanation that must ultimately be sought outside of the site itself. Ajanta's unquenchable originality can best be explained as a reflection and beneficiary of the exuberance of the Vākāṭaka empire itself, during its final flowering, when 'that moon among princes, Hariṣeṇa . . . [was] protecting the earth'[16] and rapidly was extending his empire's control over the whole of central India and from sea to sea. The growth of the empire during Hariṣeṇa's reign can be superimposed, as it were, on the growth of the site. At this time, in fact, just as the long imperium of the rival Gupta kings was in decline, the Vākāṭakas came into their own. Sustained by a '*pax* Vākāṭaka' achieved by Hariṣeṇa's power, what we might call the 'vessel of classical Indian culture' was perhaps filled fuller now than it had ever been before. The miraculously and uniquely well-preserved site at Ajanta, which must have been but one of many flourishing creative centers in the heyday of Vākāṭaka power, was a recipient of that great cultural *'pūrṇaghaṭa's'* overflow as well as a contributor to its source.

It seems clear now that the cultural crescendo that began with the early Guptas in the fourth century A.D. in north India reached its peak, not so much under the Guptas themselves but rather in the Vākāṭaka courts of Hariṣeṇa and his feudatories in the decades between *ca.* A.D. 460 and 480. The best and only remaining score by which to read that mounting music is preserved in the monuments constructed in Ajanta's valley, 'resonant with the chirpings of birds and the chatterings of monkeys' by craftsmen in those still-confident, halycon, days of Vākāṭaka rule.[17]

The startling and saddening fact, however, is that shortly before A.D. 480, such music stopped. It lingered only as poignant echoes here and there for the next half century, as a darker age, born out of Hariṣeṇa's passing and his empire's fall, subsumed the golden light so briefly mirrored on Ajanta's walls.

[16] See Cave 17 inscription, verse 21, note 3 above.

[17] See Cave 26 inscription, verse 18, note 1 above.

## Ajanta Bibliography (by date of publication)

1819 Erskine. 'Remains of Buddhists in India.' Containing a note by Morgan on the visit of the Army officers in 1819. *Transactions of the Bombay Branch of the Royal Asiatic Society* III (1819): 520.

1830 Alexander, J. E. 'Notice of a Visit to the Cavern Temples of Adjunta in the East Indies.' *Transactions of the Royal Asiatic Society of Great Britain and Ireland* II (1830): 362-70.

1839 *Bombay Courier,* containing Blake's account, reprinted in Blake. *Description of the Ruined City of Mandu, also an Account of Buddhist Cave Temples of Ajanta, Khandesh.* Bombay, 1844.

1846 Fergusson, James. 'On the Rock-Cut Temples of India.' *Journal of the Royal Asiatic Society of Great Britain and Ireland* VIII(1846): 56-60.

1851 Wilson, J. 'Memoir on the Cave-Temples and Monasteries and Other Ancient Buddhist, Brahmanical and Jaina Remains of Western India.' *Journal of the Bombay Branch of the Royal Asiatic Society* III.2 (1851): 71-72.

1862 Gill, R. *Stereoscopic Photographs of Ajanta and Ellora.*

1873-1875 Griffiths, J. Notes in *Indian Antiquary* II (1873): 152-53; III (1874): 25-28; IV (1875): 253.

1874 Burgess, James. 'Rock-Temples of Ajanta.' *Indian Antiquary* III (1874): 269-74.

1878 Mitra, Rajendralala. 'On Representation of Foreigners in the Ajanta Frescoes.' *Journal of the Asiatic Society of Bengal* XLVII.1 (1878): 62-72.

1879 Burgess, J. *Notes of the Bauddha Rock-Temples of Ajunta, Their Paintings and Sculptures and on the Paintings of Bagh Caves, Modern Bauddha Mythology, etc.* Bombay, 1879.

1879 Fergusson, James. 'On the Identification of Chosroes II among the Paintings of Ajanta.' *Journal of the Royal Asiatic Society of Great Britain and Ireland* New Series XI (1879): 155-70.

1880 Campbell, J. M. *Gazeteer of Bombay Presidency* XII, Khandesh. Bombay, 1880, pp. 480-574.

1880 Fergusson, J. and J. Burgess. *The Cave Temples of India.* London 1880, pp. 280-349.

1883 Burgess, J. *Report on the Buddhist Cave Temples and Their Inscriptions.* London, 1883.

1893 Waddell, L. A. 'Note on Some Ajanta Paintings.' *Indian Antiquary* XXII (1893): 8-11.

1896 Griffiths, J. *The Paintings in the Buddhist Cave-Temples of Ajanta, Khandesh (India),* two volumes. London, 1896.

1903 Lüders, H. 'Ārya Śūras Jātaka-mālā and the Frescoes of Ajanta' (translated). *Indian Antiquary* XXXII (1903): 326-29.

1915 Lady Herringham. *Ajanta Frescoes.* Oxford, 1915.

1919-1939 *Annual Report of the Archaeological Department of His Exalted Highness the Nizam's Dominions, 1917-18* (1919): 11-12; *1918-19* (1920): 7-8; *1919-20* (1922): 3-4; *1920-21* (1923): 14-16; *1921-22* (1926): 7-9; *1924-25* (1926): 7-8; *1936-37* (1939): 25-30; and minor references in other numbers.

1927 Goloubew, V. 'Documents pour servir a l'etude d'Ajanta, les peintures de la premiere grotte.' *Ars Asiatica* X.

1930-1955 Yazdani, G. *Ajanta.* Four parts, each with text and portfolio of illustrations. Oxford, 1930, 1933, 1946 and 1955.

1932 Shriniwasrao, Shrimant Bhawanrao *alias* Balasaheb Pant Pratinidhi. *Ajanta.* Bombay, 1932. With eighty plates of illustrations, many of them in colour and most of them heavily retouched.

1937 Kramrisch, Stella. *A Survey of Painting in the Deccan.* Hyderabad, 1937, pp. 3-69.

1939 Paramasivan, S. 'Techniques of the Painting Process in the Cave-Temples of Ajanta.' *Annual Report of the Archaeological Department of His Exalted Highness the Nizam's Dominions,* 1936-37 (1939): 25-30.

1941 Dikshit, Moreshwar G. 'An Unidentified Scene from Ajanta.' *Transactions of the Indian History Congress, Fifth (Hyderabad) Session, 1941*: 567-68.

1947 Goetz, Hermann. 'The Neglected Aspects of Ajanta Art.' *Marg* 2.4 (1947-48): 35-64.

1948 Auboyer, J. 'Composition and Perspective at Ajanta.' *Art and Letters, India and Pakistan* New Series XXII.1 (1948): 20-28.

1950 Dey, Mukul Chandra. *My Pilgrimages to Ajanta and Bagh.* Second edition. Oxford, 1950.

1954 *India — Paintings from Ajanta Caves.* New York Graphic Society, by arrangement with UNESCO. New York, 1954.

1955 Fabri, Charles. 'Frescoes of Ajanta — an essay.' *Marg* IX.1 (1955): 61-76.

1956 *Ajanta Paintings.* New Delhi, 1956.

1956 Goetz, H. 'Painting: Ajanta.' *Marg* IX.2 (1956): 86-92.

1962 Gupte, Ramesh Shankar and B. D. Mahajan, *Ajanta, Ellora and Aurangabad Caves.* Bombay, 1962.

1963 *The Ajanta Caves.* With an introduction by Benjamin Rowland. New York, 1963.

1963 Barrett, Douglas and Basil Gray. *Painting of India.* Cleveland, 1963, pp. 24-31.

1963 Mirashi, V. V. *Inscriptions of the Vakatakas. (Corpus Inscriptionum Indicarum V).* Ootacamund, 1963.

1963 Spink, Walter. 'History from Art History.' *Proceedings of the (1963) International Congress of Orientalists.* New Delhi.

1964 Haloi, Ganesh Chandra. 'Ajanta Painting, its Technique and Execution.' *Art in Industry* VII.4 (1964): 12-22.

1964 Mitra, Debala. *Ajanta.* Third ed. New Delhi, 1964.

1965 Singh, Madanjeet. *The Cave Paintings of Ajanta.* London, 1965.

1966 Begley, W. 'The Chronology of Mahayana Buddhist Architecture and Painting at Ajanta.' Ph.D. diss., University of Pennsylvania, 1966.

1967 Ghosh, A. ed. *Ajanta Murals.* New Delhi, 1967.

1967 Spink, W. 'Ajanta and Ghatotkacha: A Preliminary Analysis.' *Ars Orientalis* 6 (1967): 135-55.

1967 ________. *Ajanta to Ellora.* Ann Arbor, 1967.

1968 Begley, W. 'The Identification of the Ajanta Fragment in the Boston Museum.' *Oriental Art* XIV (1968): 25-33.

1968 Dhavalikar, M. K. 'New Inscriptions from Ajanta.' *Ars Orientalis* VII (1968): 147-53.

1968 Spink, W. 'Ajanta's Chronology: The Problem of Cave Eleven.' *Ars Orientalis* 7 (1968): 155-68.

1969 Dhavalikar, M. K. 'Sri Yugadhara: A Master-Artist of Ajanta.' *Artibus Asiae* XXXI (1969): 301-08.

1971 Schlingloff, D. 'A Battle Painting at Ajanta.' *Indologen-Tagung* (1971): 196-203.

1971 ________. 'Das Lebenrad in Ajanta.' *Asiatische Studien* XXV (1971): 324-34.

1971 ________. 'Das Sasa-Jataka.' *Wiener Zeitschrift für die Kunde Sudasiens* XV (1971): 57-67.

1971 Takata, O. *Ajanta.* Tokyo, 1971.

1972 Schlingloff, D. 'Die Erforschung Altindischer Wandmalereien.' *Christiana Albertina* 13 (1972): 32-38.

1972 ________. 'Jatakamala Darstellung in Ajanta.' *WZKS* XVI (1971): 55-65.

1972 Spink, W. 'Ajanta: A Brief History.' In *Aspects of Indian Art,* edited by P. Pal, 49-58. Leiden, 1972.

1972 Stern, P. *Collonnes indiennes d'Ajanta et d'Ellora.* Paris, 1972.

1973 Schlingloff, D. 'Prince Sudhana and the Kinnari.' *Indologica Taurinensia* I (1973): 155-67.

1974 Spink, W. 'Les Colonnes Indiennes d'Ajanta et d'Ellora' (review). *Journal of the American Oriental Society* 94.4 (1974): 483-87.

1974 ________. 'The Splendours of Indra's Crown:' A Study of Mahayana Developments at Ajanta.' *Journal of the Royal Society of Arts* CXXII (October 1974): 143-67.

1975 Schlingloff, D. 'Asvaghosa's Saundarananda in Ajanta.' *WZKS* XIX (1975): 85-102.

1975 ________. 'Zwei Malereien in Hohle 1 von Ajanta.' *Zeitschrift der Deutschen Morgenländischen Gesellschaft* Supplement III.2; XIX *Deutscher Orientalistentag* (1975): 912-17.

1975 Spink, W. 'Ajanta's Chronology: The Crucial Cave.' *Ars Orientalis* 9 (1975): 143-69.

1976 Spink, W. 'Bagh: A Study.' *Archives of Asian Art* XXX (1976-77): 53-84.

1977 Schlingloff, D. 'Die Jataka-Darstellungen in Hohle 16 von Ajanta.' *Beiträge zur Indienforschung (Veröffentlichungen des Museums für Indische Kunst, Berlin* 4 (1977): 451-578.

1977 ________. 'Der König mit dem Schwert: Die Identifizierung einer Ajantamalerei.' *Wiener Zeitschrift für die Kunde Südasiens* XXI (1977): 57-70.

1977 ________. 'Zwei Anatiden-Geschichten im alten Indien.' *ZDMG* 127.2 (1977).

1977 Weiner, Sheila. *Ajanta: Its Place in Buddhist Art.* Berkeley and Los Angeles, 1977.

1978 Begley, Wayne. Review of Weiner, *Ajanta,* in *Journal of Asian Studies* XXXVII (1978): 570-71.

1980 Schlingloff, D. 'Die Älteste Malerei des Buddhalebens.' *Studien zum Jainismus und Buddhismus, für L. Alsdorf (Alt-und Neu-Indische Studien)* 23 (1980): 181-98.

1980 Williams, Joanna. Review of Weiner, *Ajanta,* in *Art Bulletin* LXII (1980): 177-80.

1981 Dhavalikar, M. K. 'The Beginnings of Mahayana Architecture at Ajanta.' In *Madhu,* edited by M. S. Nagaraja Rao, 131-38. New Delhi, 1981.

1981 Krishna, Ananda. 'An Exceptional Group of Painted Buddha Figures at Ajanta.' *Journal of the International Association of Buddhist Studies* 4 (1981): 96-99.

1981 Spink, Walter. 'Ajanta's Chronology: Cave 1's Patronage.' In *Chhavi II,* 144-57. Benaras, 1981.

1981 ________. 'Ajanta's Chronology: Politics and Patronage.' In *Kalādarśana* edited by Joanna Williams, 109-26. New Delhi, 1981.

1982 Plaeschke, H. and T. *Indische Felsentempel und Hohlenkloster.* Leipzig, 1982.

1982 Williams, Joanna. 'Ajanta and the Art of the Vakatakas.' In *The Art of Gupta India: Empire and Province,* 181-87. Princeton, 1982.

1983 Spink, W. 'The Great Cave at Elephanta: A Study of Sources.' In *Essays on Gupta Sculpture,* edited by B. Smith. Delhi, 1983.

1985 ________. 'Ajanta's Chronology: Cave 7's Twice-Born Buddha.' In *Studies in Buddhist Art of South Asia,* edited by A. K. Narain. New Delhi, 1985.

1985 ________. 'Ajanta's Chronology: Solstitial Evidence.' *Ars Orientalis* XV (1985).

# Evidence for Artists of the Early Calukya Period

Carol Radcliffe Bolon
University of Chicago

We know that ancient Indian artists were skilled members of hereditary craft organizations. We have tended, therefore, to assume that these artists were egoless, anonymous workers, building and carving according to the requirements of the patron and the traditional iconography and iconometrics of sacred subjects, following the style of the time and place without much professional freedom. A standard summation of this position regarding ancient artists might be the following:

> Traditional Hindu society makes no allowance for the individual pursuit of self-expression. The role of the Hindu artist is to give visible form to the values of his society, rather than to communicate a personal interpretation of these values. The artist is considered an instrument by which things higher and greater than himself find expression in the forms that he creates . . . . The notion of signing a work of art is of little importance as it is believed that the artist himself does not directly imagine the work — he is 'guided' and functions only as the executor. For this reason most works of Hindu art and architecture are anonymous.[1]

While it is true that an artist's individual pursuit of self-expression would have been circumscribed by the factors mentioned, individual genius still remains recognizable in Indian sculpture. The traditional role of the Indian artist need not prevent the art historian from seeking to trace individual masters' works. While we do have more information about the patrons of temples and images than about the artists, primarily from inscriptions, more can certainly be observed about individual Indian artists, their careers, and style than so far has been customary.[2]

[1] Michell 1978: 54. The same idea is expressed in Boner 1972: xliv.

[2] Building a religious monument was a meritorious deed that would weigh favorably in one's next birth. Therefore, the patron would want his or her name known, whereas artists worked primarily for compensation. There are instances of an artist making a donation himself, for instance the gift of five entrance pillars at the *stūpa* at Velagiri in Āndhra, given by the itinerant artist Siddhārtha, who is described as the son of another artist (Misra 1975: 16). At Sāñcī, the artisan Viśvakarma, a native of nearby Ujjayini, made a gift. An architrave carved with Cadanta Jātaka of the south gate of the great *stūpa* was a gift of Ānanda, the foreman of the artisans of the King Śrī Sātakarṇi (Misra 1975: 16).

Nothing, in fact, so far has been written regarding sculptors and architects of ancient Hindu temples that takes full advantage of the existing evidence.

In the field of Indian miniature painting in recent years, investigation of questions about schools of painting and their dissemination has turned towards identifying families of artists and the study of individual artists.[3] Much more inscriptional and documentary evidence to trace an individual painter's oeuvre is available, of course, especially in the Mughal period, than there is to trace the work of sculptors and architects of the more ancient periods.

Several recent studies have admirably documented known artists of a period of temple art by reading inscriptions on temples. These studies, however, do not proceed to discuss the style of individual artists, even when abundant signed examples are available, the range of subjects undertaken, or other topics which would be of interest (Mishra 1985; Narasimha Murti 1985; Settar 1973).[4] The first step towards a full

Many artists, even in early periods, signed their work. For example, the *yakṣa* found at Parkham was made by Gomataka, a pupil of Kuṇika, and Kuṇika had other pupils known from inscriptions on other images (Misra 1975: 15). A *yakṣa* from Pitalkhora of about 100 B.C. is inscribed across the hand 'Kaṇhadāsa made it.' As to the question raised by Susan Huntington in *The Art of Ancient India,* New York, 1985, p. 84 and fig 5.35, of whether 'made it' here refers to the artist or patron, I feel that the special care given to the depiction of the necklace worn by the *yakṣa* indicates that the goldsmith carved the piece. There are other early instances of names, but this one is interesting because it suggests that an artist who primarily made jewelry also carved stone. Similarly, we know that a guild of ivory carvers worked on the stone relief of the *toraṇa* post of Sāñcī's *stūpa* I, applying their expertise in precious miniature work to the new format and material required of them. Several times, artists portrayed themselves at work on the monuments they created: at Bhārhut in about 100 B.C., at Khajurāho as they moved and carved stones (*ca.* A.D. 1000), and in Orissa in a nineteenth century copy of a rare palm-leaf manuscript which records some of the working methods and other facts about stone masonry guilds (see Boner 1972).

3 For example, Goswamy 1968; Pramod Chandra, *The Tūti Nāma of the Cleveland Museum of Art and the Origins of Mughal Painting,* Graz, 1976; Milo Cleveland Beach, *The Imperial Image, Paintings for the Mughal Court,* Washington, D.C., 1981.

4 Seshadri has gathered names of artists and has published photographs of their work but makes no observation on their particular qualities. He documents many examples of signed work of the Hoysaḷa period. Settar has concentrated on the artist Mallitamma of the Hoysaḷa period who signed hundreds of images (sixty on one temple). Settar traces his name from one monument to the next and uses this to document his movements within the kingdom but makes no observations on specific qualities of his work or of the development of his style over the period of sixty years in which his work can be followed.

study has been done, however, by this reading of label-inscriptions. The second step would be to photo-document inscribed images in detail so that a full analysis would be possible.

Now that the field of Indian art history has reached a stage of some intimacy with the history of various regional kingdoms, cultural areas, and their art, interesting and useful specific information about artists has begun to emerge. The purpose of this summary is to suggest new ways to examine evidence concerning ancient Indian artists in order to pursue a more subtle understanding of their careers and work than casual assumptions have so far allowed. Inscriptional and stylistic evidence available in fact can be brought together to give visibility to 'invisible' Indian artists.

I will attempt to demonstrate what can be gained from this working method by using the example of sculptures in the early Calukya period. Such study becomes fruitful during this period (and perhaps even more fruitful during subsequent periods) because the practice of signing one's work became a common practice in this region. I will illustrate what we know from inscriptions as well as what can be extracted and hypothesized about the artists working in this single southern kingdom, that of the early Calukyas, although such a method is applicable to other areas and periods as well.

Calukya artists of the period *ca.* A.D. 550-750 built and adorned more than 100 temples in the present states of Karnataka and Andhra Pradesh. Many names are inscribed on monuments of all phases of the period, but a name is often all that is inscribed, so that we can't be certain whether the name is that of an artist, patron, or pilgrim. Sometimes, however, the inscription adds to the name the particle 'made it' (which still is ambiguous) or a more specific name-suffix used by artists such as *'ōja.'* At Bādāmi, the Calukya capital, for instance, S. V. Padigar has recently discovered that over 200 names of artists — identifiable from the name-suffixes — were inscribed on the cliffs alongside the four famous cave-temples.[5] These cave-temples are the earliest known monuments of this period. These 'signatures' of artists, except for one beside a *garuḍa* image in Cave no. 3, are not placed on specific images or temple parts, so identifying the work of each artist is not possible. By analysis of the linguistic nature of the names and the types of script used, however, Padigar was able to draw a provocative conclusion: that

[5] S.V. Padigar, 'Craftsmen's Inscriptions from Bādāmi: Their Significance,' paper read to U.G.C. Seminar on Ellora, Nov. 18-21, 1985.

the first artists working for Calukya patrons were heterogeneous, coming from Āndhra, Karnāṭa, and even a few from north India. (After this cave-temple phase, we find artists' names inscribed specifically on images, rather than being randomly placed.)

Certainly it is possible to work beyond the limitations of the existing inscribed images. By using an inscribed image to identify an artist's style, whether or not his name recurs on other images, we hypothetically can then, by careful stylistic examination, identify other images that might represent his work. This approach has not yet been pursued for Indian sculpture or architecture, though common enough in other areas of art history.

We should want to know more about ancient Indian artists, however, than their names and style. We would want to know how they learned their craft, organized, and how they worked.[6] Were they residents of a town who worked in a shop and then shipped their art throughout the kingdom or country or were they itinerant? Logic might predict that architects would have had to be itinerant while sculptors could work either as itinerant artists, who would travel to the site of construction and carve decorative designs and major *mūrti* in situ, or as 'mass-producers' in workshops, perhaps given such an assignment as to carve so many feet of a particular molding or a certain image to fit into a niche of a certain size.

Artists of the Calukya period in fact worked both ways. The evidence for this is not inscriptional but physical: some images were carved as part of the structural masonry blocks of the temple while others were carved on panels that were then inserted into their structural framing niches. I elsewhere have discussed the likelihood that images inserted into such niches on the Saṅgameśvara temple at Kuḍavēlli in fact were made in a workshop at Aihoḷe (Bolon 1986). Both the repetition of the plan, elevation, and iconographic program of a temple *ca.* 200 miles away within the Calukya realm and the repetition of rare iconography for an image across the same distance would suggest conclusions about the working methods of the artists involved (Bolon 1980 and forthcoming). Though they were often obviously itinerant, traveling within the kingdom to different sites of temple construction, they also could have worked in at least one major resident workshop (at Aihoḷe) that we

[6] Stella Kramrisch (1956 and 1958, reprinted 1983) has combined facts gathered from rare texts as well as inscriptional information to provide a general account of the role and working methods of the ancient Indian artist.

can demonstrate exported images as well as temple models.[7] Inscriptional evidence not of the Calukya period also suggests that artists were sometimes settled. (A Pallava inscription noted by R. N. Mishra [1978: 33] for example, refers to artists paying taxes as residents.)

If we turn to specific examples of evidence that illuminate aspects of the work of early Calukya artists, several signed pieces of Calukya sculpture suggest that artists often specialized in certain types of work. An inscription on the shaft of the early Calukya proclamation pillar (Fig. A) that originally stood at the temple site of Mahākūṭa and which bears a date of A.D. 602, ends with the fact that the pillar was made by two brothers, sons of Pubesa, who specialized in such pillars.[8] Another very similar, though uninscribed, pillar in fact stands at Aihoḷe in front of the Rāvaṇa Phaḍi, a Śaiva cave-temple datable to the second half of the sixth century. A third such pillar, mentioned in a Pallava inscription, is said to have been captured at Bādāmi, but has not survived. All may have been made by the sons of Pubesa.

In another instance, the repetition of an artist's name at the site of Paṭṭadakal suggests specialization in the large, dramatic, guardian figures that flank temple doorways. A guardian of the south-porch door of the Virūpākṣa temple (*ca.* A.D. 733-44) (Fig. B) is inscribed with the name 'Baladeva' and with the information that he is the son of Duggi Āchārya.[9] This figure, remarkable for its dramatic intensity, is life size;

[7] There are several instances of images created by artists of one period and area being found installed in temples far from their origin. The Mathurā workshop of the second to at least sixth centuries, which was perhaps the most extraordinary and productive of any, disseminated its works far and wide. Mathurā images, which can readily be identified by their style and distinctive regional stone, have been found in Punjab. I am referring to recent and exciting discoveries of Mathurā *stūpa* railings with figures found buried at Sanghol (Punjab State), and of Amarāvatī style sculpture found at Vijayanagara. Elsewhere, another interesting situation of cross dynastic and cross regional aesthetic appreciation is evident: the Coḷa king, Rājādhirāja (A.D. 1044-54), was so impressed with a door guardian carved by a Later-Western-Cālukya-period artist, that he had it brought from the Later Cālukya capital, Kalyani, to be installed in his temple, the Airāvateśvara Temple at Darasuram in Tamil Nadu, and had it inscribed in Tamil 'The guardian brought by Udaiyar Śrī Vijayarajendradeva.'

[8] Mahākuṭa pillar inscription: J. F. Fleet, *Indian Antiquary* X (1881): 104, and XIX (1890): 7.

[9] For photograph see *Marg* 32 (1978): fig. 14; for inscription see *Indian Antiquary* X (1881): 168.

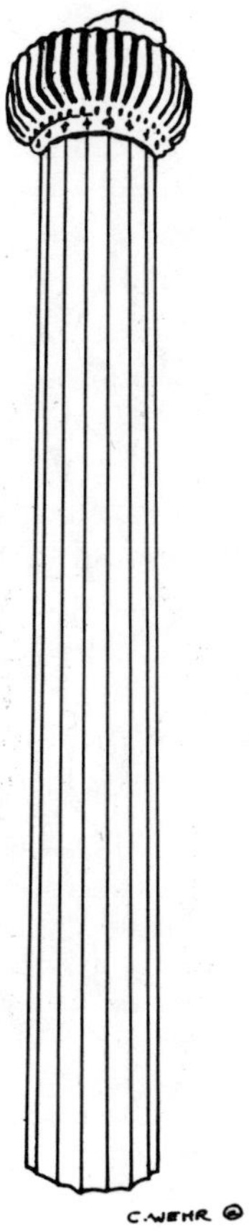

Fig. A.
Proclamation pillar from Mahākūṭa, A.D. 602, Early Calukya Period.

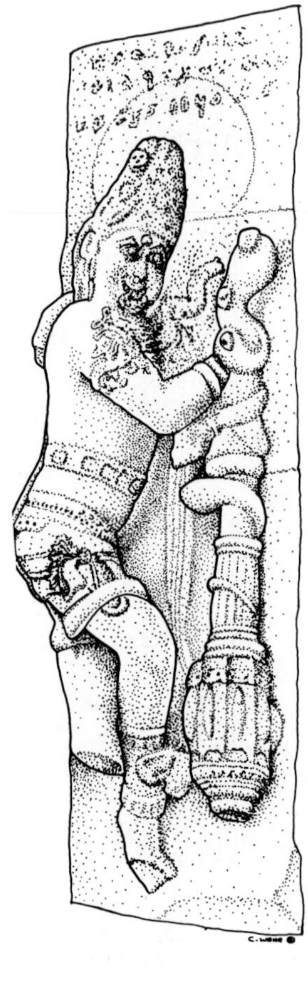

Fig. B.
Guardian, south-porch door, Virūpākṣa Temple, Paṭṭadakal,
*c.* A.D. 733-44.

he is posed realistically, as if leaning against the doorframe, and has his ankles crossed and his arms resting on top of the large mace in front of him. He is fearsome and brutal, instilling awe with his bulging eyes and fangs, and with snakes draped around his weapon. In these respects he is remarkable compared to earlier Calukya door guardians, which are unarmed and pacific beings. He is elaborately carved with jewelry and sashes and is dynamically posed. He is not a relief figure, bound to the stone, but is carved partially three-dimensionally, giving him great presence and candor.

On a second major temple at the site, Pāpanātha, the same name is inscribed above the location of a former door guardian. Unfortunately the figure was chipped off by vandals, but from the surviving outline it is apparent that this figure also was partially carved in full round. The pair to this lost figure also survives on the opposite side of the door, its style recalling that of the Virūpākṣa figure. Although unsigned, Baladeva also may have carved the excellent guardians of the north door of the Virūpākṣa temple. The invention of this type of fearsome door guardian during this period, perhaps by Baladeva, is significant because this type of figure becomes the norm for all subsequent southern guardian figures.[10]

On the same Pāpanātha temple, 'Baladeva made it' is inscribed also on the southern exterior wall on a relief depicting a *Rāmāyaṇa* scene showing Lakṣmaṇa cutting off the nose of the demoness Śūrpaṇakhā. This narrative miniature is one of many such scenes on the southern wall, which are, however, thematically unusual for temple niches during this period. The quality of carving of these scenes is quite high and each presents a dense population of figures. Similar in this regard is a ceiling panel in the Pāpanātha temple depicting the directional guardians that is inscribed 'Baladeva, [the one who is] devoid of fear.'[11] Similar to the Pāpanātha temple's *Rāmāyaṇa* scenes, which all may have been created by Baladeva, this panel is innovative in terms of its complexity of composition and the richness of its carving. Other ceiling panels in this and other temples are not as ambitious or dramatic. These distinctive qualities, which may be associated with Baladeva, suggest the possibility that he was a senior master sculptor whose individual genius has survived

[10] Often with an additional pair of arms. Chatham (1981) has studied the genesis of images of the Rāṣṭrakūṭa period from the Calukya prototypes.

[11] The iconography of this panel is fully described in S. Buchanan 1985: 415. The inscriptional reference is in Mishra 1975: 39.

in several formats: door guardians, ceiling panels, and niche scenes. At Aihoḷe his name appears again, this time as an engraver of a grant record on a stone tablet, which now stands outside the Sāraṅgī temple in the Kuntī complex.[12] The variety of his work and the fact of his frequent signature suggest that Baladeva was an active and proud artist around the middle of the eighth century A.D. One is tempted, although the evidence does not restrict us, to believe that, as an outstanding master, his preference or specialty was carving door guardians. His inscribed work, without question, stands out in ingenuity. Repetitions of this artist's name also support other evidence that all the temples on which his name appears date within a few decades of one another.

Many other images at Paṭṭadakal are signed with single artists' names that are not repeated. An image of the sage, Pulaha, for example, is inscribed 'made by Śrī Māṇdeva.'[13] Three famous Calukya ceiling panels now displayed in the Prince of Wales Museum, Bombay, originally from the Aihoḷe Huchchapayya temple all seem to represent Māṇdeva's style.[14] The proportions of figures within the composition, the detailed handling of jewelry and sashes, refined linear emphasis, and the large format of the main figures parallel aspects of the Virūpākṣa image. There are more signed images at Paṭṭadakal, which is a slightly later Calukya site (*i.e.* first half of the eighth century), than at earlier sites, suggesting a trend toward identification of artists. From the numerous names found inscribed on the large Paṭṭadakal temples, it is known that many artists worked on their abundant imagery. A linguistic analysis of these artists' names, as was done by Padigar at Bādāmi, could possibly inform us whether these artists were also a mix of local and immigrant workers, a fact that would have important implications for development of style. Was the style of the period primarily a local development or one subject to a constant influx of influences introduced by immigrant artists?

[12] Mishra (1975: 39) stresses that although a scribe would be employed to compose an inscription, it was the artist, probably illiterate, who engraved it into the stone. This explains the occurence of errors in inscribed grants and charters. Translation of this inscription was given to me by S. V. Padigar.

[13] *Indian Antiquary* X(1881): 168.

[14] Moti Chandra, *Stone Sculpture in the Prince of Wales Museum,* Bombay, 1974, figs. 125-127.

Śrī Māṇdeva may have carved these excellent ceiling panels now kept in the Bombay Prince of Wales Museum, but he was not the architect of their temple at Aihoḷe, the Huchchapayya, which bears a remarkable inscription by its architect that reads 'Hail! There has not been and shall not be in [India] any wise man proficient in [the art of building] houses and temples equal to Narsobha.'[15] Another inscription at Aihoḷe near the Jain cave-temple refers to Narsobha as the disciple of Biñjadi, proficient in preparing temples, knowing the sacred texts and images, all according to proportion. He is further described as equal to the Sun god, Sūrya, in character. 'Śrī Narsobhanna made it' is also written on a rock nearby, next to a sketch of a temple which includes plumb lines. Two earlier Calukya temples also provide their architects' names: the Bādāmi Mālegitti temple was made by Āryamenci Upadhyaya, and the Nāganātha temple was the construction of Uṛa, Avuga, and Canda. (Signatures by architects are less frequent in all periods than the names of sculptors.)

The names of artists preserved in Calukya territory all are those of men, except one found on a gateway, carved with auspicious symbols, at Ittagi. One of its uprights gives the name of king Vinayāditya, thus dating the gate to his reign, *ca.* A.D. 681-96. The other pillar lists the names of four artists, one of whom is a woman, Śrīmatī Aṇagam.[16] This is a remarkable occurence, unique, to my knowledge, in the realm of ancient Indian stonework. Although other women may have worked on temples as craftswomen, this is the only female signature surviving.

Paṭṭadakal is also rich in inscriptional information about architects and artists. Śrī Guṇḍa is referred to as the architect who 'made the temple of the Queen of Vikramāditya II'[17] in an inscription on the eastern gateway of the courtyard of the Virūpākṣa temple, which also states that the temple was constructed for Queen Lokamahādevī to commemorate her husband's conquest of Kāñcī, the Pallava capital. Guṇḍa is here described as he 'whose conversation is entirely perfect and refined, who has for his jeweled diadem and crest jewel the houses, vehicles, seats, and couches [that he constructed].' He is called the '*sūtradhāri*' of the southern country, given the title 'maker of the three

[15] *Indian Antiquary* IX (1880): 74, no. 62.

[16] M. S. Nagaraja Rao, *Progress of Archaeology in Karnataka 1956-72,* Mysore, 1978, pp. 31, 38-9.

[17] *Indian Antiquary* X (1881): 164, notes 6-10.

worlds,' and honored three times by a certain ceremony. He has the title of 'Sarva Siddha *ācārya,*' which is probably the name of a guild of architects.

Another member of this guild is hailed in an inscription on the east face of the Pāpanātha temple at Paṭṭadakal. Caṭṭare Revadi Ovajja is described as 'one who decorated the whole southern country with his temples' or, alternately, 'one who decorated the southern side of the temple.'[18] He is said to have been acquainted with the Śrī Śilēmuddas, who are thought to have been a guild of local stonemasons. The southern side of many temples has sculpture distinct in quality from the northern side and the southern wall of a temple gets strong sunlight throughout the day, enlivening the sculpture with shadow, making this the side that perhaps would be preferred by the master artist. I therefore prefer reading *'tanaka desi'* as 'southern side.' We know that groups of artists worked on the images of large temples, as is verified by the many inscribed names of artists. That the master sculptor might have preferred the southern side is an interesting sidenote on his aesthetic consciousness.

Throughout the history of Indian art, duplicate images occur. For example, a famous image of standing Buddha commissioned by a Buddhist monk named Bala in the first or second century A.D. was virtually repeated in a figure found at Maholi near Mathurā.[19] Perhaps the monk commissioned two copies from the same artist (though the Maholi figure is not inscribed) or, perhaps, seeing the first, he requested a copy. A similar example, in my opinion, are two images of Viṣṇu each still *in situ* on Calukya temples *ca.* twelve miles from one another, that were carved in the late seventh century. They are not precisely identical, but show greater similarities in style as well as iconography than any other two surviving Calukya images known to me. The two temples, the Lāḍ Khān at Aihoḷe and the Mallikārjuna temple at Mahākūṭa, both seem to have been built around A.D. 680. I assume that one artist carved both, though neither is inscribed with the name of an artist.

Another image on the Mahākūṭa Mallikārjuna temple is unusual and distinctive in that it does not represent an idealized god, but a realistic portrayal of a wise man. This iconography is quite rare, but does occur again *ca.* ninety miles southeast on a contemporary temple at

[18] J. F. Fleet, *Indian Antiquary* X (1881): 170, fn. 58.

[19] Stanislaw Czuma, *Kushan Sculpture: Images from Early India,* Cleveland, 1986, p. 28, figs. 2, 3.

Sandūr, within Calukya territory. I assume one artist carved both, on the basis of their distinctiveness and similarity. A further image of this sage, however, whom I have identified as Agastya, is carved in miniature at Ajaṇṭā within the monastery cave no. 20 (dated *ca.* A.D. 475-90). There he stands, with his mustache, bald head, staff, and pot belly, beside a seated couple carved on a doorjamb (Bolon 1982: fig. 31). This earlier occurence, during another dynastic period (Vākāṭaka), at a more northerly site, provokes a desire for an explanation. There are many possibilities. It does not seem to be a coincidental or a random repetition of iconography. If the artists involved were not related by family, a descendent of the earlier artist having migrated toward the south, then at least the Calukya artist must have seen or otherwise been aware of the Ajaṇṭā Agastya type through some portable version of it. In Indian art history, we must always be conscious of the large numbers of lost images that once must have existed and also of the profound effect cultural sharing within language areas must have had, as recently given substantial exposition by Tartakov and Dehejia (1985).

The ties of Calukya sculpture to earlier styles and iconography in fact do adhere to a region within apparent cultural borders. Along the west coast and to the north, for example, there are iconographic ties to images, such as the 'Descent of the Gaṅgā' at Elephanta, which can be compared to the nearly contemporary relief with the same subject and rare iconography at Aihoḷe in the Rāvaṇa Phaḍi cave-temple. This iconographic formula, with busts of the three rivers above Śiva's hair, can also be found north of Elephanta at Mandasor.

Regarding the two Calukya images of Agastya, I would conclude that, as near twins in iconography, style, and date and as the only two such representations within this period, they were made by a single artist. Similarity with the earlier image at Ajaṇṭā should cautiously be ascribed to cultural sharing across this region over the two intervening centuries.

From the recurrence of near duplicate images on different Calukya temples, one further senses the economics behind their creation. Many details recur on temples: pillar designs, doorway designs, windows, beam patterns, ceilings. These have been classified by George Michell, who believes that such 'standard parts' were part of a temple's 'specifications order' filled by a workshop. Artists possibly were asked by a patron to repeat certain images he had seen elsewhere, or, alternatively, artists may, if rarely, have repeated images from one to the next temple on which they were commissioned to work.

Within the Calukya period, architecturally, there also are nearly duplicate temples. These sometimes stood at the same site (for example the Mallikārjuna and the Mahākuṭeśvara at Mahākuṭa, Ālampur's Svarga Brahmā and Garuḍa Brahmā, Bādāmi's Upper and Lower Śivālaya; Paṭṭadakal's Virūpākṣa temple and the smaller Mallikārjuna to its side) or at distant sites (Ālampur's Viśva Brahmā and Paṭṭadakal's Galaganātha) (Bolon forthcoming). These are in all cases near contemporaries, and in most cases have similar, if not identical, iconographic programs. This suggests that both temples may have been commissioned, designed, and constructed simultaneously. At Paṭṭadakal, we know that the Virūpākṣa and Mallikārjuna temples were commissioned by two queens, the senior queen patronizing the construction of the larger of the two temples. A similar double commission may explain the existence of other twin temples. Building two temples at once would certainly have been more efficient in labor and time and probably more economical than separate commissions. The recognition of such practical aspects helps us, perhaps, to enter into the historical ambiance surrounding the construction of these great temples.

One can, I believe, follow the hand of a single artist from one temple to the next, as in the case of Baladeva and Māṇdeva, yet, overall, each temple site does have its own distinctive predominating sculptural substyle, however, and distinct architectural characteristics as well. It seems obvious, therefore, that some direct interchange between sites has occurred when one sees the Aihoḷe sculpture style 200 miles away on the Kūḍavēlli Saṅgameśvara temple in Āndhra, for example, or when architecturally twin temples standing at Ālampur in Āndhra and at Paṭṭadakal in Karnāṭadeśa (Bolon 1986).

The more intimate our understanding of the working methods and style parameters of individual artists becomes, the more accurate our appreciation of ancient Indian art can become. While our familiarity with ancient Indian artists is unlikely ever to approach the completeness of the record found in various areas of Western art, it certainly can become more informed than currently is the case, and the search for new evidence can provide us a rich new ground to explore.

## Bibliography

Bolon, Carol Radcliffe. 'The Durga Temple, Aihole, and the Saṅgameśvara Temple, Kūdavelli: A Sculptural Review.' *Ars Orientalis* 15 (1986): 47-64.

_________. 'The Pārvatī Temple, Sandur, and Early Images of Agastya.' *Artibus Asiae* XLII (1982): 303-26.

_________. 'Reconstructing Galaganātha.' In M. S. Nagaraja Rao, ed., *Śivaramamūrti Memorial Volume.* (forthcoming).

Boner Alice. 'Economic and Organizational Aspects of Building Operation of the Sun Temple at Konarak.' *Journal of Economic and Social History of the Orient* XIII (1970): 257-72.

Boner, Alice and Sadasiva Rath Sarma with Rajendra Prasad Das. *New Light on the Sun Temple of Konaraka.* Varanasi, 1972.

Boner, Alice and Sadasiva Rath Sarma, tr. *Śilpa Prakāsa by Ramacandra Kaulacara.* Leiden, 1966.

Buchanan, S. 'Calukyan Temples: History and Iconography.' Ph.D. diss., Ohio State University, 1985.

Chatham, Doris. 'Pratihāras from Pattadakal to Ellora, The Early Western Calukyan Basis for the Sculptural Style of the Kailāsa Temple.' In *Chhavi II,* 71-79. Benaras, 1981.

Del Bonta, Robert. 'The Hoysaḷa Style: Architectural Development and Artists, 12th and 13th Centuries A.D.' Ph.D. diss., University of Michigan, 1978.

Goswamy, B. N. 'Pahari Painting: The Family as the Basis of Style.' *Marg* 21/4 (1968): 17-57.

Gupta, S. P. ed. *Kushana Sculptures from Sanghol (1st-2nd Century A.D.) A Recent Discovery,* Vol. 1. New Delhi, 1985.

Kramrisch, Stella. 'Artist, Patron, and Public in India' (1956), 'Traditions of the Indian Craftsman' (1958), reprinted in *Exploring India's Sacred Art,* edited by Barbara Stoler Miller, 51-68. Philadelphia 1983.

Michell, George. *Early Western Cāḷukyan Temples.* London, 1975.

__________. *The Hindu Temple.* London, 1978.

Misra, R. N. *Ancient Artists and Art-Activity.* Simla, 1975.

__________. 'Artists of Ḍāhala and Dakṣiṇa Kosala: A Study Based on Epigraphs.' In *Indian Epigraphy: Its Bearing on the History of Art,* edited by Frederick Asher and G. S. Gai, 185-90. Delhi, 1985.

Narasimha Murthy, A. V. 'A Study of the Label Inscriptions of the Hoysaḷa Sculptors.' In Asher and Gai, 215-20.

Padigar, S. V. 'Note on a Pattadakal Inscription.' *Quarterly Journal of the Mythic Society* 76 (1985): 247-50.

Radcliffe, Carol. 'Early Chalukya Sculpture.' Ph.D. diss., New York University, 1981.

Sivaramamurti, C. *Royal Conquests and Cultural Migration in South India and the Deccan.* Calcutta, 1955.

Seshadri, M. 'Sculptors and Architects of Ancient and Medieval Karnataka.' *Half-Yearly Journal of the Mysore University* 29-30 (1970): 1-10.

Settar, S. 'Peregrination of Medieval Artists.' *Journal of Indian History Golden Jubilee Volume,* (1973): 419-35.

Tartakov, Gary and Vidya Dehejia. 'Sharing, Intrusion, and Influence: The Mahiṣāsuramardinī Imagery of the Calukyas and the Pallavas.' *Artibus Asiae* XLV (1985): 287-345.

# Suitable Patterning and the Indian Dyer

Mattiebelle Gittinger
Textile Museum, Washington D.C.

An examination of Indian textile patterning as preserved in actual patterned cottons allows one to sketch, albeit broadly, a temporal sequence of pattern change from the fourteenth-fifteenth into the second half of the seventeenth century. Slightly later textiles from the eighteenth century suggest that the Indian dyer, himself, was keenly aware of this 'progression' and that it was a factor in his decision-making process concerning what was suitable patterning within a given context. There is also a strong suggestion in the patterns that the dyer chose to make that textile patterning was a subtle means of communication within its original societal context, going beyond the function of decoration alone.

The textiles regarded here are those of plain-weave cotton with patterns affected by wax or mud resists, mordants, and dyes. The medium is significant because, once mastered, it imposes few restraints on design in contrast to woven patterns, which are of necessity ordered by the warp and weft.[1]

The earliest Indian cotton textiles that remain are fragments from the site of Fustat, the former Egyptian capital south of Cairo (Figs. A-E). Once a rich center of trade, the city declined when the capital was shifted to the north. Excavations at the end of the last century and subsequent archaeological work in this and other Egyptian sites have uncovered a significant number of patterned cotton fragments that were originally made in Gujarat in the fourteenth and fifteenth centuries (Lamb 1937).[2]

Even though these fragments are of inferior quality, being worked from coarsely spun and woven cotton fibers, they speak to questions of the technology and design-types of that period. They show the stamping and drawing of resists, the stamping and direct application of mordants, the use of tannin, and dyeing using shades of red and blue. A technical

[1] A more detailed explanation of the means employed by Indians to pattern cotton may be found in Schwartz 1956, Irwin and Brett 1970, and Gittinger 1982.

[2] A precise dating of these fragments is impossible at this time.

and stylistic detail not in evidence, but one that can be seen in later patterning, is that of outlining forms with a freely drawn iron mordant. This may still have been a skill in Western India at this time, however, but used in association with more expensive textiles than those found at Fustat. A more extensive range of dyes was also surely available, but not expended on these coarsely worked trade cottons.

The design elements and stylistic features found among these textiles are extremely varied, but some conventions prevail. The entire cloth surface is covered with design elements that frequently are ordered by geometric repetition. Major design fields are frequently defined by multiple guard stripes that also serve to separate framing borders filled by contrasting design elements. The design-elements have many sources. Some, such as stick dancers and mythological animals like the *gajasiṃha,* have an origin in western Indian art. Others imitate patterns found in tooled leather, Chinese ceramics, or other more expensive textile forms such as velvets and tie-dye. Many design elements arise from plant forms, flowers, tendrils, leaves, or entire trees. None of these floral elements is specific; they rather are generic statements of 'flower' or 'leaf.' This type of floral interpretation is also a feature of miniature painting in western India in this period.

This generic statement of floral form undergoes a profound change at the beginning of the seventeenth century. As Robert Skelton has pointed out (1972: 147 ff.), there suddenly appears at this time a new textile patterning convention of a realistically rendered floral form regularly spaced on a plain ground. He attributes this to Emperor Jahangir's great love of the flowers of Kashmir and to European herbals thought to have been given to the emperor.

This became a pattern type used for silks with complex technical structures and for cottons patterned by stamps and freely drawn mordants. The technical flexibility of the latter technique encouraged an accuracy of rendering and the inclusion of small details not easily achieved in the woven forms. This realism was used with dynamic effect on the tent walls and hangings of the Mughals' portable cloth cities and with studied charm on the fabrics used as clothing.

The attention to detail demanded by replicating botanical sources seems to have had an effect on other designs drawn with mordants on the cottons of this period. Details, which formerly had been hastily sketched — such as architectural features, furniture, vases, and floral forms, as those that can be seen in an early seventeenth-century curtain (14.719.1-7) now in the Brooklyn Museum (Gittinger 1982: 89-108;

Irwin 1959: 8 ff.) — become well drawn and well defined forms fifty years later, as can be seen in an Indian hanging now in the Victoria and Albert collection (Gittinger 1982: 112-13). Attention to detail and precision in draftsmanship became important criteria in the dyer's art in the course of this period.

This attention to detail led to a dissection of the floral form into its component parts of petals, sepals, pistils, and stamen, all of which became surfaces for varied decorative patterns. Over time, these structuring elements came to be reassembled in the imaginative and creative ways we now associate with chintz fashions popular in eighteenth-century Europe and which continue to be a source of design inspiration today.

This sequence of changing pattern seems to have been well known to the Indian dyer and influenced his concepts of what was suitable. Three quite remarkable textiles bear witness to this.

An Indian-made textile recently found in eastern Indonesia, now in the Museum for Textiles in Toronto, is a prime example. This textile, a detail of which is rendered in Fig. F, was probably made in Gujarat in the eighteenth century and entered into the trade for spices which flourished in the eastern archipelago at that time. It became a family heirloom and was preserved as a sacred textile, a not uncommon occurrence in Indonesia. Recent changes in values have caused some of these textiles to be sold, making them available for study for the first time. This example, approximately five meters long by one meter high, shows a striking row of Gujarati women engaged in a stick dance. The large figures, which fill the weft dimension, as well as the accompanying details of umbrellas, fans, and canopies, all relate directly in form and stylistic detail to illuminations in fifteenth-century manuscripts created in western India. These similarities include the sharply attenuated nose, protruding eye, exaggerated body posture, costume style, etc. Most important for this discussion, the patterns of the dancer's costumes are of the Fustat genre, not the realistic floral forms promoted by Mughal taste nor those of decorative chintz.

While the outlines of these figures appear to have been blocked, the selection of textile patterns worn by the figures on the Toronto textile was not dictated by carved stamps. The women's garments were patterned with freely drawn resists and the cloth was then vat-dyed in indigo. Pattern options available to the dyer were theoretically all of those outlined in the sequence traced in previous paragraphs, yet he reached back in time to match a fifteenth-century graphic style.

A second textile (Fig. G) that can speak to the question of 'suitable patterning' is a *kalamkārī* (no. 2221) in the collection of the Association pour l'Etude et la Documentation des Textiles d'Asie in Paris (Gittinger 1982: 121-27). Dating to *c.* 1660-80, the textile was probably made in the Madras region or an area somewhat to the south. The scenes depicted provide a rare glimpse of secular life in a Hindu court of South India, possibly of Tanjore or Madurai. Pictured in the upper register of the textile is a man, possibly a noble person, in dalliance with female attendants in his private apartments. In the lower section, a large ceremonial procession approaches an elegant chamber in which a man lounges, surrounded by attendants.

The style of the figures arises from the post Vijayanagar conventions developed under the Nāyak rulers of South India in the seventeenth century. Similar conventions are seen in a *Rāmāyaṇa* manuscript of 1725 which was drawn and painted in southern Andhra Pradesh (Mittal 1979). The contrast between the textile hanging and the manuscript, however, is startling. The manuscript artist invokes few textile patterns, while the *kalamkārī* artist clothes his forms with well articulated textile patterns remarkable in their precision.

With rare exception, the patterns depicted on the costumes are not each unique; rather there is a casual repetition of simple checks, stripes, zigzags, simple geometric forms, and an occasional floral repeat. Surprisingly, these are not deemed appropriate to a single sex: both men and women may use a common pattern.

Unique textile patterns are worn by the principal male shown in each major section of the hanging and a woman squeezed among companions in the third alcove on the lower left (Gittinger 1982: fig. 111). Her garment, which may not be a *sārī* as worn by the other women, shows a simple fret design. Why she has been singled out in this manner is not known. The costumes of the principal male seen lounging in three scenes in the upper register seem to be a *dhoti* draped with a large mantle.[3] The important equestrian in the lower right may wear a *jāma* over striped pajama with still another cloth wrapped about his hips. The patterns rendered on the *dhoti* and mantles are of intertwining floral vines and tendrils or schemetic 'blossoms' alternating in a grid pattern, the latter design not dissimilar to certain *paṭola* patterns. The rider's *jāma* shows small circles associated with tie-dye patterning.

[3] Lotika Varadarajan identifies this shoulder cloth as the *angavastram* in an article to be published by the Association pour l'Etude et la Documentation des Textiles d'Asie in 1986.

Patterns *not* worn by the principal figure are of equal significance. In no instance does the regularly repeated naturalistic flower associated with Mughal costume enter the costume of men depicted on the hanging, yet this mode was surely known to the dyers of the east coast at this time. The choice of pattern rendered in the *kalamkārī* may indicate that patterns could carry religious and political messages and that the floral scheme of Mughal inspiration was not suitable to the costume of a high ranking Hindu. This raises the hypothesis that we may look for meaning in the textile patterns rendered in hangings and miniatures, and expect to find a significance — an added message — in the selection that has been made.

A third textile (Fig. H) that illustrates how thoughtfully the Indian dyer clothed his forms is an altar curtain in the Armenian Cathedral of Saint James in Jerusalem. Made in Madras in 1733, the 7 x 5 m. hanging carries a large central figure of the Virgin Mary surrounded by twenty-four scenes from the life of Christ. The scenes, each framed in an architectural niche, include a wealth of human figures, delightfully rendered animals, and architectural details. The whole is embellished with minutely patterned surfaces, including richly patterned textiles.

The inspiration for the scenes on the curtain may be traced to the woodblock prints of Christoffel van Sichem, a seventeenth-century Dutch artist. Van Sichem's prints were used in the first printed Armenian Bible published in 1666 in Amsterdam. Later, these same blocks were reused in subsequent Armenian publications. The prosperous community of Armenians in Madras in the eighteenth century would surely have had copies of these and it is not surprising that they would serve as models for the curtain scenes.

In none of Van Sichem's works are the costumes patterned; they rather draw upon conventions of shading and the delineation of pleats and folds for visual interest. Therefore, while the Indian dyer used the formal scheme of the woodblock prints as a source for his compositions, he drew from his own traditions to affect the costume patterns. Some patterns rendered by the dyer seem to imitate velvet, striped fabrics are common, and there is a suggestion of *ikat* patterning. (The pattern rendered most frequently, however, defies convincing analysis and remains in question.)

Important to the present issue is the fact that the dyer of the curtain never clothes his forms with a Mughal floral scheme, nor with 'contemporary' designs (such as those suggested in the costumes worn by figures on the Paris *kalamkārī*), nor with the floral schemes being made at that time for trade to Europe. Surely all of these would have been known to a dyer having the skill and experience needed to work a *kalamkārī* of this importance. These patterns he obviously felt were not suitable to his subject.

The three hangings cited suggest that within the Indian context the patterning on costumes could often have a significance beyond that of decoration. Certain patterns were associated with particular time periods while others seem to have assumed a religious or political connotation that governed their use. We can hypothesize that the choice of a particular flower or form for a pattern could have been a means of communication, turning on a double entendre of name or legendary association. By further investigating the world of patterns, particularly in the rich field of manuscript illumination, we may find that the artist spoke with several vocabularies.

## Bibliography

Gittinger, Mattiebelle. *Master Dyers to the World: Technique and Trade in Early Indian Dyed Cotton Textiles.* Washington D.C., 1982.

Irwin, John. 'Golconda Cotton Paintings of the Early Seventeenth Century.' *Lalit Kala* 5 (1959): 8-48.

Irwin, John and Katherine B. Brett. *Origins of Chintz.* London, 1970.

Lamb, C. J. *Cotton in Medieval Textiles of the Near East.* Paris, 1937.

Mittal, Jagdish. *Andhra Paintings of the Ramayana.* Hyderabad, 1969.

Schwartz, P. R. 'French Documents on Indian Cotton Painting: (1) the Beaulieu Ms., 1734.' *Journal of Indian Textile History* 2 (1956): 5-23.

Skelton, Robert. 'A Decorative Motif in Mughal Art.' In *Aspects of Indian Art,* edited by P. Pal, 147-52. Leiden, 1972.

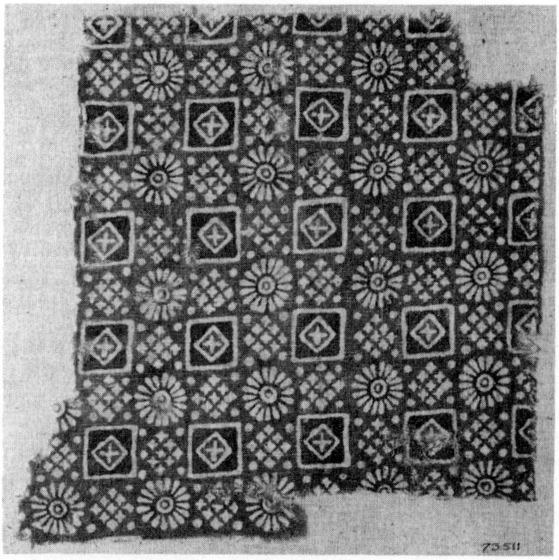

Fig. A.

An Indian-made cotton fragment found at Fustat, Egypt, patterned by stamped resists and two shades of blue dye. 25 x 26 cm. The Textile Museum, Washington D.C. (73.5111). *(Courtesy of the Textile Museum, Washington, D.C.)*

Fig. B.

An Indian-made cotton fragment found at Fustat, Egypt, patterned by stamped and drawn resists and blue dye. 50.5 x 31 cm. The Textile Museum, Washington D.C. (6.120). *(Courtesy of the Textile Museum, Washington, D.C.)*

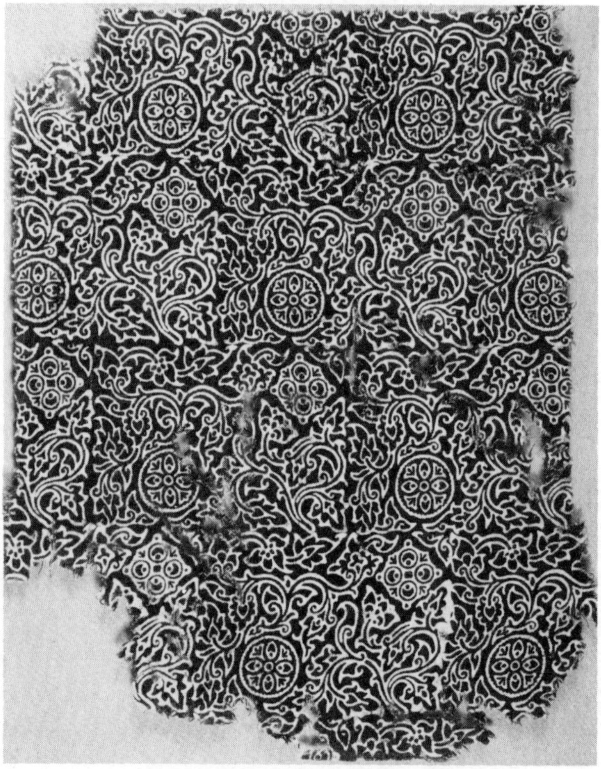

Fig. C.
An Indian-made cotton fragment found at Fustat, Egypt, patterned by stamped resists and blue dye. 37.5 x 46 cm. The Textile Museum, Washington D.C. (6.127). *(Courtesy of the Textile Museum, Washington, D.C.)*

Fig. D.
An Indian-made cotton fragment found at Fustat, Egypt, patterned by stamped resists and blue dye. 33 x 40 cm. The Textile Museum, Washington D.C. (73.232). *(Courtesy of the Textile Museum, Washington, D.C.)*

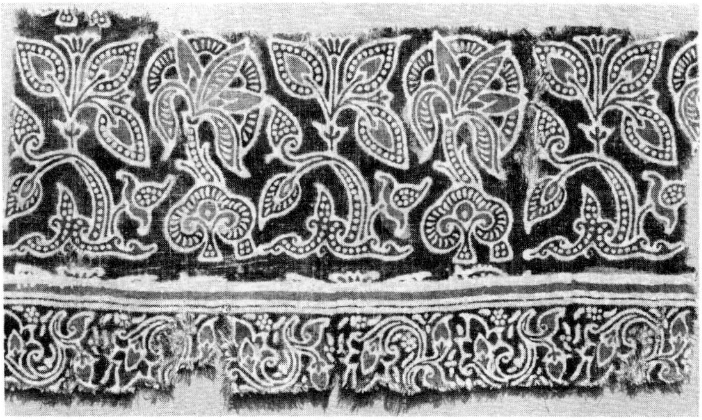

Fig. E.
An Indian-made cotton fragment found at Fustat, Egypt, patterned by stamped resists, painted mordant, red and blue dyes. 47 x 23.5 cm. The Textile Museum, Washington D.C. (73.200). *(Courtesy of the Textile Museum, Washington, D.C.)*

Fig. F.
A detail from a cotton hanging made in India and traded to Indonesia. The outlines of the figure were stamped, but details were drawn with resists and mordants. The colors are blue, red-brown, and black. 503 x 101 cm. Museum for Textiles, Toronto (R81.942).

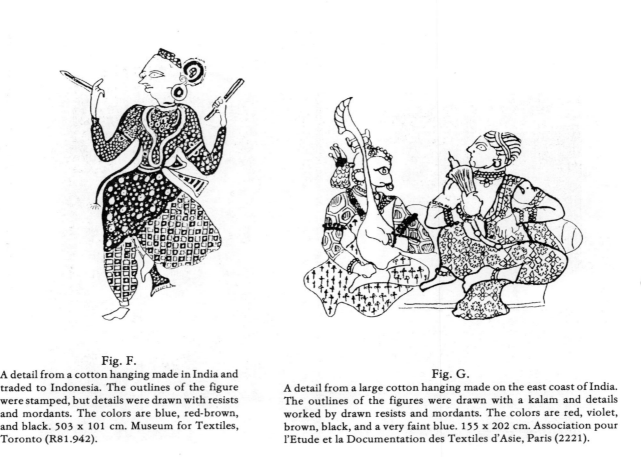

Fig. G.
A detail from a large cotton hanging made on the east coast of India. The outlines of the figures were drawn with a kalam and details worked by drawn resists and mordants. The colors are red, violet, brown, black, and a very faint blue. 155 x 202 cm. Association pour l'Etude et la Documentation des Textiles d'Asie, Paris (2221).

Fig. H.
A detail from a cotton curtain made in Madras in 1733. The outlines of the figures were drawn with a *kalam* and details worked by drawn resists and mordants. The colors are red, violet, brown, black, blue, yellow, green. Detail size approximately 73 x 83 cm. The Armenian Patriarchate, Jerusalem.

# The Mughal Artist

Milo Cleveland Beach
Center for Asian Art, Arthur M. Sackler Gallery,
Smithsonian Institution

One passage from the *Tūzuk-i-Jahāngīrī,* the official memoirs of the Mughal Emperor Jahāngīr (r. A.D. 1605-27), has been particularly influential in defining Mughal art for European and American art historians:

As regards myself, my liking for painting and my practice in judging it have arrived at such a point that when any work is brought before me, either of deceased artists or of those of the present day, without the names being told me, I say on the spur of the moment that it is the work of such and such a man. And if there be a picture containing many portraits, and each face be the work of a different master, I can discover which face is the work of each of them. If any other person has put in the eye and eyebrow of a face, I can perceive whose work the original face is, and who has painted the eye and eyebrows.[1]

The passage actually began by noting that:

On this day Abū-l-Hasan, the painter, who has been honoured with the title of Nādiru-z-zamān, drew the picture of my accession as the frontispiece to the Jahāngīr-nāma, and brought it to me. As it was worthy of all praise, he received endless favours. His work was perfect . . . .[2]

If this were not sufficient confirmation of Jahāngīr's interest in his painters, a portrait of the emperor inspecting a painting, probably in the presence of Abū'l Hasan, has recently been published.[3] (Other portraits of Mughal artists, a subject which was especially prominent during Jahāngīr's rule, have long been known.)[4] This textual stress on con-

[1] *The Tuzuk-i-Jahāngīrī or Memoirs of Jahāngīr,* ed. Henri Beveridge, trans. Alexander Rogers, Delhi (reprint), 1968, ii, 20-21.

[2] *ibid.*

[3] *A la Cour du Grand Moghol,* catalogue of an exhibition at the Bibliotheque Nationale, Paris, 1986, no. 8.

[4] See Beach 1978: figs. 4-13.

noisseurship and the importance of artistic individuality also coincided neatly with the established interests of twentieth-century art historians.

As the most complete statement of imperial involvement in artistic production, Jahāngīr's words have determined our attitudes towards patrons as well as artists. They reveal that Jahāngīr took delight in an ability to recognize the individual styles of his painters; that he, at least occasionally, spoke directly with painters; and that he rewarded artists for specific achievements. The implication, of course, is that imperial taste became the motivating force for painters, and this has resulted in extensive studies of Mughal painting that concentrate on the activities and personalities of the emperors. It has also produced an attitude best summed up by the following recent statements about Jahāngīr's father and predecessor, the Emperor Akbar (r. A.D. 1556-1605):

> Akbar was a realist .... In his studio he created a new form of reality in the world of painting .... Akbar inspired the painters who gave form to his vision. His genius worked through their sensitivity and craftsmanship .... Akbar's dynamism was given form by his painters ....[5]

One result of this attitude has been the attribution to Akbar directly of those elements of Mughal painting that seem particularly innovative within the context of Indian painting overall. Akbar, who was a prolific patron, has long been considered the first of the Mughal emperors significantly to be interested in the visual arts. There are now reasons to reassess the extent and character of innovations that can be attributed to the period of his reign, however, and this should spark reconsideration, both of his role as a patron, and of our understanding of Mughal patronage generally. Inevitably, this will force us also to reassess the range and importance of contributions made by painters themselves.

Akbar's father, Humāyūn (r. 1530-40; 1555-56), is far more important to the evolution of Mughal painting than has hitherto been acknowledged. Several works that can be reliably attributed to his reign are particularly important: the 'Princes of the House of Tīmūr,' probably by Abd as-Samad, *ca.* A.D. 1550 (with later additions), British Museum (1913.2-8.1);[6] 'Humāyūn and His Brothers in a Landscape,' probably by

5 Kramrisch 1986: xiv-xv.

6 The most recent discussion and color reproduction is in Welch 1985: no. 84.

Dust Muḥammad, *ca.* A.D. 1550, Staatsbibliothek, Berlin;[7] 'Prince Akbar Presenting a Painting to Humāyūn in a Tree-House,' by Abd as-Samad, *ca.* 1555, Former Imperial Library, Tehran;[8] 'Prince Akbar Kills a Nilgae,' *ca.* A.D. 1555, Fitzwilliam Museum, Cambridge (72.1948),[9] that depicts an event which occured on Humāyūn's arrival in Delhi in 1555 when the young Akbar killed a *nilgāe* (antelope), and its meat was saved for his father, who had temporarily renounced eating flesh;[10] 'Portrait of a Young Scribe,' by Mīr Sayyid Alī, *ca.* A.D. 1555, Collection of Edwin Binney III;[11] and 'Portrait of Abu'l-ma'alī,' probably by Dust Muḥammad, *ca.* A.D. 1556, Collection of Prince Sadruddin Aga Khan,[12] which as a work by a painter known to have been in Humāyūn's employ and the subject, one of Humāyūn's favorite courtiers — a youth who rebelled against Akbar three days after his accession — is a portrait that certainly reflects Humāyūn's interests and not those of his son.

Each of these six images depicts an historical occasion or personality and shows an intense interest in recording aspects of daily life. Such subjects should therefore no longer be considered Akbari innovations, a fact that can be confirmed also by literary sources. The *Qānun-i-Humāyūnī* of Khwandamīr, for example, is subtitled by the translator 'a work on the rules and ordinances established by the Emperor Humāyūn and on some buildings erected by his order.' As an historical account of the character of life at the court, it is an important prototype for the *Akbar-nāma* and *Ā'īn-i-Akbarī* of Abū'l Faẓl. A second history of Humāyūn's reign, written by Jauhar, is even more interesting in regard

[7] Welch 1985: no. 85.

[8] Laurence Binyon, J. V. S. Wilkinson, and Basil Gray, *Persian Miniature Painting,* London, 1933, pl. CIVb.

[9] Brand and Lowry 1985: no. 7.

[10] See Abū'l Faẓl 'Allami, *Akbar-nāma,* trans. H. Beveridge, Delhi (reprint), 1972, i. 634. This painting comes from the 'Fitzwilliam Album,' which has been fully published in Beach, *Early Mughal Painting* (1987). Two calligraphies in the volume also suggest Humāyūn period patronage: one is signed by Muḥammad Amīn Qazwīnī (who is known to have left Persia for India at this time), while a second is dated H. 953=1546-47, with additional information that it was painted 'in the capital of the Kingdom, *dar al-Sultanat,* Kabul.' This was Humāyūn's headquarters in that year.

[11] Brand and Lowry 1985: no. 6.

[12] *Ibid.,* no. 81.

to painting specifically. It recounts an episode in which Humāyūn captured a bird and ordered his painters to paint its portrait.[13] This narrative of an event in A.D. 1542 introduces a category of subject matter — that of natural history — that became a major interest to Jahāngīr more that sixty years later. In his fourteenth regnal year (A.D. 1619-20), for example, Jahāngīr recorded the gift of a falcon and noted that he 'ordered Ustād Mansūr who has the title of *Nādiru-l-'asr* (wonder of the age) to paint and preserve its likeness.'[14] Typically, he records the name and title of the painter as scrupulously as he had wanted the artist to document the bird.

While this account of a captured bird is the only reference to painting in Jauhar's text, there is no suggestion that the episode was in any way unusual. There are other passages in histories of Humāyūn's reign that help further to build a sense of the emperor's interest in painting, however. Khwandamīr mentions the *Bisat-i-Nishat* (Carpet of Mirth), a round carpet with astrological significance. He continues:

> Sometimes while people were seated . . . they used to throw dice on various sides of which figures of persons in different postures were painted by the creative pen; and whichever figure turned up on the throw from the hand of a person, he assumed the same position in his circle . . . if the reclining position turned up, he lay down and even went to sleep.[15]

In another passage, the same author describes a moveable palace made of wood:

> This marvellously decorated palace was adorned in various colours by the most skillful painters . . . [and] the chamberlains of the throne, the nest of religion, had covered it with curtains of seven colours, made of cloths from Khotan, Turkey, and Europe.[16]

These references to European textiles are frequent; in Khwandamīr alone we read specifically of European *kimkhabs* (brocades), woolen

[13] Jauhar, *The Tezkereh al Vākiat,* trans. Major Charles Stewart, New Delhi (reprint), 1970, p. 43.

[14] Beveridge, ii. 108.

[15] Khwandamīr, *Qānun-i-Humāyūnī,* trans. Baini Prasad, Calcutta, 1940, p. 81.

[16] *Ibid.,* p. 46.

cloths, and velvets[17] that seem to have been lavishly displayed. One typical reference describes the marriage feast of Mīrzā Hindal:

The nobles and the ministers built *Chahar Taqs* (a type of tent) in the royal garden .... They were adorned with Turkish and European cloths, and with embroidered and seven coloured cloths. The artists and tradesmen decorated all the streets, while the shops were so beautifully adorned as to be the envy of the Chinese picture galleries ....[18]

In a separate account of this event, Gulbadan Begam, Humāyūn's aunt, refers specifically to 'Portugese cloth' among the decorations;[19] but equally interesting is her reference to China. Such phrases are known, too, in Akbari annals. At the death of Daswanth, Akbar's favorite painter, for example, the *Akbar-nāma* states that 'his paintings were not behind those of Bīhzad and the painters of China.'[20] Thus, not only is one of the standards of excellence for painters in the Akbar period based on established Humāyūn-period criteria, but Humāyūn himself was clearly a cosmopolitan connoisseur in touch with distant regions of both Asia and Europe. The more that is learned of Humāyūn period painting, the more it seems certain that his artists were aware of European and Chinese images. (It has already been suggested elsewhere that Akbar's artists may have had contact with European prints before the emperor himself found them of interest.[21] Here, too, we must question assertions that it was Akbar who provoked the mixture of styles from which Mughal painting evolved.

This placement in the Humāyūn period for interests long thought to have been initiated by Akbar suggests that we may have somewhat misunderstood both patrons, but it need not change our ideas about patronage in general. For these we must examine how painters worked. Though we have few contemporary references for this, paintings themselves are particularly informative.

17 *Ibid.,* pp. 37, 46, 49 and 64-65.

18 *Ibid.,* pp. 64-65.

19 Gulbadan Begam, *Humāyūn-nāma,* trans. Annette S. Beveridge, Delhi, 1972, p. 129.

20 *Akbar-nāma,* iii. 651.

21 Milo C. Beach, 'A European Source for Early Mughal Painting,' *Oriental Art* 22.2 (1976): 180-88.

Mughal painting distinguishes itself as a tradition from Safavid Iranian painting as well as from contemporary Indian styles particularly be the presence of historical subject matter. Daily events of the court and portraits of leading personalities inevitably have been cited as new and distinctive subjects for artists. While individual portraiture of a type very close to Mughal works of the early Akbar period was known in Safavid Iran,[22] painting as a chronicle of actual events was certainly newly emphasized in Mughal India. However, for painters, no major change was necessary. Even the painting, 'Prince Akbar Kills a Nilgāe,' mentioned above, has been based on a well established compositional type (repeated for a quite different purpose in the great *Ḥamza-nāma* manuscript begun for Akbar about A.D. 1562).[23] Painters used familiar formulas for hunting or battle scenes, for example, whether the literary reference for the scene was historical (as in the scene of Akbar hunting) or purely imaginary (*e.g.,* the *Ḥamza-nāma*). Moreover, close examination of the first known illustrated *Akbar-nāma* manuscript (of about A.D. 1590 or earlier) shows that the specific events illustrated are frequently reworkings of scenes 'recording' quite different events in the earliest known historical manuscript, the *Tīmūr-nāma* of about A.D. 1580. It is possible to propose, therefore, that painters conceived scenes according to a repertoire of types (*e.g.,* the siege of a fortress, crossing a river, an audience or battle scene). When specific subjects were assigned in volumes such as the *Akbar-nāma,* most artists went first to these established compositional types, which they reworked or adapted, with minor modifications. Change came slowly, and within these accepted procedures.

This suggests that tradition exerted great control over what was painted — which is hardly surprising. With this in mind, we should reconsider another frequently cited passage in the *Ā'īn-i-Akbarī* Akbar's historical chronicle. The author is discussing painting specifically:

His majesty, from his earliest youth, has shown a great predilection for this art, and gives it every encouragement .... Hence, the art flourishes, and many

[22] See especially Stuart C. Welch, *Wonders of the Age,* Cambridge, Mass., 1979, nos. 72 and 80. Idealism in Iranian portraiture seems to have been misunderstood. Usually presented as a trait of the overall tradition, idealism and realism may instead be functions of the social statements being made in the work, or of the level or purpose of the patronage. By limiting concern to the highest imperial levels of quality, therefore, scholars have produced a very limited understanding of the overall tradition.

[23] *Ḥamza-nāma* (facsimile), Graz, 1982, vol. 2, plate 27.

painters have obtained great reputation. The works of all painters are weekly laid before His Majesty by the Daroghas and the clerks; he then confers rewards according to excellence of workmanship, or increases the monthly salaries.[24]

It is important, but so far unnoted, that there is no evidence here that Akbar spoke directly with painters. While this is precisely what is indicated in the passage from Jahāngīr's memoirs cited above, we cannot honestly make the same assertion about Akbar's involvement with artists. Tradition, therefore, may have been more important than imperial will in determining the character of Mughal works of the Akbar period.

Painters usually created new compositions only when no prototypes existed, and only a few artists were capable of such invention. Just as painters were controlled by tradition, so too their work was coordinated by the increasingly hierarchic organization of the imperial studios. Manuscripts made before about A.D. 1580 have a distinctive individual character, but no overall unity, and this suggests that the imperial workshops were not yet under the tight control of a single master artist. During the Lahore period (A.D. 1585-98), however, illustrations for all manuscripts were standardized. While we can recognize individual artist's styles during these years, the styles of workshop directors — those men who controlled directly how and what painters painted — become equally important. Their power to control the assignment of subjects and the character of style is evident.

Many forces were therefore at work, and paintings can be as informative about individual painters' styles as they are about the direction given by project directors or the taste of patrons. In the period of Jahāngīr's rule (A.D. 1605-27), manuscripts became less important than individual pictures, suggesting that the complex organization of the painting studios was no longer so necessary. In fact, Jahāngīr, with his personal involvement, may have functioned effectively as the head of the studio. This would, however, have been a unique situation, hardly typical of Mughal painting as a whole.

It is essential, therefore, that we recognize the role that painters, as well as artistic tradition, played in the evolution of Mughal style, and to do this properly we need to know far more about the organization of artistic workshops than we currently know. We should not associate the power and visibility of emperors with an ability to override the force of

[24] Abū'l Faẓl 'Allami, *Ā'īn-i-Akbarī,* Calcutta, 1939, iii. 113.

tradition nor assume that they could make the kinds of artistic decisions that remain the province of artists alone.[25]

## Bibliography


Beach, Milo Cleveland. *Early Mughal Painting.* Cambridge, Mass., 1987.

__________. *The Grand Mogul: Imperial Painting in India — 1600-1660.* Williamstown, Mass., 1978.

Brand, Michael and Glenn D. Lowry. *Akbar's India.* New York, 1985.

Brown, Percy. *Indian Painting Under the Mughals.* Oxford, 1924.

Chandra, Pramod. *The Ṭūṭī-nāma of the Cleveland Museum of Art and the Origins of Mughal Painting.* Graz, 1976.

Kramrisch, Stella. *Painted Delight.* Philadelphia, 1985.

Simpson, Marianna Shreve. 'The Production and Patronage of the *Haft Aurang* of Jami in the Freer Gallery of Art.' *Ars Orientalis* XIII (1982): 93-119.

Welch, Stuart Cary. *The Art of Mughal India.* New York, 1963.

__________. *India!* New York, 1985.


[25] The ideas expressed in this talk are discussed more fully in my *Early Mughal Painting* (1987).

# Itinerant Kashmiri Artists: Notes on the Spread of a Style

Karuna Goswamy
Chandigarh, India

A major problem in Indian art is that of diffusion. While most of us have adopted, for the sake of convenience, dynastic or regional labels to describe styles, there are always odd works — sculpture, paintings, or monuments — that keep sticking out uncomfortably because they do not fit necessarily into a region, if region is taken as the basis of style, or into a period, if styles are spoken of in terms of chronology alone.

Classification raises endless problems, and it is seldom possible to develop a consistent pattern. This is certainly the case in Indian painting, and apparently also the case in sculpture. If we have a situation in which works in a more or less similar style turn up from areas which are very far removed from each other either in point of time or in point of date some explanation needs to be found.

Of late one of the explanations that has started receiving wide and serious notice is that of artists that migrate from one region and settle down in another.[1] Such patterns of migration are difficult to establish and factual data are rather slender. Whatever has come out, however, especially in a field such as painting with which I concern myself most of the time, is exceedingly interesting. We have an impressive body of evidence, even if illustrative rather than exhaustive, in which we see families of artists that split at certain points of time — their members having learned to work in the same style together — deciding to leave their home to settle elsewhere, to pursue their craft at a different court in a different region.

Members of one Pahārī family of artists — that of Pandit Seu — for instance, have clearly been demonstrated to have worked not only at Guler (which was their family home) but also in Basohlī, Nūrpur,

[1] A conference held at Gwalior in 1981 addressed itself to precisely this question in the context of the development of regional styles in Indian sculpture. Attended as it was by art historians, sociologists, archaeologists, and historians, it brought different perspectives to the question. The proceedings of this conference which was held at the Jiwaji University are, however, yet to be published.

Chambā, Kāngra, and even in distant Lahore and Garhwāl.[2] For this kind of migration we also have historical antecedents. One hears of artists that migrated from Gujarat into Rajasthan and Central India, as Stella Kramrisch has recorded.[3] At an earlier time we hear of a large number of artists from outside who settled in Tibet and Ladakh.[4] Professor Tucci has recorded a tradition (and taken pains to document) that the style of Tibet in the western region at one point was influenced by the importation of Kashmiri artists invited by the Tibetan ruler in order to produce paintings and sculptures for his monastries.[5]

There are other bits of evidence, I am sure, from other regions and other times, that would also lead us to the conclusion that migrations among artists were quite common.

Artists moved from one place to another — with what frequency we cannot say — and carried with them the style that they had been groomed from childhood to work in. This must be our best explanation for the appearance of a particular kind of work at a place where we did not expect it to be.

I wish to draw attention particularly to a further possibility I have considered in the work I have been doing in the area of Kashmiri painting. I refer to artists who do not migrate permanently or semi-permanently but who are professionally itinerant, making their living *through* being on the move. While working on Kashmiri painting, an area that to my regret is little known and rather poorly understood in terms

[2] See B. N. Goswamy (1968). The spread of the style of this family of artists seems, interestingly, to have been graphically represented through the figure of a many-armed goddess spreading her hands in different directions, as if she were a spider weaving a fine cobweb.

[3] The connections between the craft traditions of these three contiguous areas are far better explained through these movements across space. One sees this especially in the metalwork and woodwork in all the three areas spoken of here.

[4] These migrations go back to the eleventh and twelfth centuries according to traditional Kashmiri sources.

[5] Giuseppe Tucci (1949).

of its quality,[6] I came upon the phenomenon (almost a pattern) that, while it was easy to identify the broad Kashmiri style, I kept on turning up works in the same style in places that were quite far removed from Kashmir.

Kashmiri paintings are essentially illustrations to texts, mostly occuring either at the beginning of chapters or of new texts within the same bound volumes *(gutkā)* and were found frequently in works in association with different scripts.[7] This was somewhat puzzling. I came upon Kashmiri style illustrations in Sanskrit texts inscribed as having been executed in Varanasi on the one hand as well as in texts in Śāradā on the other hand.[8] I even found one text in Pushto with Kashmiri illustrations (in the Victoria Memorial Library, Calcutta, but obviously made somewhere in the Afghan region).[9] There were also works in Persian, apparently made in Kashmir itself (illustrations to the *Shāhnāmeh,* the *Gulistān,* or a Persian version of the *Mahābhārata,* the *Rāmāyana,* etc.).

In the plains of Panjab there are a large number of manuscripts that turn up almost everywhere: in the collections of local pandits, in temples or monastic establishments, or even with well-to-do people who pos-

[6] There is scarcely a book on Kashmiri painting that one can find, and whatever has been published of Kashmiri painting so far has been so indifferent in quality that it almost seems to deserve the reputation that it has. However, some distinguished work in Kashmiri style was done right into the nineteenth century and the reputation of Kashmiri painting needs to be examined in the light not of routine work, but of its best products. I have seen some quite remarkable Kashmiri paintings in the collections of the National Museum, New Delhi, the Shri Pratap Singh Museum, Srinagar, and of the late Dr. Alice Boner.

[7] One has only to examine a major collection like that of the National Museum, New Delhi, to discover the range of works, in different scripts, that contained illustrations in the Kashmiri style. From large-sized *Janam sakhis* in Gurmukhi, to medium-sized *Shāhnāmeh* illustrations in Persian, to truly tiny, pocket-sized *gutkā*-type prayer books in Sanskrit one finds Kashmiri artists contributing to these. When one sees a small compendium of texts, for daily recitation like the *Bhagavata Gita,* the *Viṣṇu Sahastranam,* the *Gajendramokṣa,* the *Śiva Mahimnastotra* all bound together in one handwritten volume, one almost naturally assumes that the illustrations would be in a Kashmiri hand.

[8] Reference unavailable.

[9] Interestingly, I chanced upon a Pushto manuscript with Kashmiri illustrations also in the Historical Museum at Bern in Switzerland. That manuscript had come in a group with a Swiss traveler of the nineteenth century who toured Afghanistan.

sessed and kept manuscripts for their own private needs.[10] In the collections of many libraries in the Panjab and Harayana, and at several places in Himachal which I have had occasion to visit, one turns up manuscripts in a fairly similar, even sometimes identical, style.[11] The spatial extent over which this style spreads (if one can term it a unified style) is quite impressive. And this may only be a part of the evidence. From Afghanistan in the northwest to Banaras is no small distance, nor is the distance from the plains of Harayana around Kurukshetra and Kaithal to the valley of Kashmir. The explanation for this spread of a style does not seem to me simply the migration of artists, but rather their professional itinerancy.

The explanation for this phenomenon lies, perhaps, in the footloose nature of Kashmiris as a community; among them there is a well-known tradition of being on the move in order to make a livelihood. In the world of scribes and calligraphy, this tradition has already been documented and published.[12]

Pandit Sthanu Dutt, a learned Sanskrit scholar of Kurukshetra, has said that he remembers from his childhood (at the turn of this century) that practically every year, in the village to which he belonged, a small group of three or four persons, all Kashmiris, would arrive with little bags *(bastās)* slung from their shoulders. They would enter the precincts of the village and give out a shout, like a hawker's, saying *'Kātib, Kātib'* (meaning 'scribes') to announce that the scribes have arrived. Occasionally, the group was even larger, consisting of four or five persons: the shout that then went up as they entered the village was *'Kātib mai Mussavvir'* meaning 'scribes, together with a painter.' These professional

10 In the small district of Gurdaspur alone, I have seen manuscripts with Kashmiri illustrations at numerous places, ranging from the large Vaiṣṇava establishments at Pindori and Damtal to the relatively small but influential Śaiva establishment at Jakhbar, and the private possession of minor *jyotiṣis* and priests at local temples with no major influence. This situation, one can be certain, obtained elsewhere also throughout this region.

11 The Panjab University Library at Chandigarh, the Kurukshetra University Library at Kurukshetra, and the Dogra Art Gallery at Jammu possess manuscripts with Kashmiri work in some numbers. In Himachal Pradesh, I have consulted manuscripts in the collections of Sir Nathu Ram at Nurpur, Pandit Bhudev Shastri at Sujanpur, Sri Priyavrat of Wazir family at Mandi, etc.

12 See B. N. Goswamy (1971).

scribes came to the village and offered to copy any manuscript for a negligible fee. Anyone who wanted a manuscript copied would ask the scribe to stay, the manuscript would be pulled out of the family box or borrowed from a friend or a *pandit* (it could be the *Bhagvad Gītā,* a Śaiva Tantra, a Kavacha from the *stuti* of Devī, or even a whole rendering of the *Bhāgavata Purāṇa)* and handed over to the scribes along with a little bit of oil (meant apparently to be burnt to midnight). The scribes took the manuscript with them to the inn *(serai)* at the edge of the village where they stayed. They had everything else with them (paper, writing instruments, ink, and the like) and all the members of the group were trained scribes, practising an almost similar hand. They would work through the night and bring back the folios they had copied to the owner or patron in the morning.

The entire manuscript was not handed over at one time to the scribes. Only a few *patrās* (folios) were given at one time as a prudent precaution lest the Kashmiris, who were not known to everyone, might make off with the manuscript. The next batch would then be handed over, and this would go on till the work was finished. At the end of the assignment payment was made and the scribes would move on to the next village.

When there was a painter with the scribes, he went about his job in the style he had mastered and grown up with. The hand of the scribes was rigorously trained, stylized, and conventionalized, as also was the style of the painter who accompanied the group. His style met a standard he brought with himself, not something he developed locally under the influence of work seen there. Scribes went apparently around as Pt. Sthanu Dutt reports, especially in the winter season.[13] This is interesting because the winter season even now is associated in the plains of the Panjab with a virtual invasion of Kashmiris (not scribes, who are no longer needed because of the printing press, but other traders and craftsmen — embroidery-wālās, and carpet-sellers who come down at a time when their valley is cold and covered with snow). It is much simpler in that season for the enterprising among Kashmiris to ply their trade elsewhere. This goes also for middlemen who bring woodwork, semi-precious stones, or *namdahs.*

[13] Pandit Sthanu Dutt's memory in this respect is remarkably clear. He spoke thus of these parties of scribes walking about in *bukkals* — heavy wraps around their bodies — indicating winter, when he first saw them.

Even more interesting are the *paṇḍas* of Mattan (the priests who keep records of the visits of pilgrims to Kashmir) who appear at the doors of their clients every winter with their *bahīs* on their shoulders (and good words on their lips).[14] In winter the *paṇḍas* go (as they say) on their *'jajmānī'* for collecting money from their *'yajamānas'* and clients.

Pandit Sthanu Dutt has also mentioned that there were two different rates of payment for the scribes — one for ordinary copying and the other for *'hartal-ki-likhai'* (writing that has been corrected by the putting of some *hartal* or yellow orpiment as a correcting fluid on words wrongly inscribed). He did not fully realize himself that 'Mussavvir' in Persian meant painter; all he remembered was the sound of the words as he had heard it as a child.

According to Pandit Sthanu Dutt, these Kashmiri scribes were not truly literate. Some of them could barely read and write and all they did was copy precisely what they saw in the manuscript in front of them onto sheets of 'Kashmiri' paper that they carried with them, including all the manuscript's errors and imperfections. This is all of interest.

These scribes, according to Pandit Sthanu Dutt, were skilled at more than one script. We in fact have manuscripts inscribed in scripts ranging from Persian, Pushto, Gurumukhi, and Devanāgarī to the Śāradā script that still was dear to the hearts of the learned people of Kashmir in the nineteenth century.[15] The range of script and language within the Kashmiri scribe's control is thus as impressive as the spatial extent over which the Kashmiris roamed. The style of painting, however, found in such manuscripts varies very slightly, and the two major strands I have been able to discern I call currently 'Hindu' and 'Muslim' for want of better terms. (This is neither the time nor the place to talk about these matters; my concern at the moment is a different one, the painters themselves.)

To come back to the painters: limited as the scope of oral information is, it is of significance because it makes such eminent sense in terms of the spread of manuscripts showing similar hands over so large an area.

14 There are *paṇḍas* at a number of major pilgrimage centers, including Haridwar, Benaras, Allahabad, and Gaya but it is the *paṇḍas* of Mattan in Kashmir alone who travel regularly visiting their clients in true Kashmiri tradition. For *paṇḍas* and their records in general see B. N. Goswamy (1966).

15 As a native of the region, Śāradā was widely read and written as a script in Kashmir over a long period of time, but is sadly falling into disuse now. Interestingly, however, the *paṇḍas* of Mattan still keep their records in Śāradā and naturally still read and write it.

Painters may well have been only of marginal importance to the itinerant group of scribes because the text was more important for the patron. Yet through their itinerant link to patronage, the painting style became mobile. In relation to other art forms and other areas, it may not be difficult to conceive of craftsmen likewise moving from place to place, not necessarily hawking their wares and skills in the same way, but certainly doing work at the bidding of a patron or on their own for sale. The possibilities of 'itinerant' as distinguished from migrating artists influencing sculptural styles may have been less than in the field of painting but cannot be ruled out. I see the Kashmiri case as a possible model that might have obtained, with some modification, even in areas far removed from the Kashmiri hamlet.

It is easy to concede that in respect to itinerancy the Kashmiri may have had an unusually strong tradition. We know that Kashmiri Pandits (second only to Pandits from Kāśī) were greatly in demand all over northern India.[16] There are several surviving accounts of Kashmiri Pandits being called in to preside over some ritual, to be present at the time of the *pratiṣṭhā* of some temple, etc. We also have evidence to indicate that throughout Kashmir there was a decided measure of cultural diffusion. Hermann Goetz, who wrote some of the few words so far published on Kashmiri painting, made reference to an 'Afghan-Kashmiri style' in painting,[17] meaning possibly Kashmiri work practised for Afghan patrons (something I have had occasion to see for myself through friends who have lived in Afghanistan). English travellers (such as Forster[18] in the eighteenth and Moorcroft[19] in the early nineteenth

[16] Starting initially as pandits, many families of Kashmiris settling in Northern India gradually went into different professions, often of the learned kind. One knows of Kashmiri pandits at the court of Ranjit Singh in Lahore, as well as Cooch-Bihar in Eastern India.

[17] See H. Goetz (1962-63).

[18] George Forster (1798).

[19] Apart from his travels in the Himalayan provinces, which is the published account of his journey through India and Central Asia, William Moorcroft has a long account of the craftsmen of Kashmir in his *Journals,* now kept in the India Office Library in London. Thus in mss. *Ens. E 113,* he speaks of the manufactures of Kashmir with great enthusiasm. 'The Nuqqashes or painters (of Kashmir) employed in this business,' he says, 'are an intelligent set of men and might readily be induced to acquire any other mode of applying their pencils, as painting on china for which they would be well adapted and give to European works the Asiatic character in a style of execution, superior to that of Chinese artists . . . .' (p. 91).

century) record a great deal of coming and going in the Kashmir region, but this 'itinerancy' need not be true only of Kashmir; it might have obtained elsewhere, even if in a lesser measure.

There is yet another possibility for understanding what may have happened in centuries before ours. Between the professionally itinerant artist and the artist who could be persuaded to migrate is a further category, that of the artist who is *temporarily* on the move. Once again I refer to evidence surviving about Pahārī painters. One ordinarily thinks of painters as permanently and lazily settled in one place, born there and dying there, set in a given situation attached to a specific court, favorites of a particular patron and plying their brushes for his sake at a single center,[20] but this in fact runs somewhat counter to reality. Painters moved out of their areas from time to time, not to settle at another place permanently, coming back eventually to their own native place. This whole business of mobility within Indian culture is something that still has not been worked out as fully as it needs to be. The institution of pilgrimages (one tangible and measurable form of mobility) has begun properly to be explored only in the last few years.

Within these common social patterns of mobility, artists, like everyone else, also moved from place to place and went on pilgrimages. A considerable body of published evidence now shows that painters from the Pahārī region visited Mattan in Kashmir, Kurukshetra and Pehowa in Harayana, and Haridwar in Uttar Pradesh, when they came out of their retreats.[21] A different set of circumstances brought them to these places each time: a death in the family, the entourage of a Rājā, the wish to take an old father on a long pilgrimage to Vārāṇasī and Gayā. I see this movement also as a possible source of diffusion of the styles in which these people worked. There is no precisely recorded evidence, but one can imagine the possibility of artists going on a long pilgrimage, spending months away from their homes, but also carrying the tools of their trade with them — papers, brushes, pigments, burnishers — preferring not to remain idle and perhaps paying their way as they went along. It is quite possible that many of them found work at points along the route they followed from their hometown to places of pilgrimage as far removed as

[20] This seems to be the assumption behind the writing of most art historians who speak of styles identified not only with regions but with given centers, as if the situation were fixed and unmoving.

[21] Evidence to this effect is adduced in B. N. Goswamy (1968).

Jagannath Puri in Orissa or Gaya in Bihar. It would be natural for artists, who often moved in the company of artists from other families, to seek out other craftsmen wherever they went. This could have led to exchanges of all kinds. It is also possible that when they were out at a place for a few days, let us say Haridwar, the *paṇḍas* or some local chief who had come to know of their arrival might commission them to do some work there. That is certainly one possible explanation for the amount of work done in the style of the Panjab plains in the nineteenth century on walls of important *havelis* at Haridwar and Kankhal.[22] Painters may have been specially sent there by some Panjabi patron for a favoured priest, but it also seems possible that groups of painters, arriving there with their tools of trade, could have been asked by some local patron to do work on a contractual basis. Once the work was finished, the painters might then have moved on to another town along their route of pilgrimage, perhaps to more work. As with the murals at Haridwar, so also murals at places on the Panjab plains such as Pindori could have been painted by a visiting Kāngra artist at the asking of a Mahant.[23]

Some years ago O. P. Sharma published an interesting bit of evidence that might support what I am saying. He discussed a manuscript of the *Bhāgavata Purāṇa,* now in the National Museum, that, while not especially attractive, still recognisably is painted in 'high' Kāngra style. The colophon is somewhat damaged, but there is fair certainty that it records this work having been completed for a given patron by some artist trained in the Kāngra style at 'Marut,' a place that could be Meerut. It is likely that the artist passed through this town on his way to somewhere else, stopping for a few days to complete work for a casual patron. This evidence is typical of the stray bits that turn up now and then from different sources. In this context, I wish to suggest that the possibility of the casually itinerant artist (not professionally, but rather socially and privately, itinerant) must be taken into account when we consider the diffusion of styles over broad areas.

Nothing, of course, is conclusive (nothing is ever conclusive). I do not have slides of Kashmiri artists with *bastās* slung on their shoulders and writing instruments in their hands, moving about from village to village. That is a thing of the past. Nor do I have slides of painters at

[22] Some of this work can still be seen on *havelis,* although much of this is fast deteriorating. An important *haveli* with frescoes is that of *Mangalabandi* at Kankhal.

[23] See Usha Bhatia.

places of pilgrimage painting for unknown patrons who casually have engaged them. There also are obvious differences between the craft of painting and that of sculpture. The former takes much less time than the other to accomplish and therefore the possibility of sculptors casually itinerant in the fashion of painters may be discounted by some scholars. Yet the evidence I have gathered might point to the 'dynamics' of a situation, even in that field, that so far has been thought of primarily in static terms.

## Bibliography

Bhatia, Usha. 'Painting in the Hindu Monastic Establishments in the Panjab.' Ph.D. thesis, Panjab University.

Forster, George. *A Journey from Bengal to England.* 2 vols. London, 1798; Patiala, 1970 (Indian reprint).

Goetz, H. 'Two Illustrated Persian Manuscripts from Kashmir.' *Arts Asiatique* IX.1-2 (1962-63): 61-72.

Goswamy, B. N. 'On Two Accounts of Manuscript Writing.' *Proceedings of the Panjab History Congress.* Patiala, 1971.

__________. 'Pahari Painting: The Family as the Basis of Style.' *Marg* XXI.4 (1968): 17-62.

__________. 'The Records Kept by Priests at Centres of Pilgrimage as a Source of Social and Economic History.' *Indian Economic and Social History Review* III.2 (1966): 174-84.

Tucci, Giuseppe. *Tibetan Painted Scrolls.* 2 vols. Rome, 1949.

# Architects and Architecture of Kerala

Murray Libersat
Austin, Texas

The traditional architecture of Kerala is predominantly made of wood, and therefore little dates back more than 600 years. Buildings are not monumental and magnificent, as found in many parts of India, but are simple, elegant, and intricately carved. Predominant features are the large curved wooden roofs.

The three major architectural texts in Kerala are the *Manuṣyālaya Candrikā,* the *Tantrasamuccaya,* and the *Śilparatna.* The *Manuṣyālaya Candrikā* deals almost exclusively in residential construction; the other two relate predominantly to temples, idol making, and temple functions. These works detail the principles of an architectural system using mathematical formulas to give proportion and size to every element of construction, including wells, furniture, etc. I have for years worked closely with a traditional architect in Kerala, and my following comments are based on what he has taught me directly in a traditional fashion.

The basis for all traditional architecture of Kerala is spiritual, stemming from ancient Vedānta philosophy. Its very conception is said to have been laid down by sages who intended that it give a direction and means for the individual to rise spiritually. The whole of the architectural experience is related to the individual's development, rather than to a collective experience as in Europe. It is totally related to the concept of *dharma* which can be taken on any level according to the capabilities of each individual to experience it.

The mathematical principles still in use by traditional architects in Kerala are based largely on astrology and on a proportional system much like that of the 'golden mean' of the Egyptians and Greeks. A basic concept is that of creating harmony and compliance with the natural order of the universe. The use of measurement is primarily employed in the perimeter of a structure. The perimeter is used because it defines space.

To try to simplify these concepts, the basic calculations are *yoni* (source), *ayam* (income), *vyayam* (expenditure), *nakṣatram* (star), and *vayasu* (age). There are others, but these are the most dominant. The *yoni* is related to a circle which represents the directions. There are eight directions, the four cardinal directions being the most auspicious to use. The unit of measurement is the *kol,* which is supposed to be based on the diameter of the earth through the east-west axis. This measurement varies within Kerala in order to compensate for the bulge of the earth at the equator. According to the tradition in Kerala, these measurements must be strictly adhered to in order to preserve the prosperity and inner development of individuals who use the space. Measurement is based on human form, and even the names of architectural elements are descriptive of human anatomy. The primary element in both house and temple is the *arudam.* It is a member of the roof that is made in such a way that if it is cut or damaged it will affect the whole roof and subsequently the building. It is defined as 'that which is created' and symbolizes the higher self in man. Its measurement is the most important and must reflect the *yoni* in which the house faces. The other elements must be in a good *yoni* complimentary to the *arudam.* Because this is a wood technology, most of the primary elements are in the roof construction and beams.

The following is a paraphrasing of a commentary written by N. G. Kartha Panavally, who was my teacher in the study of Śāstric architecture:

*Yoni* is related to the reason of a thing; reason for the real feelings. *Kalam* or time cannot be really divided into night or day, but the division is formed by the imagination of man gained through his experiences in this world and is translated according to the individual's unique instincts. This imaginative tendency when expanded is called *karma* and is time. So time and place react on the man and the building. The rules for *yoni* are related to the eight directions. Only the four cardinal directions are correct to the *dharma* and are related to life. The corner directions (NE, SE, SW, NW) are said to be where two cardinal directions meet and therefore each contains the combined aspects of both directions, which is not good for the *dharma* of the house or individuals who live there. In the body, life exists as a whole. The life force is thus related to *yoni.* If the life force is not in a part, that part quickly decays. Therefore, this principle is used in construction of the house. The idea of the *yoni* is that the life of the building pervades each part of the house and each part must be in a *yoni* related to all other parts. If one part is in a bad *yoni,* then it gives rise to disharmony, disease, and loss to the inhabitants.

The measure of *yoni* is *kols* (unit of measurement), which is a representation of matter itself. If there is matter, then it has a measurement. This measurement is most important in the perimeter because it defines space. The measurement remains in knowledge, and matter remains as itself. Matter has a beginning — germination, then growth, decay, and death. For all matter in existence, there is a lifespan; so also for its measurement.

In the traditional view, matter may not be related to an exact moment of conception because all things are in a constant state of change. One is not always able to see the relativity of these things. The way of existence is in the cycle of birth and death. This cycle is always going on in the universe. Thinking in these terms, the architect can achieve some idea as to the proper age or stage of change that will be best for the situation.

*Bhejam* (seed) is the beginning and is masculine. The plot or the thing that accepts the seed is considered feminine or *kṣetram.* This literally means 'to allow to grow.' So the plot is considered to be female. To place the seed is the work of the masculine. The placing of the foundation stone is a ritualized or symbolic representation of the fertilization of the egg. From this seed or foundation stone grows the house. That growth is the work of man and so *gṛham* is man *(puruṣan).* This is the way of *dharśana* relating to the plot and building. One tries to choose all those characteristics which will uplift and cause the inhabitants to prosper.

The plot is like the human body and is said to have *marmams* or vital points as laid down in the Ayurveda medicine. To touch this point can cause a sensation or even discomfort felt throughout the body. The *marmams* or *mayyam* of a house are related to these points in the body. To disturb this point or area in a house can cause bad effects, just as this point can cause a reaction in the human body. There are twelve of these *marmams* or *mayyam.* It is said that these are related to the change of the sun at a critical point in a *rassi.* The sun passing through one *rassi* is one month. Since there are twelve months, there are twelve *mayyam* in a house. The change between these months or time is a critical moment.

For example, in a house, if the length of a beam has been determined, then it can be divided into eight parts. The lines to make these divisions are called *mayyam.* If eight is used in the length, four is used in the width. This adds up to twelve *mayyam.*

Therefore the four main *yoni* are *dvajayoni* — which is said to be of Brāhmaṇ *varna.* Jupiter is its ruling element. It faces west and is mild in nature. Siṁhayoni-Kṣatriya is the *varna* with Mars as the ruling planet. It faces north and has some *tamasic* tendencies. Its aspect is that of the attribute relating to desire. Gajayoni-Vaiśya is the *varna* with Mercury as the ruling planet. Powerful in nature, it gives good things. It faces south. Vṛṣayoni-Śudra is the *varna* and is ruled by Saturn. Prosperity is its nature, and it faces to the east.

The plot of ground is always divided into a square. The land, if it is regular, is divided into a square and the remainder is not used for building purposes. The plot has four sides and is called *vāstu,* or earth. The plot is symbolic of the whole earth. The plot is considered to be a microcosm of the earth. The center of this square is called *brahmastānam,* or the place of *brahman.* It is considered static or beyond movement and without time. Therefore no life can exist there, because there is no movement. The house and auxiliary buildings are never built here. The house is moved away from this point to cause the forces of the plot to act upon it and cause movement or life. Symbolically, the earth is thought of in mythology as being a boiling mass in its beginning ruled by an *asura* called Vāstupuruṣa. The gods, it is said, felt that no life could exist while this *asura* ruled. Therefore the gods jumped upon this *asura* and subdued him. The *asura* fell with his head toward the northeast and his feet toward the southwest. The place where the gods jumped upon him is given divisions, and *pūjās* are done there to each god as a means of propitiating this act. In this context, *asura* literally means 'that which does not allow life to proceed in a sober way.' It is symbolic of the *asura* in man and is that element which keeps one from realizing one's true self.

It is said that the great sages of the past wrote the *śāstras* and *purāṇas* as a means of passing on wisdom and a means to help man rise spiritually. Therefore, these architectural texts have many levels of meaning according to the capacity of the person to understand, from the carpenter to the *sthāpati* (architect). The texts pass on technical data which is necessary to build a house correctly but also symbolize the concept of the universe according to Vedānta.

The plot of the traditional houses of Kerala represented the whole microcosm of the universe so that all needs would be met in a way that would also symbolize spiritual growth. The house and compound were a whole unit which provided for every need of the expanded family unit that dwelt there: the family deities, bathing tank, cow shed, well, grain storage, etc., all had a position according to this symbolic representation.

The *śāstras* for temples are said to be based upon man. The foremost symbolism is said to be that of the *yogaśāstra.* Temples and their construction are based on the betterment of the individual and the community that builds a temple and worships there. It is related to the *dharma* of the individual, in every realm to uplift him. By worship to the *deva* or god one is lifted up to realize the light or *caitanya* that is within himself. It is said that the idol represents that light that is within the individual, or *ātma.*

The temple is a symbolic representation of man in a yogic sense as well as physical. The temple compound has nine doors that relate to the nine doors to the human body; *i.e.* the eyes, ears, mouth, nose, etc. The idol is the life in the body. The elements are arranged in a linear fashion from the flagstaff to the *śrīkōvil* where the idol is installed. The six doors are said to represent the six *cakras* or yogic centers of the body. The temple compound is divided into three distinct areas which represent the three worlds within man. They are *devalokam, bhūlokam,* and *patala-lokam.* The head is the part of the body called *devalokam.* The torso is said to be *bhūlokam,* and the legs and feet are said to be *patalalokam.* The *deva* literally means that which lives in *light.* The head is where the light of knowledge illumines. It is also where the eyes and the sense perceptions take place. Therefore, it is the region where the *devas* dwell. The torso is *bhūlokam* or where Brahmā dwells as the controller of life. Here is where the food is burned by the digestive juices *(agni)* and purified to carry on the higher functions of thought, perception, etc. In the temple, this is where the *pūjās* are performed and where food is offered ritualistically to the god. The lower region is *patalalokam* or *serpalokam.* The meaning here is that which has *serpana* or movement. In the temple it is symbolized as the outer portion where *pradakṣiṇā* or walking around the deity is performed.

The plot for the temple is divided or made into a square as in the residential plot, but with the exception that the *śrīkōvil* or inner sanctum of the temple is placed in the center or *brahmastānam.* Every element of the temple is built radiating away from this spot. Each element is shifted slightly to the right from the central axis to signify the movement of the universe. This movement is called *gamanam.*

The architect or *sthāpati* is therefore the keeper of the knowledge. By tradition, it is strictly passed by the teacher to his students. It is the architect's responsibility to make the calculations for a house or temple and to insure that the carpenters and masons execute it in a precise way. The *sthāpati* must be a learned man both in the *śāstras* of architecture and astrology. He is called upon to make additions to older temples and to give the proper times for major festivals and *pūjās* at a temple. It is his intuition and experience that allows him to judge the values of a plot and the best structures to harmonize with the natural elements of the plot. Some of the renowned *sthāpatis* used the ancient science of *nimata* to go into subtle aspects of location not visible to the eye.

In summation, the *śāstras* of architecture and the tradition of oral knowledge passed on generation after generation in India remains one of the most remarkable systems of architecture in the world. It is remarkable in that it perpetuates the idea of *dharma* as relevant to every sphere of the construction of a building. This is passed down to every worker who is laboring on the building. The carpenters, masons, painters, artists, etc., perform an act of worship in each action. This philosophy permeates the whole structure and is visible in the few remaining examples of Kerala architecture being built. The unfortunate aspect is that such traditional architects and many of the arts and trades they practice may not survive beyond this generation.

## Bibliography

Acharya, P. K. *Mānasāra* series. Vols. 1-7. London, 1928-46.

Bernier, Ronald M. *Temple Arts of Kerala: A South Indian Tradition.* New Delhi, 1982.

Kramrisch, Stella, *et al. The Arts and Crafts of Kerala.* Cochin, 1970.

Mallaya, N. V. *Studies in Sanskrit Texts on Temple Architecture (with special reference to Tantrasamuccaya).* Annamalainagar, 1949.

Meister, Michael W., ed. *Encyclopaedia of Indian Temple Architecture,* Vol. 1, pt. 1. Philadelphia, 1983.

Nambhudiripad, Kanippayyur D. *Manushyalaya Chandrika* (Sanskrit text elucidated in Malayalam). Kunnamkulam, 1927.

Nambhudiripad, Kanippayyur D. *Tantrasamuccaya* (Sanskrit text elucidated in Malayalam). Kunnamkulam, 1927.

Rajan, K. V. S. *Temple Architecture in Kerala.* Trivandrum, 1974.

Sarkar, H. *An Architectural Survey of Temples of Kerala.* New Delhi, 1978.

Vaidyanathan, K. R. *Temples and Legends of Kerala.* Bharatiya Vidya Bhavan, 1981.

# Craft Production in an Agrarian Economy

David Ludden
University of Pennsylvania

On a spectrum of manufacture, art lies at one end, where producer, product, and consumer interact intensely as individual entities. Industry expands at the other end, where producer, product, and consumer have no individuality whatever. Craft production fits near the center, because even though crafts are utilitarian objects and are produced in great number, craft workers make their products by hand and thus retain technical decision-making power, imparting to the product something of the maker's individuality, a quality that is visible and valued in the aesthetic of craft consumption. Moreover, the utility of crafts creates potentially widening avenues of market demand, and the commercialization of craft production 'industrializes' craft labor, because investors use their capital to control production, standardize products, limit the decision-making power of producers, expand the physical and social space over which products move through markets, distance producer from consumer, and diminish the identification of producer with product. Whole populations of producers and thus whole regions are differentiated in this process, because all products do not find equal markets — weavers, for instance, may be subjected to commercialization more universally than potters — and some regions move into industrial craft production more heavily than others because of proximity to markets or demand for particular items or both. Commercialization therefore moves craft workers across the spectrum of manufacture from the artistic toward the industrial.

This movement underlies the history of non-agricultural labor in South Asia and is the subject of this paper. Using data mostly from the Indian peninsula, and referring mostly to textiles, I will argue that by 1800 many craft workers had moved well into the realm of industrial labor and that by 1900 few craft workers should be imagined as village artisans making products for local patrons but rather most were already anonymous workers in towns and cities, bashing off standard commodities for mass markets.

My historical baseline is the medieval period, *c.* A.D. 900-1330, when peninsular India was an archepelago of tiny agricultural core zones in river valleys. In this localized economy, long-distance trade had minimal impact on work, which was dominated by local demand. Some locales were big consumers — courts, armies, and temples — but craftsmen worked almost entirely in rural settings, for local commissions, organized by caste. Within most such agricultural islands, dominated by landowning castes, craft producers either farmed, themselves, or exchanged local products for food. There were exceptions, one of which is important here: Kaikkolar weavers formed armed contingents for long-distance trade. These disappeared in post-medieval centuries, replaced by caste organizations in towns.

In the post-medieval era, *c.* A.D. 1300-1550, militant migration in the north generated similar migrations by warriors, peasants, and craft workers elsewhere and transformed India's economy. Migrants settled on land around and between old core areas, expanded agricultural production, formed territories of control centered on fort towns, introduced new technologies, and generated demand for agricultural and craft products. Rulers like the Vijayanagar kings held coercive power that boosted their consumer power, and recipients of their largesse experienced a similar boost.

Growing demand after A.D. 1500 slowly, unevenly, but steadily commercialized and urbanized craft production. Rural production for local consumers remained the norm for centuries, but in the south five important craft groups — goldsmiths, blacksmiths, carpenters, masons, and brass workers — formed by the 1500s one large caste group called Kammalar as a result of the special attention paid to them by rulers who sought to attract them to royal centers. The increasing value of craft production spurred 'right'- and 'left'-hand caste conflict between land-controlling and craft-controlling groups seeking royal patronage. Kaikkolars became an elite weaving caste with privileges in many temples; royal patronage, caste organization, and commercial activity set Kaikkolars apart but stimulated specialization and urban concentrations among many craftsmen in towns throughout the subcontinent.

After 1600, growing demand in royal centers in India was enhanced by growing demand for Indian crafts from Europe; this accelerating demand brought more and more craftsmen — most importantly, weavers — into commercial production as it made town-based craft production both more common and more distinctive.

In the countryside, durable, uniform practices had developed around rural artisans by the eighteenth century, when an inscription from near Vijayanagar lists twelve vital servants of the village — accountants, headman, carpenter, washerman, purohit, barber, shoemaker, goldsmith, watchman, waterman, blacksmith, potter — who were paid according to status from the harvest, which could mean being given plots of land. Mark Wilks has given a similar list of village servants supported by land grants in rural Mysore at the turn of the nineteenth century — headman, accountant, taliary, watchman, waterman, astrologer, smith, carpenter, potter, washerman, barber, and silversmith — paid by land or a share of the harvest (Chicherov 1971: 24). A similar system has also been described for Andhra, Maharashtra, Gujarat, Panjab, and Hindustan; it produced a degree of self-sufficiency for many villages.

No textile workers are, however, listed as village servants. By 1750, textile production had become distinct from other village artisan activities and had absorbed growing masses of labor because of the growing value of Indian cloth in overseas markets.

Indian textiles dominated world markets by 1700 because of their high quality, because Indian labor was cheap compared to European labor due to the low subsistence costs found in the agriculturally advanced regions of production, and because India had a large pool of specialized, technically skilled producers for preparing thread, cloth, dyes, and patterns, because major production regions had large pools of merchant capital and expertise accumulated over many years and committed to the cotton cloth-trade. The four export production regions were the Panjab, where textiles served the overland demand from Persia and Central Asia and also travelled by river to ports from Sind to Maskat, Kung, and Basra; Bengal, whose major outlet had been upper India but where 'European trade . . . had the effect of shifting the balance radically in favour of the seaborne trade' so that the 'textile industry . . . not only expanded to keep pace with the increased demand but . . . fully adjusted its output to the special specifications required for selling in Europe' (Chaudhuri 1978: 247); Gujarat, where weavers could supply Red Sea ports at lower cost than other parts of India; and the Coromandel (Andhra-Tamil Nadu) Coast, which had major markets in Southeast Asia.

The overseas cotton-textile trade affected politics through its influence on the distribution of economic power. Major textile export-centers became nerve centers of Company Raj; and Europe — not upper India — became Bengal's chief trading partner in the 1700s, reducing the flow of exchange to finance Mughal state-revenue. Textile production in northern and western India centered on provincial capitals and towns on caravan routes to Delhi and Agra, and this fed urban markets and sustained urban economies, among which Delhi was the largest, with 35,000 troops and a population nearly the size of Paris, so that economic and political decline of these urban centers after 1820 dislocated the entire economy of North India.

In the south and east, economic pressure to urbanize the eighteenth-century textile industry was partly offset by lower transport costs along rivers and coastal waterways, by lower subsistence costs in old core agricultural zones, by the practice of weaving long warp threads under the shade of village groves, and by the importance of physical mobility for weavers. The weavers' most powerful weapon was their ability to move from one patron or one town to another. The Madras Council reported that 'the weavers when disgusted leave lighted Lamps in their Houses and remove to some other part of the Country, so that whole Towns are deserted in a Night' (Chaudhuri 1978: 252-3).

Everywhere in eighteenth-century India, forces propelled weavers into towns and encouraged merchants and rulers to make it desirable for them to stay, or impossible to leave. Political insecurity brought weavers to town for protection, as in Madras, Bombay, and Calcutta. Famine produced flight to towns. The weaver's commitment to his village appears strong in times of agrarian plenty and weak in times of distress. Growing availability of urban employment would have hastened his decision to head for town to find work during times of hardship in the village.

Weavers also relied on town merchants. Specialization in textile production encouraged weavers to deal with wholesale dealers. In most other crafts, the craftsman completed many if not all stages of production, but textiles required a coordinated effort by growers, carders, spinners, weavers, dyers, cutters, sorters, packers, and others. Weavers reduced their costs and risks by selling unbleached cloth to wholesalers, who arranged for its further processing and sale. Specialized craft-production depended on markets outside the locality of production, and to reach these, craftsmen had to rely on merchants, who controlled the level and type of output. Merchants also provided much of the working capital for weaving.

Merchants had strong incentives to concentrate producers in compact areas, where they could both control production and more easily solve three problems: (1) the obtaining of capital for advances, (2) assuring proper storage and timely delivery of goods, and (3) maintenance of quality control and product standardization. For capital, merchants relied on bankers and on European companies, who controlled access to overseas markers and used that leverage to shift the risk of default by weavers to Indian merchants. Timely delivery required that weavers fulfill their contracts on time, which meant they had to be carefully supervised. Quality control meant even closer watching. Weavers could put merchants in a bind by taking advances and running away or by not delivering the goods on time. The specialized nature of foreign demand reduced the likelihood of a domestic market for cloth made for export, so if a foreign company rejected the cloth, Indian merchants could be stuck.

The mobility of weavers, their capacity to fall back on village employment, and the existence of alternative bidders for their products — Dutch, French, or English companies and Indian elites — put weavers in a position to maintain considerable independence. Subsistence crises, merchant monopoly, and political insecurity, however, made weavers less independent and pushed them into towns where their production fell increasingly under the control of merchant capital. Wars, famines, and expanding English East-India-Company power after 1740 brought weavers to town, where they could be supervised and the cost of their employment reduced. Already by the 1760s many weavers in the export centers of India had come close to the status of wage laborers. Only Bengal seems to have escaped this trend.

In the countryside, the artisan produced for a share of the harvest; when he entered a system of cash advances he entered a vertically organized system of coordinated commercial production in which integration and control were exerted from the top down by the power and needs of merchants. When demand was steady and their social and political context gave them security, weavers could maintain their autonomy, but when demand fluctuated wildly and instability threatened, both weavers and merchants sought to form a new relation between each other. Working for wages assured the weaver income; at the same time, it ended his autonomy and gave the merchant more power to benefit from the ups and downs of the market. This shift in India did not lead to large scale industrial organization on European lines. The specialization of functions involved in textile production would have been very costly to modify to bring all the specialists under one central management, but weavers in commercial centers did move along the spectrum of manufacture toward the industrial end through the creation of a system of central management involving networks of commercial capital and the urbanization of export production.

Similar forces brought other kinds of craftsmen to town: blacksmiths, founders, copper-workers, jewellers, and other metal workers were important not only to elite urban consumption but also to the military establishment. Swords, guns, arrows, stirrups, saddles, ships, and even forts had to be produced in large quantities and demand for them was concentrated in towns. States logically sought to control the producers, using as leverage state powers to tax, coerce, protect, and buy. The Mughals as well as other Indian rulers as far afield as Musulipatnam and Golconda had *kārkhānās* to produce paintings, weapons, and other products. There also were private workshops, the best known perhaps those that produced Kashmiri shawls.

Two pillars of craft independence prevented craft workers from being absorbed entirely into an urban proletariat: (1) agrarian resources — land, shares of the harvest, and their ability to fall back on agricultural labor for support — provided subsistence security; (2) caste specialization limited intrusions by capital into the organization of craft work. One Englishman complained in the eighteenth century that the artisans 'will never be put off their old way of working; and should you ever be desirous of instructing them, or showing them a more expeditious method, they will plead the custom of their forefathers, for which they have so great a veneration that they were never known even in a single (detail) to depart from it' (Chicherov 1971: 83).

This complaint was anachronistic by 1800. Commodity production in cloth had brought many non-traditional weaving castes into the industry. An early nineteenth-century account from Bengal says that weaving had been taken up by farmers who moved into weavers' settlements, and J. A. Taylor noted that goldsmiths, barbers, and even *kāyasthas* had taken to weaving in Dacca, so that with the decline of weaving after 1800 many of these non-weaving families had 'abandoned the town' and given up weaving (Chicherov, pp. 83-4).

After 1800, competition from English machine-made cloth drove many of these non-specialist weaving-caste families back onto the land; expanding agricultural production in this period, however, created new opportunities for increased craft production for a domestic market, and the handloom industry in Madras Presidency survived the onslaught of mill cloth in good shape. From 1850-1880, imports of English machine mill-products actually stimulated increases in Indian handloom weaving by lowering the cost of thread. After 1880, the Indian handloom industry began to grow even faster due to increasing demand both at home and abroad. Demand for Madras Presidency cloth came in particular from southeast Asia and Africa.

After 1900, handlooms in Madras Presidency multiplied rapidly as the industry responded to technical innovations. Synthetic dyes made Madurai a dyeing center and drove natural dyes off the market. The fly-shuttle was introduced in 1901. By 1912, 20,000 looms could boast the new device; by 1917, 100,000; by the mid-1930s, 70% of the Presidency's looms. Weaving centers diversified to meet local and regional as well as export needs.

Two factors shaped the modern handloom industry: the low cost of entry into business and the centrality of marketing. Low fixed capital and skill requirements for coarse cloth production meant that people could go into weaving temporarily, in times of hardship. The most difficult part of the handloom business was marketing and those with skill, knowledge, and resources to organize marketing thus tended to dominate the industry.

These factors produced a peculiar relation between labor supply and consumer demand: lower-cost laborers flocked into the industry for work specifically at times when the agricultural economy was depressed and local consumer demand weak. It therefore took substantial capital and expertise for a capitalist in the industry to adjust supply to demand to sustain profits. The 'putting-out' system became the classic organizational form in the handloom and other petty industries, in which capitalists would decide what would be made, supply materials and working capital to craftsmen, take back the product, and convey it to market. In bad times, the capitalist could cut off the worker and had no obligations to support a labor force or permanent plant. As times improved it was easy to mobilize producers again because craftsmen were in debt to capitalists.

The structure of the industry differentiated centers of handloom production. Centers producing fine cloth for export had independent weavers with premium skills, working in small shops with master-weavers and yarn-merchants from the same community. In these centers, local caste organization would have at least some aspects of a craft guild; both capitalist and caste were likely to provide relief in bad times, and in some cases, caste organizations would sponsor technical education for weavers' sons.

In centers where coarse cloth was the main product, weavers would form mixed-caste communities, including a variety of weaving castes along with people from other service and merchant groups and agricultural and laboring *jātis.* Craftsmen were considerably less independent, organized in large groups of 200-1,000 under master-weavers or big yarn-merchant capitalists.

The handloom industry in Madras Presidency changed in the twentieth century as handloom capitalists responded to the unprecedented instabilities engendered by both the two world wars and the great depression. Capital, adapting to new conditions, also changed the character of handloom labor. Six trends after 1900 helped define the craft economy and handloom industry as we see it today in South India.

(1) Coarse cloth production increased much faster than fine cloth production and many weavers moved from finer to cheaper grades of production. The ranks of coarse cloth weavers were also swollen by migrants from the countryside during periods of agricultural distress, especially in the 1930s and 1940s.

(2) Control over working capital engaged in the handloom industry became concentrated in fewer hands. There always had been magnates, but instability scared capital away from smaller operators. Large stores of personal wealth enabled magnates to mobilize production quickly when markets were good and to hold stocks when markets collapsed. Salem and Coimbatore became major centers in Tamil Nadu, with individual magnates controlling looms producing Rs. five lakhs per year.

(3) Concentrations of capital produced concentrations of weavers under the putting-out system. Even independent weavers were tied into larger financial nets through debts that averaged about Rs. 180 per weaver by 1930. Surveys in the 1930s and 1940s found that many weavers had lost what little independence they had, particularly as they moved from the production of fine to the production of coarse goods.

(4) The industry tended to concentrate in towns rather than villages and in big towns rather than small ones, partly because being in a town gave weavers better access to merchant capital and partly because the government began to provide welfare services — most importantly, food rationing — only in larger towns during World War II. The urbanization of the industry did not generate factories with assembly lines because market insecurity encouraged capitalists to diversify into landowning, the film industry, mill-cloth trade, and other lines of business, and it encouraged weavers to look for other ways to make a living in bad times. In Madras, weavers reportedly flocked to become bus conductors; in Salem and North Arcot they went back to the farm to harvest — and to the mills to process — groundnut in the 1940s. Mobility remained critical for both capital and labor, making the small shop and the putting-out system the most practical and popular type of industrial organization.

(5) Fearing economic disruption and political unrest, government increasingly intervened in the industry. Madras reorganized the Handloom Weavers Provincial Cooperative Societies in 1942. Collective

Weaving Centers were established where weavers made goods for state needs and for the market. In an attempt to prevent speculation, the government appointed a yarn commissioner to issue licences to all dealers and to oversee the movement of yarn in the province. In 1947-48, when mills returned to normal production, the market for handloom goods crumbled. Deeply committed to the Cooperative Societies and the handloom weavers who had formed battalions of protesters during the Non-Cooperation and Quit India movements, the Congress had quickly to protect the industry. In 1836, there were thirty cooperative societies; in 1946, there were 336, with 65,286 members and Rs. 374 lakhs annual turnover; in 1953, there were 1,191, with 222,619 members, Rs. 394 working capital, and Rs. 538.53 lakhs turnover per year. By 1950, the handloom industry depended entirely on the government for its survival.

(6) The agrarian economy after 1900 generated more wage laborers and pushed workers into towns to find jobs. A long expansion of agriculture had bolstered the craft economy through the first world war, but during the depression, both internal and external markets for farm products collapsed, forcing capital out of agriculture into machine mills and workers off the farm into urban labor markets. After 1920, there was also a steady decline in the land sown with food crops in Tamil districts, as those farmers with firm control of land, labor, and village capital sought to maximize their returns by concentrating on higher-value commercial crops. The biggest decline was in millets, the food grains of the rural poor — *kambu, ragi, korra, varagu, samai* — whose share of sown acreage fell from 22% in the 1910s to 13% in the 1940s. While the population of Tamil districts rose 80%, acreage devoted to millets that fed the bulk of the poor fell by more than a third.

This meant that the crops that had provided food security in the village vanished and workers had to seek wages in order to buy more expensive food crops in town, thus altering the historic interaction of urban and rural populations. Migration to towns became permanent, as had never been the case before. The growth of petty industries under the putting-out system, and of welfare services under government control, made urban centers increasingly attractive, and government also intervened in the management of major urban industries to safeguard employment and law-and-order. The population of Madras increased by 82%, crossing the one-million mark in the 1940s.

The movement of the poor to towns resembled that during war and famine in the 1700s, but was of infinitely greater magnitude, and for the first time seems permanent. It swelled the labor force in petty manufacture and entrepreneurs invested eagerly in industry, but learned quickly that markets were restricted by the limits of the rural economy and the international markets. Industries that emerged to dominate that urban economy of South India after 1947 were, first, factory industries, mostly involved in processing natural products with relatively simple technology in small production units, with management based on family organization and with a very low ratio of fixed to working capital, and, second, modified versions of traditional handicraft industries, characterized by intermittant operations, a reserve of cheap labor, and a putting-out system. The second type was by far the more important, becoming the mainstay of urban exployment for the poor. Most of these petty manufactures were organized in a fashion similar to the handloom industry, but without government protection. Though these submitted to the rhetoric of traditional crafts production, 'the towns of Tamilnad were rapidly becoming workhouses for the rural poor' (Baker 1984: 414).

## Bibliography

Baker, Christopher John. *An Indian Rural Economy: The Tamilnad Countryside, 1880-1955.* Oxford, 1984.

Bayly, Christopher A. *Rulers, Townsmen, and Bazaars: North Indian Society in the Age of British Expansion, 1770-1870.* Cambridge, 1983.

Chaudhuri, K. N. *The Trading World of Asia and the English East India Company, 1660-1760.* Cambridge, 1978.

Chicherov, A.I. *Indian Economic Development in the 16th-18th Centuries: An Outline History of Crafts and Trade.* Moscow, 1971.

Krishnamurthy, J. 'The Occupational Structure.' In Kumar, ed., pp. 533-52.

Kumar, Dharma, ed. *The Cambridge Economic History of India, Volume Two, c. 1757 – c. 1970.* Cambridge, 1983.

Ludden, David. *Peasant History in South India.* Princeton, 1985.

Mines, Mattison. *The Warrior Merchants: Textiles, Trade, and Territory in South India.* Cambridge, 1985.

Twomey, J. Michael. 'Employment in Nineteenth Century Indian Textiles.' *Explorations in Economic History* 20, 1 (1983): 37-57.

# Textile Production and Trade in Seventeenth-Century India

Manju Parikh-Baruah
College of St. Benedict, St. Joseph, MN

## I.

The production and trade of Indian handloom textiles in the seventeenth century provide a good vantage point to understand the nature of India's 'pre-modern' economy and the impact of British colonial rule. Immanuel Wallerstein (1985) has recently reconstructed the history of the integration of South Asia into the 'capitalist world system.' The Indian subcontinent before 1750, according to him, was a 'zone largely external to the operations of the then Europe-based capitalist world-economy.' While he recognizes that the preceding 150 years (A.D. 1600-1750) in India showed remarkable commercial vitality, it constituted only the beginning of the process that brought about the integration of South Asia into the world economy. Wallerstein's argument is based on his view that a major expansion of the world economy took place around 1730 or 1740, and that the sources of this expansion were internal to the European economy. During this period of expansion, between 1750 and 1850, not only South Asia but also the Indonesian archipelago, the Ottoman Empire, the Russian Empire, and parts of West Africa and America were incorporated into the capitalist world economy.

In this paper, I will raise some questions about Wallerstein's thesis in light of the history of the seventeenth-century Indian textile industry. I specifically will examine the organization of production and trade of textiles in two major regions of seventeenth-century India: Gujarat and Coromandel. The organization of textile production was intricately linked to an extensive overseas trade. The export of textiles was part of an international network of exchanges which linked India with markets in Southeast Asia, the Middle East, and East Africa. The profitability of importing Indian handwoven textiles into England and re-exporting them to Europe and parts of the New World, with its rising demand in the seventeenth century, motivated the European East-India companies to attempt to capture and gain a monopoly over the trade. Competition from Indian handwoven textiles, I argue, was an important stimulus to the development of a modern textile industry in Britain and other parts of Europe.

## II.

Records of foreign travellers and accounts of the officials of European trading companies have made it possible to reconstruct the essential features of textile production and trade in the seventeenth and eighteenth centuries. Gujarat and Coromandel were two major areas with extensive overseas trade linkages in the seventeenth century. In Gujarat, most production was in or around urban areas. In the Coromandel region, it was mainly in villages (Chaudhuri 1978: 249-50; Curtin 1984: 122-24; Irwin and Schwartz 1966: 28-33). The major center of textile production in Gujarat was Ahmedabad, the capital of the province. There were also a number of smaller textile producing centers in the proximity of Ahmedabad and road networks connecting these textile centers to Surat and Cambay, the two major ports on the coastline of Gujarat (Gillion 1968: 29; Gokhale 1969: 187-90; Naqvi 1972: 124-25).

In Coromandel, the bulk of textile production was carried out in villages along the coast. When the export of textiles expanded in the later part of the seventeenth century, weaving and printing establishments emerged around inland towns such as Trichinopoly, Tengapatam, Tanjore, and Madurai. The Coromandel textiles were exported from several seaports along the coast, including Masulipatam, Pulicat, Negapatam and, later on, Madras and Porto Novo (Bal Krishna 1924: 23-26; Davies 1961: 82-85; Irwin and Schwartz 1966: 30-33).

The most notable aspect about the merchant communities in the two regions was their inherited and specialized skill in trading. Typically, business was organized around the members of a family and handed on from one generation to the next. In Gujarat, merchant communities engaged in textile trade were mainly Hindu and Jain *vāṇiās,* a caste traditionally associated with trade and finance. The *vāṇiās* were known for their business acumen and frugal habits. Among these communities, the most prominent were the *sarāfī* families, who were indigenous financiers. They wrote *huṇḍis* (checks which could be encashed over long distances), exchanged foreign currency, and provided loans and insurance. Through the backing of these financiers, merchants could engage in long distance trade despite the risky journeys of caravans and ships (Mehta 1982: 3-4, 11-12; Spodek 1969; Gillion 1968: 16-18; Naqvi 1972: 119-21).

In the Coromandel region, the two prominent trading communities engaged in the textile trade were the *komati* and the *chetti* merchants. '*Chetti*' is a title which could be used by a number of non-brahmin castes who engaged in trade and finance. Amongst these, the most prominent are the *nattu kottai chettiars.* Like the *sarāfs* in Gujarat, this sub-caste of *chettiars* constituted a community of indigenous financiers. Their scale of operations ranged from small-scale moneylending and joint-stock banking to running an indigenous banking system. Many *chetti* merchants migrated from southern India to Ceylon, Burma, and the Malaysian peninsula (Arasaratnam 1966; Chaudhuri 1978; Ito 1966; Raychaudhuri 1962: 11-12, 144).[1]

The production of these textiles necessitated cooperation of many different types of craftsmen such as spinners, weavers, bleachers, dyers, and printers. The production of textiles could constitute full-time work or seasonal employment for peasant communities during the slack period in agriculture (Chaudhuri 1978: 253-54). The most specialized varieties of textiles were produced by castes whose skills were hereditary. In Gujarat, these weaving castes were usually the *vankars, bhavsars, gandhis, dheds, khatris, tais, momins* and *bohras* (the last three belonging to the muslim community) (Choksey 1968: 226-27; Desai 1978: 29; Pearse 1930: 18). In the Coromandel region, the weaving castes were *salies, devangas,* and *patnulkars.* Each of these sub-castes specialized in producing distinct varieties of cloth (Raju 1941: 166; Alaev 1982: 317-22).

The production of cotton and silk fabrics involved a number of stages — weaving, bleaching, dyeing, printing, even painting — demanding specialized skills. As many as eleven categories of workmen were employed in the manufacture of certain fine varieties (Chaudhuri 1978: 254; Gillion 1968: 27).

Piece-goods intended for sale abroad entered the market by two channels. Either they were sold directly by independent weavers producing traditional patterns or by merchants who organized production of special types to satisfy specific markets. These merchants made advance payments to weavers, who bought the raw material and used the leftover cash to support themselves during production. Merchants were assured of a definite supply of products in this way (Chaudhuri 1982; Desai 1978: 27-28).

In port cities like Surat, Cambay, Masulipatam, and Madras as well as in towns like Ahmedabad, Agra, or Delhi, it was common to find a colony of foreign merchants such as Arabs, Armenians, Turks, Moors, or Persians. Among them, Arab merchants played a vital role in the

[1] Other references useful to this issue are Jain (1929): 30; Naidu (1941); Thomas (n.d.).

exchange of commodities between India and Europe (Pires 1944: 42-46; Chaudhuri 1978: 247; Davies 1961: 91; Gokhale 1969: 188).

The dominant pattern of the overseas trade was a triangular exchange in which South Asian textiles played a central role. Ships owned and manned by Arabs first arrived with bullion from Red-Sea ports and the Persian Gulf to purchase textiles from ports in Gujarat and the Coromandel region. These textiles were then carried to the Malayasian Peninsula where they were exchanged for spices. Finally, these ships returned to Mediterranean ports. Italian merchants purchased spices at enormous value and re-exported them to other parts of Europe.[2]

With the arrival of European traders in the Indian ocean at the end of the fifteenth century, the demand for textiles in Europe increased enormously. It is difficult to gauge accurately the volume of textile exports, since no complete records are available. What we have are estimates computed from the registers of shipping companies and the records of purchases by the East-India companies. In 1610, European and Asian ships already were carrying about ten million yards of cloth to Southeast Asia and the Middle East, plus a few thousand samples to Europe. By 1625, the volume within Asia had increased two-fold (Bronson 1983: 17).

By the 1630s, the demand for calicoes — the trade name for Indian cotton piecegoods — went up sharply as English traders began to use them to trade for slaves in West Africa. Calicoes first went to London through the English East India Company, which sold them to the Royal African Company, whose ships sailed to West Africa where they exchanged calicoes for slaves, then carried the slaves and the remainders of the textiles to the West Indies, where slaves and textiles were exchanged for sugar and tobacco. These were then brought to England for re-export to other European countries (Irwin and Schwartz 1966: 12).

By the 1650s, the Asian trade had begun to level off at around 25 and 30 million yards, several million exported to Europe and Africa. In the late 1660s, European imports had crossed the ten million mark and continued to rise steadily. In England and other countries of Europe, calicoes became fashionable among the affluent classes. In 1667, the English East India Company had imported 160,000 yards of calicoes and

[2] One of the main reasons for the use of textiles to obtain spices was the inadequately monetised character of the economy of the Spice Islands. Indian handwoven fabrics were exchanged to meet their basic needs for everyday garments (Chaudhuri (1982): 386; Meglio (1970): 118-21; Irwin & Schwartz (1966): 28-29).

30,000 yards of silk piecegoods. In the early 1680s, the volume of imports ranged from 35 to 40 million yards. In 1684, the English East India company's purchases amounted to 45 million yards. If we add exports carried by other European companies and by Indian and Arab traders, one can roughly estimate a total of 100,000 million yards. There are very few complete estimates available in terms of value for these imports. One source gives the value of imports in a peak period from 1697-1702 as 1,053,725. By the end of the seventeenth century, cotton piecegoods constituted about two-thirds of the total volume of imports of the English East India Company and demand continued to grow until the middle of the eighteenth century (Furber 1976: 240; Khan 1975: 11, 163; Irwin and Schwartz 1966: 11-13; Pearse 1930: 18).

These figures indicate a phenomenal increase in the export of Indian textiles in the seventeenth century. During this period, 'India was the major supplier of textiles — not just fine clothes, but everyday wear for the masses' in Southeast Asia, Iran, the Arab countries, East Africa, the West Indies, as well as Europe. It was the most stable item of exchange in international transactions (Raychaudhuri 1968: 85; Chaudhuri: 205, 238; Davies 1961: 83; Irwin and Schwartz 1966: 11, 28).

## III.

What changes did European participation bring to India's textile trade and production? Prior to the arrival of the European East-India companies, the area between the Indian Ocean and the South China Sea was a zone of ecumenical trade, linking several port towns to inland caravan centers and five or six major ports to forty or fifty smaller ones (Curtin 1984: 127-28). The trading between different communities of merchants was conducted through free competition in the sense that no nation or group of traders had gained exclusive control over the markets through non-economical means (Raychaudhuri 1964: 127-28). Although some communities were more successful in trade and navigation in specific regions (Gujaratis in the Indian Ocean, Arabs in the Persian Gulf and the Red Sea, Chinese between China and Malaya, Malay and Javanese in Indonesian waters), in general, trade was open to all. European arrival in the Indian Ocean, however, forced significant 'changes in the ground rules by which Asian trade was conducted' (Curtin 1984: 135, 119-31).

The pattern of trading first established by the Portuguese was later adopted by the Dutch in Southeast Asia and by the English and French in South Asia. Asian trade prior to Portuguese entry was conducted with fairly low protection costs. Most ships were lightly armed and 'sea borne canons were virtually unknown' (Curtin 1984: 137). When the Portuguese gained entry in the Indian Ocean, they first built fortified trading posts and then began to seize control of sea routes. They demanded that Asian merchants pay them fees for sailing in the zones under their control and those ships that failed to purchase permits were confiscated. The Portuguese also blockaded ports to extract exclusive trading privileges from local Indian rulers. Dutch and English East-India companies adopted similar methods to gain monopoly control over trade routes (Chaudhuri 1982: 382-84; Raychaudhuri 1964: 68).

What changes ensued from European participation in the Asian trade? Historians have been very cautious in their assessments of these changes, primarily because older patterns of exchange continued to persist for the first 150 years after the entry of the Europeans (indeed the scale of commerce seemed to increase with the growth of new markets). Long-established patterns of trade exchanges continued to survive, yet some significant qualitative changes did result from the consolidation of the position of European trading companies in the Indian Ocean (Dasgupta 1982: 425-31).

One group of merchants who lost their earlier privileges were the Arabs, who could not match the military power of the Portuguese and Dutch. However, Indian merchants in the sixteenth century succeeded in maintaining their portion of the trade because they cooperated with the Portuguese authorities, their trading operations were better organized and financed, and they had an insider's knowledge of the markets (Dasgupta 1970: 207; Raychaudhuri 1964: 68).

But as the East-India companies consolidated their strength in the seventeenth century, the traditional patterns of trade were destroyed. There was decline in Indian participation in Southeast Asia trade as it was captured by the Dutch East India Company. The Indian merchants were only left with the Red Sea and Persian Gulf markets. Yet, they managed to make enormous profits throughout the seventeenth century because trade as a whole had expanded as a result of the many new overseas markets. During this period, Indian merchants continued to retain control of the West Asian markets in spite of stiff competition from the English East India Company. But this did not extend into the eighteenth century, following decline of Mughal rule. In the earlier period, whenever Indian merchants were beleaguered by the military strength of the European traders they could seek help from Mughal authorities. In 1711, however, the English successfully maneuvered exclusive privileges from weakened Mughal authorities (Dasgupta 1982: 429-31; Raychaudhuri 1964: 73-75).

How did the increasing trade and growing influence of the European East-India companies effect production relations in the handloom textile industry? The major innovation that these trading companies introduced was the institution of a modern firm: an abstract impersonal organization that functioned independent of time and personnel. These joint-stock companies were the precursors of modern trans-national firms dealing in multiproduct operations in varied markets.

The most significant consequence of this innovation was the establishment of hierarchical control over production and distribution systems in the textile industry (Chaudhuri 1982: 404). Prior to European participation, textile production and distribution had operated through a system of multifarious agents who mediated between the craftsmen and the overseas traders. Such a system granted autonomy to individual actors and protected their customary privileges. It was a fiercely competitive universe, however. 'There was no impersonal law, efficiently administered, which would encourage merchants to seek a wider cooperation. In fact, cooperation in business was unpopular' (Dasgupta 1982: 425).

The European trading companies not only created a hierarchy of brokers who became in effect employees of the companies but also subordinated the weavers, who produced now exclusively for them. The weavers previously had depended on a system of advance payment. The growing monopolistic influence of the East-India companies, with their enormous resources, changed this situation. The new relations of production now made the weavers virtually wage workers for the companies (Arasaratnam 1980: 280).

What is the link between Indian handloom imports and the modern British textile industry? The profitable global trade of hand-woven Indian textiles now included the import of Indian textiles into England by the East-India companies and was an important stimulus to the growth of mechanised textile production in England. In the late seventeenth century, British textile manufacturers vigorously agitated against the import of Indian textiles. This agitation was supported by wool merchants and by wool and silk weavers, who sought to persuade Parliament to impose tariffs on imports. Advocates of tariffs used merchantilist arguments to decry against the loss of bullion, and the imposition of high tariffs on Indian imports in 1700 and 1710 served to curb domestic consumption of these textiles while permitting companies to continue trade for re-export.

The most notable consequence of this agitation was protection for the emerging cotton and silk industries in Britain, and manufacturers used this period to imitate dyeing and printing technology used in India, in order to exploit the enormous popularity of bright coloured, delicately printed, and washable calicoes. In a short period, British manufacturers were able successfully to reproduce many varieties of Indian cotton piecegoods to be sold extensively in the colonies in Europe. By 1785, with technological advances brought on by the Industrial Revolution, Britain could produce cloth for mass consumption more cheaply than Indian textile weavers and, early in the nineteenth century, machine-produced English textiles had captured the Indian market (Bal Krishna 1924: 261-65; Furber 1976: 241).

## IV.

Neither the involvement of the English East India Company in the trading of Indian textiles nor the tariffs imposed against Indian imports at the instigation of English manufacturers supports Wallerstein's view that India was peripheral to the European world-economy or that the motivation for the growth of capitalism was entirely internal to Europe. The profitability of India's textile trade and the existence of its expanding export markets were both important stimuli to the development of mechanization in the British textile industry, which was the progenitor of British capitalism.

It could be argued that, in the long run, modern capitalist organization of textile production would, in any case, have driven out handloom production. However, from the perspective of the sixteenth and the seventeenth centuries, even while Europeans could utilize efficient organizational methods and greater resources, Asian merchants continued to compete because of their thrift, lower costs of operations, and an insiders' knowledge of trade. When the Indian textile trade finally began to decline, it was not because Indian textiles ceased to be competitive, but rather because the collapse of the Mughal empire resulted in the loss to traders of guaranteed access to the home market. In overseas markets, Indian imports were curtailed through non-economical means, such as tariffs and quotas.

The rise of a modern textile industry in England was embedded in patterns of world trading through which the fates of South Asia and England already were intertwined. Not only competition in production technology but also political manipulation over a long period of time finally brought about Western hegemony. History could have taken another turn. A recent author has marvellously conceived such an alternative scenario:

If things had worked out only slightly differently, the Industrial Revolution might have taken place in India. We could now be living in a world where Indian tourists complained constantly about the squalor of England and where Europe and North America would be underdeveloped quasi-colonies whose main function was providing raw materials for the insatiable factories of Bengal and Gujarat . . . . (Bronson 1983: 23)

## Bibliography

Alaev, L. B. 'South India.' In *The Cambridge Economic History of India,* I. Cambridge, 1982.

Arasaratnam, S. 'Aspects of the Role and Activities of South Indian Merchants *c.* 1650-1750.' In *Proceedings of the First International Conference Seminar of Tamil Studies,* 1, pp. 582-96. Kuala Lampur, 1966.

__________. 'Trade and Political Dominion in South India 1750-1790: Changing British-Indian Relationships.' *Modern Asian Studies* 13 (1979): 19-40.

__________. 'Weavers, Merchants and Company: The Handloom Industry in South-Eastern India, 1750-1790.' *The Indian Economic and Social History Review* 17 (1980): 257-281.

Bagchi, Amiya. 'De-industrialization in the 19th Century: Some Theoretical Implications.' *Journal of Development Studies* 12.2 (1976): 135-64.

Bal Krishna. *Commercial Relations Between India and England 1601-1757.* London, 1924.

Barbosa, Duarte. *The Book of Duarte Barbosa.* 2 volumes. Edited by M. L. Dames. London, 1918-21.

Brennig, Joseph J. 'Chief Merchants and the European Enclaves of Seventeenth Century Coromandel.' *Modern Asian Studies* 11.3 (1977): 321-40.

Bronson, Bennett. 'An Industrial Miracle in a Golden Age: The 17th Century Cloth Exports of India.' *Field Museum of Natural History Bulletin* 54.1 (1983): 12-25.

Chaudhuri, K. N. 'Foreign Trade.' In *The Cambridge Economic History of India,* I. Cambridge, 1982.

Chaudhuri, K. N. *The Trading World of Asia and the English East India Company, 1660-1760.* Cambridge, 1978.

Choksey, R. D. *Economic Life in the Bombay Gujarat, 1800-1939.* Bombay, 1968.

Commissariat, M. S. *A History of Gujarat.* Vol. 2. Bombay, 1938-57.

Curtin, Philip, D. *Cross-Cultural Trade in World History.* Cambridge, 1984.

Dasgupta, Ashin. 'Indian Merchants and the Trade in the Indian Ocean, *c.* 1500-1750.' In *The Cambridge Economic History of India.* Cambridge, 1982.

Dasgupta, Ashin. 'Trade and Politics in 18th Century India.' In Richards 1970.

Davies, D. W. *A Primer of Dutch Seventeenth Century Overseas Trade.* The Hague, 1961.

Desai, Neera. *Social Change in Gujarat: A Study of 19th Century Gujarati Society.* Bombay, 1978.

Furber, Holden. *Bombay Presidency in the Mid-Eighteenth Century.* London, 1965.

__________. *Rival Empires of Trade in the Orient, 1600-1800.* Minneapolis, 1976.

Gillion, Kenneth. *Ahmedabad: A Study in Urban History.* Berkeley and Los Angeles, 1968.

Gokhale, B. G. 'Ahmedabad in the XVIIth Century.' *Journal of the Economic and Social History of the Orient* 12 (1969): 187-97.

Gopal, Surendra. *Commerce and Crafts in Gujarat: 16th and 17th Centuries.* New Delhi, 1975.

India (Republic), All India Handicrafts Board. *Indian Printed Textiles.* no date.

Irwin, John and Margaret Hall. *Indian Painted and Printed Fabrics.* Ahmedabad, 1971.

Irwin, John and P. R. Schwartz. *Studies in Indo European Textile History.* Ahmedabad, 1966.

Ito, Shoji. 'A Note on the 'Business Combines' in India with Special Reference to the Nattokotai Chettiars.' *The Developing Economies* 4 (1966): 367-80.

Jain, L. C. *Indigeneous Banking in India.* London, 1929.

Khan, Safaat Ahmad. *The East India Trade in the XVIIth Century.* New Delhi, 1975.

Kling, Blair B. and M. N. Pearson, eds. *The Age of Partnership: Europeans in Asia before Domination.* Honolulu, 1979.

*Madras District Gazeteer: Coimbatore.* Madras, 1966.

Meglio, Rita D. 'The Arab Trade with Indonesia and the Malay Peninsula.' In Richards 1970.

Mehta, Makrand. *The Ahmedabad Cotton Textile Industry: Genesis and Growth.* Ahmedabad, 1982.

Meilink-Roelofsz, M. A. P. 'Trade and Islam in the Malay-Indonesian

Archipelago Prior to the Arrival of the Europeans.' In Richards 1970.

Naidu, B. V. N. 'The Nattukottai Chettiars and their Banking System.' In *Rajah Sir Annamalai Commemoration Volume.* Annamalainagar, 1941.

Naqvi, Hameda Khatoon. *Urbanisation and Urban Centers Under the Great Moghuls.* Simla, 1972.

Pearse, Arno. *The Cotton Textile Industry of India.* Manchester, 1930.

Pires, Tome. *The Suma Oriental of Tome Pires: An Account of the East from the Red Sea to Japan, Written in Malacca and India in 1512-15.* Ed. and trans. by Armado Cortesao. Vol. 1. London, 1944.

Raju, A. Sarada. *Economic Conditions in Madras Presidency: 1800-1857.* Madras, 1941.

Ramsay, George D. *English Overseas Trade During the Centuries of Emergence.* London, 1957.

Raychaudhuri, Tapan. 'European Commercial Activity and the Organization of India's Commerce and Industrial Production 1500-1750.' In *Readings in Indian Economic History,* edited by B. N. Ganguli. New York, 1964.

__________. 'A Re-Interpretation of Nineteenth Century Indian Economic History?' *The Indian Economic and Social History Review* 5 (1968): 77-100.

__________. *Jan Company in Coromandel 1605-1690: A Study of the Interrelations of European Commerce and Traditional Economies.* The Hague, 1962.

Richards, D. S., ed. *Islam and the Trade of Asia: A Colloquium.* Oxford, 1970.

Spodek, Howard. 'Traditional Culture and Entrepreneurship: A Case

Study of Ahmedabad.' *Economic and Political Weekly* (Feb. 1969): m-27.

Thomas, P. J. 'Nattukottai Chettiars: Their Banking System.' In *Rajah Sir Annamalai Commemoration Volume,* 840-54. Annamalainagar, 1941.

Wallerstein, Immanuel. 'The Incorporation of the Indian Sub-Continent into the Capitalist World-Economy.' Paper delivered at the Seminar on the Indian Ocean, New Delhi, 1985.

# The Craft and Commerce of Oriental Carpets: Cultural Implications of Economic Success and Failure

Brian Spooner
University of Pennsylvania

What we recognize now as oriental carpets, especially pile-carpets, are currently made in most of the countries of the Middle East, North Africa, and southwest and Central Asia, including of course Pakistan and India, as well as China. The technique originated before 500 B.C. somewhere in the area that later became the culturally Irano-Turkic part of Asia. Royal patronage under the Sasanians (if not earlier empires) raised carpet production to the status of high art. The most highly regarded carpets have continued to come from Irano-Turkic areas (including the Caucasus). Carpets made to the west and south of these areas have remained derivative in both technique and design, and less admired, though sometimes of objectively excellent craftsmanship. (The Chinese tradition is also derivative but developed independently.)

Like other textiles, a pile-carpet begins with weaving on a loom set up with warp threads, the ends of which usually provide the fringe at either end of the finished product. The webbing at the beginning and end of the weaving may be simple weft on warp, but may be elaborated by one or another of a number of flat-weave techniques. The body of the carpet is produced by tying rows of knots around overlapping pairs of warp threads. Each row of knots is held in place by the insertion of one or more weft threads before the next row is added. The ends of the knots are cut evenly to constitute the pile. In a fine carpet they are cut very close to the base. In order to achieve the desired degree of tightness and evenness of weave and density of knots, after every few rows — before the cutting — the weavers beat the weft threads and the pile back towards them with a comb-like implement, the teeth of which fit over the warp threads. This action also has the effect of making the pile of traditionally handwoven carpets incline permanently in one direction, towards the end the weaver started from. For this reason, throughout the life of the carpet, light strikes the ends of the knots at different angles according to the position of the viewer and, in the case of some qualities of wool (and especially of silk), makes the colors appear different from different angles, contributing to the overall appeal of the product.

We do not know the origin of the craft or at what time it became an integral part of the material culture of the rural sector of Irano-Turkic society, but from the time of the earliest evidence onwards, there appear to have been two separate but related traditions of carpet-weaving: tribal carpets, made with household materials for household purposes (whether or not they later found their way onto the market), and urban carpets, made for and financed by the market, with materials provided by it. It is useful to represent the history of the craft and the trade in terms of (1) tribal (female) weavers working in the home on horizontal looms with their own materials, among whom the relations of production emphasized the structure of the family and the symbolism of the carpet elaborated the meanings of the family and community life; and (2) urban weavers (mostly minors and males) working outside the home on vertical looms for wages under a master. Between these two traditions there evolved very early on a grey area of rural producers, living close in, who worked for gain and were financed to varying degrees by local or regional businessmen.

Oriental carpets (both tribal and urban, and their imitations) are, despite their variety, immediately recognisable by their design, which is composed by using different colored wools for the knots that constitute the pile. While their is a broad range of designs, they fall easily into two types: figurative and geometric. Urban carpets are mainly figurative, while many tribal carpets favor geometric motifs. The figurative designs of classic urban carpets can easily be traced back to such elitist inspirations as royal gardens. It is possible that the geometric designs of tribal carpets go back to similar origins. Other aspects of the relationship between village and city, or between desert and sown, in the history of the Middle East suggest that tribal carpets are likely to be in large measure derivative of urban forms. The historical success of the craft is due to the fact that it was developed under royal patronage while it continued to be practiced in rural and nomadic communities for household use. This social range and variation in the relations of production has been responsible for the great variety that we associate with oriental carpets.

Apart from wood for the simple horizontal loom, all other materials for the tribal weaver could be generated locally, for the most part within the household, and it was feasible for each family to provide all of its production needs. For example, the typical Turkmen carpet (a perennial favorite with collectors) was until recently made entirely of wool, except perhaps for a little cotton or silk to provide a color, especially white, that was rare or difficult to achieve with their own karakul breed of sheep. The fact that the weaver, typically a daughter or wife, was closely associated in everyday life with the flock manager, typically the household head, was important. A good carpet required wool spun differently for three different purposes (warp, weft, and pile). A good warp is so fine and strong that the unaccustomed observer may fail to recognize it as wool. The secret lies in the choice of the longer fibers from the fleece, in the carding as well as the spinning. For each purpose, the weaver selects wool sheared at a particular season from a particular part of animals of a particular age. There is much in such a technology that is easier to organize in a household that manages all the operations, from animal husbandry to carpet production, than with the division of labor and relations of production typical of a more complex economy. Moreover, independent household production encourages a particular type of personal and communal association with the product and with its design, which is reflected in the artistic dynamism and integrity of the product. In the household mode of production, the carpet has intense symbolic value for the producers — which dissipates as the productive process is drawn into the larger economy. There are also practical considerations. A weaver who accepts wool from the market loses the ability to control quality and to differentiate types of wool for different purposes. But there are also benefits in centralisation. Dyeing, for example, can be done more efficiently on a large scale.

The urban (or factory) type of carpet has changed little as the result of modernisation. Some of the most exquisite carpets known to us were produced for the Safavid court in Iran in the sixteenth-seventeenth centuries. But they may have been no better than those at the Sasanian court in the third-seventh centuries. The only significant difference in today's carpets of the same type may be some improvement in the lot of the weavers and a decline in quality, which has led to a situation where many of the better modern products (the famous Persian carpets, such as Nains and Kashans) have been priced out of the international market.

The tribal or household type of carpet, on the other hand, has been almost entirely drawn into the grey area of urban (or international) dependency. The process began gradually with the diffusion of artificial dyes in the second half of the nineteenth century, accelerated in the second half of this century with the increasing economic demand of the Western world, and was finally completed by the unstabilising effects of severe drought, especially in Afghanistan, in the early 1970s.

Although we know little about the early history of the production of oriental carpets, we have a reasonable amount of information about the recent history of international consumption, about how oriental carpets came to be an integral part of the material environment of the Western world. Once they had become an object of royal patronage and manufacture, they became also an object of long-distance trade. As the trade moved westwards, the oriental carpet influenced the textile production of the West. Eventually, in the nineteenth century, imitation oriental carpets began to be mass-produced in Europe and America. Consumers sought them because of their interest in *objets* that were not only highly functional but exotic (in fact they were not commonly used for floor-covering in the West until the eighteenth century.) By including an oriental carpet in his home a man made a statement about himself to his community. He sought distinction (Bourdieu 1984). A well-chosen oriental carpet on the floor suggested that the personal significance of the owner transcended the affairs of the local community, both linking him to another category of people with whom he wished to be associated and giving him a distinctive image among them. *I* represent my criteria for choosing the carpet I display in terms of its authenticity. I distinguish myself by projecting my concern for distinction into my reconstruction of the social and cultural provenance of the carpet. As economies expand and demand increases, more and more people wish to make such statements about themselves — even people who are less experienced in the social game of distinction or who cannot afford authenticity. These people may be happy to buy Western imitations.

Although oriental carpets found their way into Europe very early, on the scale we are familiar with today the trade essentially began with the mechanisation of textile production in the West in the middle of the nineteenth century. A little later, in the second half of the nineteenth century, oriental carpet production was drawn irrevocably into the world economy, initially through the attraction of chemical dyes. By the turn of the century there had been a quantum increase in the numbers of oriental carpets reaching the West, and a qualitative change (caused by the influence of the West-dominated world economy) in the production process. Until this time, although it would probably not be true to say that production was untouched by any influence from the international market, such influence had been relatively slight. Since then, and even more since about 1975, the demand of the international market has increased to the point where it dominates all considerations of production even in the most isolated Asian rural communities.

The international carpet trade has been exceptional in economic history both for its stability (what other product has enjoyed consistent and expanding demand for at least 2,500 years?) and for its reliance on the mutual interdependence of culturally different producers and consumers in different parts of the world who had no direct communication with each other. The merchandise worked its way through chains of dealers in Asia, the Mediterranean, and Europe — especially Bukhara, Istanbul, Venice, and London. What the Iranian or Turkic weaver wanted to produce and what the Western consumer wanted to buy coincided only by chance — though the odds were increased by Western interest in exotic authenticity. Neither had any idea of the other, or of the social or cultural conditions that shaped their conception of the ideal carpet. During the second half of this century, however, the situation has changed, and continues to change at an increasing rate, as a result of global changes in technology and communications.

In the 1970s the supply of both old and new carpets increased significantly. In Afghanistan, in particular, the economic difficulties caused by the Sahelian drought had the effect of flushing out onto the market priceless heirlooms that would otherwise never have been sold. In the mid-70s even antique carpets could sometimes be found at bargain prices. At the same time, orphaned children were trained to weave carpets for the Western market in factory-type situations. Prison inmates were similarly employed. Most significantly, financiers and dealers from the eastern end of the trade network were able and encouraged to visit the West and see for themselves the consumption of their products and to communicate directly with the consumer, making their own deals instead of working through multiple intermediaries. For the first time, producers saw the opportunity to open up new markets by adapting production to satisfy demand.

This process was encouraged by the accelerating expansion of demand. Oriental carpets had become important accessories in fairly routine interior design. Every department store displayed them. This new type of demand has generated a need for a new type of production: an oriental carpet that would compete with the factory-produced imitation from Western as well as other Asian countries. It was no longer just the best oriental carpets that were in demand but the whole range of quality and value. Instead of one Western criterion of assessment, the connoisseurship of authentic craftsmanship, there were two: to the collector's criteria of connoisseurship were added those of modern interior design. The two did not always coincide. The result of this recent accelerated process (based mainly in England and Germany) has been some instability and change in the connoisseurship of older carpets (some types of carpet, such as Baluches, that were ignored by collectors twenty years ago are now highly valued), and considerable modification of designs, mixing of motifs, and experimentation in colors in current production.

By filling this new market niche with products from the lower end of their quality range, many traders from the Middle East have made new fortunes, but there have also been significant commercial failures. Afghan producers in particular (especially Turkmen, the generic merchants of Central Asia) have for the first time tried to capitalise directly on their new opportunity to produce for the expanding Western market by assessing Western taste themselves, redesigning their product, and undercutting Western imitations. They seem unable, however, to understand the dynamics of Western taste, either the Western quest for authenticity or the criteria of modern interior design. The commercial problems they have run into are now exacerbated by the recent U.S. Congress' withdrawal of 'most favored nation' status from Afghanistan. The Indian and Pakistani dhurrie is presently more successful than Afghan products at the lower end of the market for exotic floor covering. Dhurries are simple loosely woven throws, often wool weft on cotton warp, with minimal decorative embroidery. They are simpler and easier to produce and to redesign, and require relatively little investment in training or materials, than pile carpets. It is worth noting that the dhurrie is produced by Pakistanis and Indians who have had 150 years of experience adapting to Western tastes. Afghans do not have such experience.

The trade in oriental carpets was successful on a relatively large scale in a particular period, roughly 1870 to 1970. The top of the market continues to be held by antique and old 'authentic' pieces. The craft (which for the time being will survive on the local and regional demand which has always been its main support) is losing the competition for the middle and lower sectors of the international market, which currently are held by imitations and derivative work from the periphery and by the dhurrie.

This present evolution of the relationship between producer and consumer in the international trade in oriental carpets carries with it some lessons for our study of inter-cultural communication generally. As long as there were chains of intermediaries between the two poles of a culturally distant economic relationship, the relationship worked, but it worked at a relatively low volume of trade. Only a small proportion of the total production of oriental carpets was consumed in the West and the consumers were 'up-market.' Now that producer has met consumer and attempted to move down-market in order to increase sales, acquire more control of the market, and to deal directly across what may be an unprecedented cultural distance, the relationship is no longer working. We tend to put this type of failure down to straightforward economic factors, but these factors themselves are due to the cultural inability of producers to 'read' the consumers. Although producer and consumer interact and communicate about the tastes of the consumer and the abilities of the producer, somehow the producer does not satisfy the consumer. When the consumer could not interact with the producer, 'authenticity' itself supported the trade. Direct demand for specific, objective, products across the same cultural gap (and where authenticity no longer is a factor) does not work.

Anthropologists have long studied cultures in contact, but they have emphasized the processes by which people in neighboring cultures modify their values, interpretations, and their interaction in order to understand and live with each other. In the study of acculturation (which has been the study of the process of the breaking down of cultural barriers) we have taken it for granted that cultures in contact will adapt to each other, that mutual understanding (like ecological adaptation) is bound to come about, and that the cultural barriers to understanding will always break down. Even if this is inevitable in the long run, it may be more relevant that it does not occur in the short term. Based on the experience of the last decade or so, typified by the Afghan carpet producer in America but equally true for other visiting, immigrant, refugee groups, immediate social accommodation in some degree may be the norm, but cross-cultural understanding does not necessarily occur.

The success of the dhurrie typifies the public culture of a pluralist world. We live in the age of the dhurrie. The Western market is interested in products with exotic flair that are not too durable or too expensive. The success of the dhurrie in competition with even the less expensive varieties of handwoven oriental pile-carpets is a phenomenon instructive in demonstrating the problems and processes of cross-cultural communication in the modern world, which differ from the past because of the rate, quantity, and complexity of such communication today.

## Bibliography

Bahnassi, Afif. 'Authenticity in Art: Exposition, Definition, Methodology.' *Cultures* 6 (1979): 65-82.

Benjamin, Walter. 'The Work of Art in the Age of Mechanical Reproduction.' Reprinted in Walter Benjamin, *Illuminations,* New York, 1969.

Bourdieu, Pierre. *Distinction: A Social Critique of the Judgement of Taste.* Cambridge, Mass., 1984.

Irons, William. 'The Place of Carpet Weaving in Turkmen Society.' In *Turkmen: Tribal Carpets and Traditions,* edited by Louise W. Mackie and Jon Thompson, pp. 23-38. Washington, D.C., 1980.

Schurmann, Ulrich. *Central Asian Rugs.* London, 1969.

Silver, Harry R. 'Calculating Risks: The Socioeconomic Foundations of Aesthetic Motivation.' *Ethnology* 20 (1981): 101-14.

Spooner, Brian. 'Weavers and Dealers: The Authenticity of an Oriental Carpet.' In *The Social Life of Things, Commodities in Cultural Perspective,* edited by Arjun Appadurai, pp. 195-235. Cambridge, 1986.

# Mithilā Painting

Mary C. Lanius
University of Denver, Colorado

Mithilā painting was first revealed to outsiders as a distinct and unequalled artistic expression because of an unfortunate quirk of nature. In 1934, an earthquake of devastating proportions ravaged the Madhubani District of northern Bihar. In several of the particularly hard-hit villages, fragile mud walls cracked and disintegrated, revealing inner rooms and verandas richly adorned with paintings. The once smoothly plastered walls, which had been all but hidden from casual view, were covered with intricate diagrams and figures. Upon closer investigation, it was found that the drawings and paintings had been done by village women to celebrate a variety of seasonal festivals and rituals. Some of the most intricate of these auspicious symbols were for the interior walls of the *kohbar ghar* or marriage chamber and the *gosiar ghar* or room of the gods. The young district official who had been sent by the government to direct relief operations after the earthquake was William G. Archer. Some years later, Archer himself became well known as a noted authority on Indian painting.[1] During the relief operation, there was no time to make even a preliminary survey of the wall paintings. Several years later, however, Archer made two extensive tours in the region. On each of those occasions, he made numerous photographs of murals *in situ* and collected examples of 'memory' pictures done on paper. The majority of these photographs and paintings on paper are now in the India Office Library, London.

No one knows how ancient this traditional form of wall painting is. In the *Rāmcaritmānas,* a vernacular version of the *Rāmāyaṇa* written by Tulsīdās in the second quarter of the seventeenth century, there is, however, a reference to paintings on houses in the Mithilā region. Several episodes of this great epic poem are set in Mithilā, since Sītā, the wife of the hero Rāma, came from this ancient kingdom. This is the first ascription that we have, but may reflect a common literary connection of the time, rather than a reference to true painted designs on the houses.

[1] After Independence, Archer became Keeper of the Indian Section, Victoria and Albert Museum, London.

Painting on paper is relatively new. In the past, 'memory' pictures — small versions of wall paintings — were done on paper, usually in pen and ink, and given to a young bride when she left her village for the village of her husband. These 'memory' pictures were patterns to aid her in reconstructing the often complex designs of the wall paintings that she had learned to make as a child and young woman; now she must make them in her new home in conjunction with the many festivals and ceremonies that will punctuate her life there.

The idea of transferring such designs to paper for display and/or sale was introduced by another outsider, this time an Indian, Upendra Maharathi, a noted designer and scholar. Maharathi was greatly impressed by the wall paintings and diagrams that he had seen on several tours of the Madhubani District. He held a series of exhibitions in the late 1930s that were made up of wall-painting motifs and floor designs *('aripans')* that had been recorded by the village women on paper. In the 1950s, he began to distribute handmade paper among the women of various villages where wall painting survived. In 1955, he held an exhibition of some of these works on paper at the Folk Art Museum in Patna. During this exhibition, such paintings were seen for the first time by the head of the All India Handicrafts Board.

Several years earlier, in 1949, Archer already had published a richly illustrated article in *Marg* entitled 'Maithil Painting,' which introduced this distinct style of wall painting to a large international audience. Even with all of this recognition and acclaim, the tradition of wall painting and floor diagrams was very much on the decline in the entire Mithilā region in the mid-fifties.

Modern Mithilā covers an area of some 22,000 square miles and extends north from the Ganges river to the foothills of the Himālayas. Somewhere around twenty-five million people live within this isolated expanse of the Ganges plain. The ancient kingdom of Mithilā flourished long before the time of Aśoka, and it was here that legendary king Janaka, father of Sītā, reigned.

A severe drought in 1966-67 left most of the villagers within the Mithilā area destitute and without any way of making a living. Pupul Jayakar of the All India Handicrafts Board remembered the paintings on paper she had seen at the exhibition in Patna as well as the remnants of wall decorations that she had seen on a tour of the district with Maharathi. In hopes of finding a new means to support the drought-stricken villages, she sent a young artist by the name of Bhaskar Kulkarni to Mithilā with handmade paper and paints to distribute. At first he was rebuked and turned away. He eventually found a village where he could at least talk to the men and tell them about the government drought-relief project. The idea was to have the women start painting on paper and give their work to Kulkarni, who would then deliver them to the Handicrafts Board for sale in their various emporia. In the beginning, he had little if any contact with the women who actually made the paintings, but as time passed, he was accepted by the villagers and began to give advice on composition and color. For the first time, traditional painting themes of Mithilā were seen outside the mud-walled villages of northern Bihar. Since then, painting on paper has become a very important part of life for many of the villagers close to the towns of Madhubani and Darbhangha. In fact, painting on paper has now been taken up by several men including two *tantrics,* basically because it is so lucrative, although it is not a steady means of income. Several of the finest Maithil-brahmin women-artists now have the assistance of sons or husbands who work alongside of them filling in the flat area of color. The development of these family ateliers is an interesting phenomenon worthy of further study.

The first large-scale exhibition of paintings was held in New Delhi in the winter of 1967, and the following summer a sampling of them was placed on display at Expo '67 in Montreal. Since then, Mithilā paintings have been shown in Paris, Expo '70 in Osaka, the University of Texas, Austin, the University of Denver, and various art exhibitions in New York, Chicago, St. Louis, Madison, Rio de Janeiro, Munich, and Switzerland.

There are three general types or styles of painting, and these appear to have developed along caste lines, long before painting on paper became fashionable. A composition using strong black outlines and bold flat areas of color typifies the work of the Maithil brahmins. In contrast, the Maithil kāyasths, the caste of clerks and scribes, do extremely fine line-drawings often using only one or two colors, usually black and dark red. The harijans, the lowest ranked caste, have developed a distinct painting style of their own. They also do inventive sculpted walls on the outside of their houses. Originally, the outlines of harijan paintings were made with a cow dung/water substance. After it had dried, the soft brown line was reinforced by a series of black dots. Only then was the painting ready to have the flat colored areas added. A rich palette is used in these paintings, and certain color combinations are favored by particular artists.

Before painting on paper became a commercial activity, the colors used were all natural, derived from vegetable and mineral sources. Today, colors are mostly chemical, purchased in the bazaar and dissolved in goat's milk or gum paste.[2] Brushes are made from slivers of bamboo frayed at the ends or pieces of rag tied around a twig. Often old fashioned steel-nib pens are used for fine-line drawings. The only mechanical aid is a bit of twine and a stick used to form a simple compass to make the circles for diagrams. Handmade wood-pulp paper is now used for most of the paintings. This paper is not made locally, but comes from Pune. If a larger surface is called for, however, anything is acceptable; all kinds of papers are used, regardless of quality or suitability.

Originally, painting was based on a communal group activity. It was rooted in tradition, and was an integrated part of village life. The paintings on walls and floor patterns *(aripans)* were done entirely by the women of the household as an everyday domestic act. Individual ceremonies required particular paintings, and sometimes they were made as integral parts of the ritual.

Somewhere around thirty annual festivals are organized and performed by women in the Mithilā region. Women's rituals, unlike those of the men, take a rather free form. They are often conducted concurrently, but separate from those of the men. Painting is a part of the culture, the painters are all amateurs, and until recently the women painted according to family tradition.

Even though the great majority of painting themes are traditional, the artists do not always follow orthodox Hindu iconographic canons. Inconsistencies in the mythology and colors associated with certain deities are common. Śaktism dominates the area and Kālī and Durgā are ever popular manifestations of female power. The *Rāmāyaṇa,* the great epic Sanskrit poem, is the single most popular subject for paintings by both the brahmins and the kāyasths. Divine couples such as Rādhā and Kṛṣṇa, and Gaurī and Mahādeva are also often portrayed. The harijans have developed a lively body of folklore of their own based on the exploits of 'Lord Salhesh,' a semidivine historic character who was a *dacoit* or robber bandit. His exploits and those of his companions are the subject of much of their painting. Unfortunately, little is known about this localized tradition outside of the Mithilā sphere.

A relatively recent phenomenon is the development of distinct individual styles among the more gifted painters. With a bit of study, the various works of individual artists can now easily be discerned. Notable

[2] Several of the artists have recently begun using natural colors, notably Karpurī Devī and Śaśikalā Devī, both of Ranti Village.

divisions still persist along caste lines, however, but even these are breaking down. Certain generalities can still be made. Kāyasth painters usually do flat complex designs that crowd the entire composition. Emphasis is on the quality of line. Color is of little importance; often only black and red or one other color is used. Borders are generally made up of intricate repeat designs, which frame the entire composition with bees, fish, flowers, and geometric forms. In contrast, the Maithil-brahmin painters define their forms with bold, forceful black lines and fill in the broad areas between with flat vibrant color. Forms are simplified, often with distorted contours. The figures are related by color and linear forms, with color often used for its own sake and not symbolically. There is no attempt to relate figures and objects naturally. Forms often float and there is little if any scale relationship. The picture plane is flat and every available bit of space is filled. Some of the painters have begun to render their figures in a slightly more natural way, which is probably due to outside influences. There is a certain naiveté about Maithil painting that has undoubtedly enhanced its popularity among collectors both in India and abroad.

Although there are several hundred people painting in the Mithilā area, there are only a handful or so that can be classed as artists. Sītā Devī is probably the best known of the artists. She began painting in 1966. Before then, she had spent long hours making grass baskets to supplement her husband's meager income. In 1975, she was given the President's Award for Master Craftsmen. The following year, Sītā Devī and her son Sūrya Dev, who does the coloring, travelled to Washington, D.C., to attend the Folk Life Festival there. On that trip, she also visited New York and East Berlin. Over the years, she has spent many months in Delhi working on various commissions, among them the VIP lounge at the Delhi airport and the Madhubani room of the Akbar Hotel. Bauā Devī is the mother of six children. Her maternal grandfather was recognized as a fine painter in his village. The coloring of her paintings is often done by her husband, and they make a rather successful team. Her work has been exhibited in a number of Indian cities and she has done several commissions. Like Bauā Devī's husband, Lalitā Devī's also helps her with the coloring. As a young child, she was orphaned and brought up by her grandmother who taught her many songs. Sometimes she interprets the story line of a song into her paintings. Mahāsundarī Devī comes from Ranti village and is a friend of Gaṅgā Devī. In 1973, she was given the highest award of the State of Bihar, the Rajkīya Pratham Puruṣkar. She, too, has done a number of commissions, the most prominent being a large painting for Parliament House, New Delhi. Gaṅgā Devī and Mahāsundarī Devī are both kāyasths and work in a very fine linear style. Gaṅgā Devī has taken *dikṣā* or initiation vows, and is considered an ascetic, or a holy person. She has also won the President's Award for Master Craftsmen. Most recently, she was in Washington as a part of the 'Aditi' exhibit. Yamunā Devī, a harijan, is in her early fifties. She has won a number of state awards and has done many commissions at various places in India. Her paintings as well as sculpture were displayed at Expo '70 in Japan. Like several of the other artists, her husband Rāmji does the coloring for her.

For centuries, Mithilā has been a most important center for Sanskrit learning and culture. The paintings done by the women on walls and paper are not new statements, but a continuation of a number of ancient expressions. Styles of painting were learned rather than individually developed. Mithilā painting has a subtlety and an ancient cultural basis that are not seen in tribal or village folk art, and it is this that sets it apart. Mildred Archer, in her book *Indian Popular Painting,* says this about Maithil artists: 'the result is a body of work which while firmly rooted in the former styles and as such is still essentially 'popular' in character, has also made a new and sophisticated contribution to modern art in India' (1977, p. 91).

During the past twenty years, painting in the Mithilā region has changed markedly. Wall painting and floor designs are still very much a part of everyday life, and it would be unthinkable to hold a ceremony or festival without the proper diagrams. However, painting on paper as a commercial activity has overshadowed these traditional expressions. It has developed into a very important source of income, and some twenty or so talented painters have become prosperous because of it. The status of many of the artists has changed for the better, and their families have attained a new financial independence. Over the years, the development of a new maturity among the best of the artists can easily be seen. They now work with the surety and confidence of professionals. Even though they continue to paint in a traditional idiom, they have developed distinct styles of their own and deserve to have their work judged as popular painting and not simply as folk art. 'In the best art, there is an inescapable element of strangeness, the sense of a novel wonder, a mystery burning at the heart of life, and it is the strangeness, this incandescence, which above all the painting of Mithila transmits' (W. G. Archer: 1949, p. 33).

## Bibliography

*Aditi: The Living Arts of India.* Washington, D.C., 1985.

Anand, Mulk Raj. *Madhubani Painting.* New Delhi, 1984.

Archer, Mildred. *Indian Popular Painting in the India Office Library.* London, 1977.

_________. 'Domestic Arts of Mithila: Notes on Painting.' *Marg* 20.1 (1966): 47-52.

Archer, William G. 'Mithil Painting.' *Marg* 3.3 (1949): 24-33.

Brown, Carolyn Henning. 'Folk Art and the Art Books: Who Speaks for the Traditional Artists?' Review of *The Art of Mithila,* by Yves Vequaud. *Modern Asian Studies* 16.3 (1982): 519-22.

Huyler, Stephen P. *Village India.* New York, 1985.

Jain, Devaki. *Woman's Quest for Power.* Delhi, 1980.

Jayakar, Pupul. *The Earthen Drum: An Introduction to the Ritual Arts of Rural India.* New Delhi, 1980.

_________. 'Paintings: Form of Gay Abandon.' *Marg* 22.4 (1969): 47.

_________. 'Paintings of Rural India.' *The Times of India Annual* (1975): 53-62.

Jha, Ratnadhar. 'Mithila Painting.' In *Lesser Known Forms of Performing Arts in India,* edited by Durgados Mukhopadhyay, 38-44. Calcutta, no date.

Kramrisch, Stella. *Unknown India: Ritual Art in Tribe and Village.* Philadelphia, 1968.

Mathur, J. C. 'Domestic Arts of Mithila.' *Marg* 20.1 (1966): 43-46.

Owens, Raymond L. 'Master Craftsmen's Association of Mithila.' (unpublished report).

Thakur, Upendra. *Madhubani Painting.* Atlantic Highlands, N.J., 1982.

Vequaud, Yves. 'Colors of Devotion.' *Portfolio.* (Feb.-Mar. 1980): 60-67.

__________. *The Women Painters of Mithila.* London, 1977.

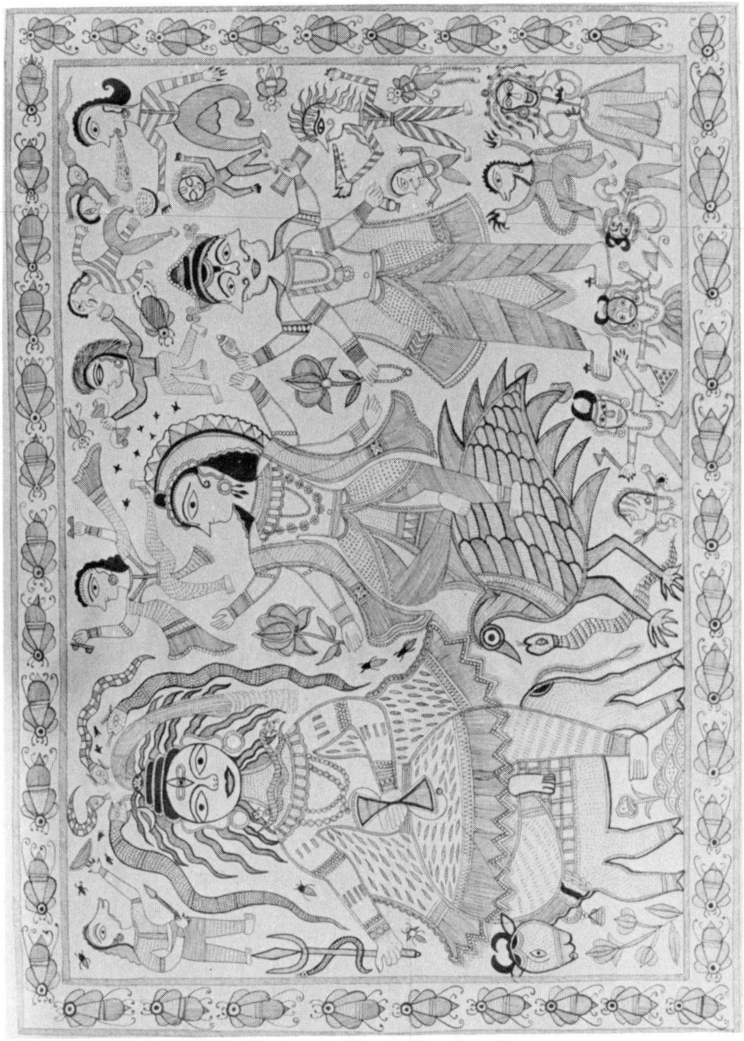

Fig. A.
'Marriage Party of Śiva,' by Karpuri Devi, Ranti village.

Fig. B.
'Two cows Belonging to Lord Salhesh,' by Shanti Devi, Leheriagunj village.

Fig. C.
'Rama and Sita Riding on a Peacock,' by Jagadamba Devi, Jitwarpur village.

# Adaptation and Change in Rural Indian Material Culture

Stephen P. Huyler
Camden, Maine

As an ethnologist documenting rural Indian material culture, I find that all parts of a village are important. Craftsmanship, broadly viewed, includes all things simple and complex made by the hand of man. The role of an Indian craftsman encompasses production of his craft, his socio-economic setting, and the value his product has for him, his community, and his environment. My field work attempts to record material culture objectively, but my broader focus is on the relation of contemporary products to historical traditions, seeing change as a product of history as well as a necessary ingredient for the future.

Westerners and often educated urban Indians tend to view rural India as remote, medieval, and rather backward. Villages are thought to be repositories of stagnant traditions offering some glimmerings of worthwhile crafts, such as Kutch embroideries, Mithilā paintings, Dhokra bronzes, Orissan *ikat* saris, etc. — but these crafts are believed to come from specific, creatively fertile regions, their products gaining an importance disproportionate to the dull villages which surround them.

My experience is that every part of rural India is rich in crafts — each subtly and suitably adapted to its environment and its function. If one considers the whole of India, the diversity is staggering. The people living in India's 560,000 villages account for one seventh of humanity. The Indian census defines a village as a community having a population of less than 5,000, but an average village contains only 635 people. Every village in India has several full-time craftspeople residing in it, but in ethnological terms that number is much higher when all the people in each village who make something by hand at one time or another are considered. In my research, a clay-slab grain-storage vessel built by a farmer's wife for her own use is just as integral to the study of rural material culture as a silk brocade wedding sari woven by a professional weaver.

Adaptation is fundamental to traditional Indian rural society. India's geographical extremes are a primary cause of its cultural diversities. Each rural community has learned, through centuries of living in one specific area, to adapt its customs, technologies, and products to the demands of its environment. While changes from one village to the next may seem slight, each village, when viewed closely, interprets its environment and its traditions differently. Viewed broadly, the whole composition of rural communities changes from one region to the next. These often subtle adaptations combine inherent wisdoms often with innovative techniques for adjustment to changing environment. While social requirements are important, prevailing winds, annual rainfall, the position of the sun, location of water sources, altitudes, variations in terrain, agricultural resources, and availability of building materials also are essential factors governing the layout and construction of villages. Today, modern villages often ignore such traditional considerations in their desire to conform to more widely accepted modern conventions. In doing so, they produce communities which are impractical for the local environment and economy and which are at odds with local aesthetics, further encouraging social fragmentation.

In the traditional Indian house, every element is important, everything fulfills a necessary function. Houses and their components are built of locally available materials and vary from village to village depending upon the climate. In the rocky Deccan, walls are built of stone slabs, in tribal jungles they are wood, and in the alluvial plains they are dried mud. Where clay is accessible, roofs are often tiled, the shapes of the tiles changing throughout the country. Many roofs are thatched, using a myriad of materials: palm fronds, leaves, reeds, cane, wheat or rice straw, etc. In Bengal, where the annual rainfall is heavy, roofs are steeply pitched, with inverted eaves to aid in runoff. In hot and humid Kerala, the ridges at the gable-ends of roofs curve upwards and are open to enhance ventilation, while exterior walls may be made of removable mats to take advantage of the prevailing winds. In contrast, roofs in the dry regions of northern Karnataka are flat rammed earth supported by wooden beams, the terraced surfaces used for drying vegetables and for sleeping while providing good insulation to keep interior rooms naturally cool. Throughout India each traditional house uses practical materials in a way ideally suited to its specific needs.

Contemporary Indian houses frequently are built of imported materials in designs ill-suited to the environment. This contrast can best be exemplified from my field experience by describing conditions in coastal Andhra Pradesh in 1978. I traveled through a region which just two weeks before had suffered such severe hurricane damage that the government had received U.N. disaster funds. I expected in my travels to meet desolation everywhere. Instead, the traditional villages I passed through were already entirely rebuilt. Devastating winds are so common in this area of eastern India that houses customarily are built with low-lying mud walls and roofs of local thatch supported separately by wooden posts. Chronically strong winds periodically blew off the easily replaceable roofs, still leaving the walls and interiors intact. On the other hand, towns and modern village houses were left in ruins. The cement and brick walls, with flat, terraced roofs, popular throughout India today could not withstand a hurricane; their owners were already in debt from the initial construction; cement was, as usual, in low supply; and houses had to wait months or even years to be rebuilt.

A new consciousness in America encourages people to recycle waste. Indians always recycle everything. There is no litter in rural India. Nothing is wasted. When a piece of clothing is worn out, its remnants are saved and used for patchwork or as the basis for embroidery. The paper from newspapers and magazines is used to wrap parcels or made into bags. Old rubber tires are converted into shoe soles or cut into strips to wrap threads in the dyeing process. Torn plastic from buckets and containers is used to patch holes and bind seams. Glass is always recycled and metal melted down. Pierced-steel oil drums serve throughout India as protective planters for seedling trees, or, when opened and cut into shape and hammered, they become the cooking utensils one sees used everywhere. In Tamil Nadu, the walls of a house on the edge of a factory that manufactures high-voltage electrical insulators is composed of that plant's discarded large porcelain products cemented with mud. In Orissa, the walls of houses in a potters village are built of stacked pots similarly cemented. Both provide cool interiors in hot climates.

Villagers are highly aware of the properties and uses of natural elements surrounding them. Local knowledge of herbs and medicinal plants is often both advanced and practical. Plant and flower derivatives and ground clays and minerals are used for paints and dyes as well as for medicines. Even manure has many uses: as fertilizer, as a building compound when mixed with mud, and as a primary source of cooking and heating fuel throughout the subcontinent. Animal urine is used as a mordant to fix dyes and as a base in clay slips for cleansing houses. Canes, reeds, sticks, and bark fibers are woven into baskets and mats. Leaves are stitched together, either flat or bent into shapes, to make disposable plates and cups. Gourds and pods are dried as containers. Wood is cut, bent, and carved into myriad utilitarian shapes, and stones are used in construction as well as for mortars and pestles and a variety of tools. India's many soils and clays become walls, floors, furniture, vessels, decorative reliefs, religious icons, and toys.

In a country as overpopulated and economically impoverished as India, often the most sophisticated solutions to everyday problems are found in the simplest cottage industries. For example, a very common vessel in which tea is served in India is the low-fired unglazed clay teacup. Made by potters everywhere, it varies slightly in shape from one locality to the next. Each person who orders a cup of tea is given a new cup, and therefore no diseases can be passed. When the tea is finished, the cup is thrown on the ground and crushed, readily biodegradable. Many even believe such clay cups improve the taste of tea. Today, plastic tea cups are rapidly replacing terracotta ones. Comparing the two, machine mass production gives jobs to very few. Reuse as well as poor sanitary conditions greatly increase the risk of contagious diseases. When finally discarded, plastic cups are non-biodegradable and difficult to recycle, and in them the tea taste seems worse than before.

Modern mass production threatens crafts and inherited customs everywhere. Many new products are good. Certainly a farmer would prefer a gas-driven steel sugar mill to a bullock-driven stone grinder or a steel plow-bit to a wooden one. Improved irrigation and better hybrid crops are revolutionizing agrarian production, helping India at last to be able to feed her massive population without resorting to world aid. But change must be tempered with a better understanding of indigenous wisdoms and techniques before wholesale erradication of traditional methods results in a nation of communities ill-suited to their environments. Some subtle changes are occuring. Until six years ago, western-type plastic buckets with straight sides and metal handles were rapidly replacing brass, copper, and clay water-carrying pots throughout India. Their improvement over previous models was obvious. They were cheap, durable, and much lighter to carry. Indians, however, usually carry water on their heads and these western buckets were impractical for that purpose because their flat bottoms were difficult to balance and their open tops allowed water to spill easily. Today plastic water carriers which duplicate the sensible curved sides, lip, and rounded bottom of the traditional *lotā* are in use everywhere. Inherent wisdom has been combined with contemporary methods in a practical product.

Craftsmanship in traditional India is a tribute to the gods. In making an item of daily or seasonal use, one honors the deity associated with that function. Decoration enhances a craft: it makes it more pleasing to the god or goddess. In rural India, everything is shaped by hand or decorated with symbols. Often even the simplest tools will be formed artistically as a tribute to the deity. In this way, walls are painted, doorways and wooden trim carved, vessels shaped, and cloth woven. Usually all the elements of even the poorest village are designed in harmony with one another. Western distaste for India's 'squalor' is based upon urban, not rural, conditions.

Traditional artistry is unselfconscious. Although villagers may be proud of their finished product — and of the creation and use of a beautiful or well-functioning object — artistic ego as found in the West is rare. Art and craftwork is never signed; it would occur to few artists to do so. The highest ideal for a craftsman or artist in India has been to reproduce precisely the object's prototype, which was learned from the artist's father and grandfather. In practice, however, many objects are unconsciously imbued with the craftsman's personal sense of design, a traditional factor as well contributing to the vitality of Indian folk art.

As elsewhere in the world, the contrast between rural and new urban aesthetics is stark. With the exception of those belonging to a very wealthy and artistically sensitive class, most modern Indian houses are surprisingly bare of decoration. They are utilitarian and comfortable, their furnishings influenced by Western designs, but when compared with traditional Indian homes they seem sterile. A villager's whole life is overlaid with religion and ritual. He and the craftsmen of his community create every aspect of his material culture, each of which to some measure is affected by religious spirit. The city or town dweller, however, lives in a world dominated by the impersonal, surrounded by mass-produced merchandise. His house is built by people outside his social circumference and usually is furnished with items that have no connection to his heritage or spirit. Handmade goods become more and more rare in urban markets each year. Despite the influence of Gandhian politics, cottage industries represent to many the products of a backward nation. The new, educated, urban consciousness likes to associate itself with the products of a modern society, emphasizing technology and industrialization, and a new aesthetic (perhaps similar to that which evolved in the U.S. in the 1950s). Most rituals for the modern householder, in fact, now take place outside of the home — in the temple, street, or ancestral village where he returns for marriages and some festivals. For many, the traditional link between householder and home has been broken.

Despite this escalating vogue for modern housing, furnishings, and lifestyles, the last several years has seen a tremendous change among the attitudes of some educated Indians. Whereas eight years ago very few were interested in the study and documentation of folklore and folk art in India, today there are universities, schools, museums, and government agencies all over the country in the midst of in-depth research. Many organizations, such as the Crafts Museum in New Delhi, are continuously involved in bringing an awareness of regional diversities in material culture and ritual arts to a wide audience. Books and articles are now being published in all major Indian languages. Even the existence of this seminar, 'Making Things in South Asia: The Role of the Artist and Craftsman,' is evocative of a change in consciousness and academic regard towards the importance of traditional Indian material culture. If this interest can be maintained and can gradually infuse the broader Indian public with an awareness of the innate sensibilities and sensitivities of much of their inherited traditions, then India may indeed evolve a positive future, which blends indigenous potentials with the prospects provided by international technological innovation.

## Bibliography

Critchfield, Richard. *Villages.* New York, 1983.

Devi, Pria and Richard Kurin. *Aditi: A Celebration of Life.* Washington D.C., 1985.

Doshi, Saryu, Jan Piper, and George Michell, eds. *The Impulse to Adorn: Studies in Traditional Indian Architecture.* Bombay, 1982.

Dube, S. C. *Indian Village.* New York, 1967.

Durrans, Brian and Robert Knox. *India: Past and Present.* London, 1982.

Fisher, Eberhard, Sitakant Mahapatra, and Dinanath Pathy, eds. *Orissa: Kunst und Kultur in Nordost-Indien.* Zurich, 1980.

Fisher, Eberhard and Haku Shah. *Rural Craftsmen and Their Work: Equipment and Techniques in the Mer Village of Ratadi in Saurashtra, India.* Ahmedabad, 1970.

Hobson, Sarah. *Family Web.* Chicago, 1982.

Huyler, Stephen P. *Village India.* New York, 1985.

Jayakar, Pupul. *The Earthen Drum: An Introduction to the Ritual Arts of Rural India.* New Delhi, 1980.

Kramrisch, Stella. *Unknown India: Ritual Art in Tribe and Village.* Philadelphia, 1968.

Mandelbaum, David G. *Society in India.* 2 vols. Berkeley, 1970.

Maloney, Clarence. *Peoples of South Asia.* New York, 1974.

Marriot, McKim. *Village India: Studies in the Little Community.* Chicago, 1972.

Mitter, Partha. *Much Maligned Monsters: A History of European Reactions to Indian Art.* Oxford, 1977.

Mohanti, Prafulla. *My Village, My Life. Nanpur: A Portrait of an Indian Village.* London, 1973.

Pal, M. K. *Crafts and Craftsmen in Traditional India.* New Delhi, 1978.

Saraf, D. N. *Indian Crafts: Development and Potential.* New Delhi, 1982.

Singer, Milton, ed. *Traditional India: Structure and Change.* Austin, 1976.

Watt, Sir George. *Indian Art at Delhi, 1903.* London, 1904.

# Making and Breaking: Craft Communities in South Asia

Stephen R. Inglis
Canadian Museum of Civilization, Ottawa, Canada

The products of Indian craftspeople have fascinated visitors since their earliest contact. 'It was not only the gifts of its soil, but also the work of its artisans which perpetuated India's reputation throughout the centuries' (Bougle 1909: 164). Recent 'Festivals of India' in the U.S. and Europe demonstrate that this still is true.

Two widespread popular images of the craftsman persist in a variety of writing in India and elsewhere. The first conjures up what Coomaraswamy called the 'high orders' of craftsmen of the 'great periods' whose work had been governed by 'immutable,' 'eternal,' and 'absolute' laws (Coomaraswamy 1913: 33) for which sources can still be found in *śilpa* texts. The second is that of the craftsman as a humble, anonymous, and organic part of rural life. My favorite expression of this is Birdwood's image of the 'Dakhan potter' as 'useful,' 'respected,' and 'content' with 'little food and less clothing': 'as little affected by the coming and going of religious or political revolutions . . . as a rock by the rising and falling of the tide' (Birdwood 1880: 230-301).

These two conventional ways of approaching craftspeople consign them to either the highest or lowest rank of prescribed behavior, overlooking the turbulent and often contentious ambiguity of status in actual social life. In the assertion of a constant and unchanging approach by craftsmen to their work, either through strict textual rules or numbing manual repetition, these views also fail to take into account the changes in technique, style, use, and meaning that constantly occur or the craftsman's dynamic position within cultural change.

It is remarkable that in a country such as India, with possibly more working craftspeople than any other in the world, there have been few detailed studies of the living traditions to which such static and idealized images of craftsmen could be compared. This is partly because Indian craftsmanship has often been approached as something of the past and also because of Western fascination with 'products' (crafts as objects). The material remains are objective data, however, only in a limited sense, for objects are part of activities and processes. Indian craftsmanship, as such, is only partly about objects. The meaning of any object must include its manufacture, its use, and its fate, a fact that becomes crucial in the study of the vast range of objects made for temporary use.

Anthropology, with its emphasis on process and on community, offers an approach that complements those guided by contemplation and classification. The strongest present work on art and anthropology seeks better to understand how art both realizes and produces culture, how craftspeople bring cultural ideas into the open to be encountered, challenged, and incorporated.[1] The case study I present here involves temporary products that rarely are studied, collected, or considered, partly because their destruction is part of their meaning. My concern is not only for meaningful form but also for meaningful time — not only 'making things' in South India but also breaking them.

**Background**

The craftspeople I introduce are potters living in the countryside around the ancient Tamil city of Maturai (Madurai) where I conducted fieldwork in 1980 and 1981.[2] I have benefited from data drawn from archaeology, epigraphy, textual sources, and the observations of others but focus here on my own observation.

Tamil Nadu's approximately 150,000 potters are known officially by the title Kulāḷar and colloquially as Kusavaṉ. More specific caste titles are used in particular regions and among people with whom they interact frequently, as well as among themselves. The most common of these, like Uṭaiyār and Ceṭṭiyār, are used by a variety of castes. In central and southern Tamil Nadu, (Tamiḻnāḍu) a common potter title is Vēḷār, usually prefixed with the name of one of the regions of the classical kingdoms: Cōḷa, Cēra, or Pāṇḍya. I worked with a large endogamous group (or sub-caste) of Pāṇḍya Vēḷār, most of whose approximately 2,000 members live in forty-two villages. The territory comprised of these villages (referred to as *nāḍu*) encompasses Madurai and runs South-east along both banks of the Vaikai River into Ramnad District.

1 My thinking in this regard has been inspired by Goldwater (1973), Geertz (1976), and Fabian and Szombati-Fabian (1980).

2 This research was supported by a Doctoral Fellowship from the Social Sciences and Humanities Research Council of Canada. A full account of this community is contained in my dissertation, 'Creators and Consecrators: A Potter Community of South India,' University of British Columbia, 1984.

The Pāṇḍya Vēḷār consider themselves indigenous to this region of Tamil Nadu and this is fundamental to their status and their work. Other groups of potters, who also live in and around Madurai and are self-admitted migrants to the area, are socially and economically insecure in comparison to the Vēḷār. Various potter groups, although living in close proximity to one another, have virtually no contact. The other groups employ a pottery technology different than that of the Vēḷār, follow different social patterns, and in several cases speak a different language.

The Vēḷār orient themselves toward the great city of Madurai, described in Tamil mythology as the 'indestructible centre of the universe' (Shulman 1980: 70). Vēḷār periodically worship at the famous Mīṉākṣi Sundareśvara temple, and in fact maintain that they were priests there before these duties were usurped by brahmins. An intriguing piece of evidence toward this claim is that potters, among all other castes, high or low, are given the privilege of worshiping first *(mariyātai)* during the three most important festivals in the Mīṉākṣi temple calender (Appadurai and Breckenridge 1976). The Vēḷārs also draw the Goddess Mīṉākṣi into their local sub-caste and community festivals, build small temples to her, and worship by fire-walking and dragging carts with impaled hooks (as well as with milk, incense, and flowers). The Vēḷār have active traditional associations with other great temples within the orbit of Madurai, for example those at Aḻkar Kōyil and Tirupparaṅkuṉṟam.

Contact with Madurai is balanced by the orientation of the Vēḷār toward the countryside. While relationships with the city are maintained mainly through individual choice and through formal sub-caste representatives, the ties to the countryside feature the hereditary right of particular Vēḷār lineages to serve and receive compensation from particular communities and their patrons. These service rights include the provision of clay pots, clay images, and priestly services in return for ritual gifts of cloth, coins, and other substances and substantial amounts of grain, other foods, and money.

The large village of Ārappāḷaiyam, just to the north-west of Madurai, is home to four major Vēḷār lineages who actively serve nearby rural areas. The members of these four lineages have been joined in Ārappāḷaiyam by members of twenty-two other Vēḷār lineages, most of whom maintain some service rights near their original villages at some distance away or have given them up completely to work in mills, do other jobs, or make pottery for cash.

### Vessels

The basis of the Vēḷār role in village life is their supply of vessels throughout the year and the busiest time is during the harvest in January. In the rural areas, the grain comes in and farmers prepare for the Poṅgal celebration, during which many of the household vessels are discarded and replaced with new ones.

The Vēḷār prepare the volume of vessels they know will be required and stack them ready for distribution. People come to Ārappāḷaiyam from nearby villages to buy the pots they need and each lineage distributes ritually specified sets of pots to the leading men of the villages they serve, most often Vēḷāḷar and Tēvar landlords. The Vēḷār prepare dozens of types of products in addition to pots for use by the populations of the areas they serve. Replacing clay vessels is not only a necessary part of the renewal of the agricultural cycle, but also of the life-cycle and the Vēḷār must prepare special pots for each birth, maturity, marriage, and death. The members of all castes in the service area call on the potters of the lineage that serves them throughout the year to provide these special containers.

Pots are not only containers of food and water, but also of the divine presence of local deities. Clay vessels are appropriate for all these purposes because they are formed of the earth of the area in which they are used and in which the crops are grown. Members of each Vēḷār lineage draw their raw clay from the area which they serve and the broken shards dissolve back into that earth. The life of pots, as of humans — which in so many contexts they represent — are part of a closed circuit: every life is predicated on a death. Potters refer to their special god, Brahmā, the archetypal potter who moulded men (Hocart 1950: 14; Zvelebil 1973: 76), but with the knowledge that their ancestor Kulāḷaṉ was attracted to this work because Brahmā, his father, was able to create *and destroy* things daily (Thurston 1909, IV).

The new pot, purest of objects, quickly becomes the used pot, a symbol of pollution. Every creation is built on the refuse of those that went before. In Tamil Nadu, the creative process, like birth itself, involves pain and danger and the potter faces the danger, absorbs the pollution, and passes on the merit associated with creative activity. He remains, of necessity, an ambiguous figure. Tamils bring to their use of pots these patterns, categories, and inferences in the course of everyday life. Pots become a focused expression of a sense of the constant cycle of nature and human life.

**Images**

In addition to making pots, many Vēḷār lineages model images during much of the year. I use the example of a village in the service area of Ārappāḷaiyam lineage, which has fixed a date in early February for its annual festival. This village has four temples for which new clay images are installed during the festival.

Well in advance of the festival date, a messenger from the village that is planning the festival comes to Ārappāḷaiyam and pays a formal visit to the head of the appropriate lineage. He offers gifts of initiation, betel nut, fruits, and a token prepayment and announces the proposed dates and needs of the villagers. Most importantly, he brings a handful of earth *(piṭimaṇ)*, from the floor of the main temple in the village, that includes the remains of previous images. This is mixed with the clay from which the new images will be modelled. This handful of earth is a vital expression of the power of place and of cycle essential to the annual continuity of imagemaking.

The lineage members set to work, making images of deities for the appropriate temples, horses for the deities to ride, and small votive images to be offered to the deities by individuals. The size and number vary from year to year according to the particular needs of the villagers and the success of the harvest.

The first day of the festival usually begins with the late afternoon arrival in Ārappāḷaiyam of 200-300 people from the host village. They have come to collect the new images of the deities and offerings, to carry back in procession to their temples. The Vēḷār lineage members set the newly modelled images in the courtyard of their houses and dress them in the new cloth and flower garlands brought by the villagers. At an auspicious moment, the Vēḷār perform the eye-opening ceremony by which the deities descend to inhabit the images, and with the courtyard echoing with the cries of the villagers, they offer the first worship. Like their mythical ancestor, Cālivākaṇaṉ, who brought his images to life and defeated an invading army, only the Vēḷār can prepare the vessels and the circumstances under which they can safely be inhabited by the capricious and powerful local deities. After initial worship, the images are carried away to the host village, accompanied by dancers and fireworks. There, on the village square *(mantai)*, they are worshiped during the night and distributed to the appropriate temples.

On the second day, in the main temple area of the host village, the farmers and other villagers come to worship and to offer gifts of fruit, paddy, and sacrificial animals by means of the Vēḷār priest. Although they share in the agricultural system and possess many of the social characteristics of the 'right-side' land-based castes and the 'kingly model' of behavior (Beck 1970; Stein 1980), the Vēḷār are often at odds with the values, wishes, and generosity of their farming patrons. Although the Vēḷār own no land and have no control over the means of production, they are crucial to the 'means of reproduction' (Plaffenberger 1982: 69) and to the fertility and well-being of the land and its inhabitants. Disputes between the Vēḷār and patrons can lead to the suspension of a festival and even the abandonment of a cycle of worship. A local deity who has no proper vessel in which to become manifest, no occasion to receive honour, and no hereditary priest to offer worship can wreak havoc. The Vēḷār may be forced away, but the consequences for the patron can be fatal.

The Vēḷār lineage members who have the right to supervise activities during the current year (this right is rotated among lineage members on an annual basis), and who come from Ārappāḷaiyam to conduct *pūjā* in this temple every Tuesday and Friday, now supervise worship for the entire three days of the festival, eating and sleeping at the temple. Most Vēḷār, even those who do not model clay, work as priests at some time during their lives.

Although the Vēḷār wear the sacred thread, maintain a Vāttiyār system of caste-priests for their own life-cycle rites, and until recently shared many of the outward fashions of brahmins, they have little actual contact with other priestly castes and carry on a lively internal debate about the role of brahmins. The Vēḷār, like many other groups of craftsmen, including the Kammāḷar (McGilvray 1983), feel they are superior, both because they predate brahmins as priests (they are Ādhi-brahmin) and because they have different and superior powers demonstrated in confrontation with brahmins. These include magical powers *(māntirikam),* which are bound up with the Vēḷār priesthood. In their close association with active creativity, blood sacrifice, and local ceremonies, the Vēḷār are also at odds with many characteristics of 'left-side' castes and priestly patterns of emulation. That they claim, along with most groups of craftsmen, a social origin in a mixed brahmin/non-brahmin marriage contributes to their ambiguous status.

On the third day of the festival, many village caste-groups come to the temple in procession. Some of these groups feature god-dancers *(cāmiyāṭi)* in a possessed state. Many festivals require the Vēḷār to dance as part of their hereditary right, and the houses of the various lineages in Ārappāḷaiyam are full of costumes and accoutrements. The deities speak through their possessed priests, and the Vēḷār are expert at rendering their bodies as vessels in a way similar to providing images in clay. The line between a human and a clay vessel is a fine one. In Vēḷār mythology, not only do clay images 'come to life,' but people, especially women who have suffered injustice, frequently die and are transformed into clay images by lying down among the pots on the firing ground. The pot firing ground *(cūḷai),* like the cremation ground to which it is frequently compared (especially by other castes), is a place of transition and liminality, of fear and hope.

One of the most popular events during the final day of a festival is the 'bull-tie' *(erutu-kaṭṭu),* where leading village landlords sponsor fighting bulls and young heroes display their courage by baiting them. By the next morning, however, all is quiet at the village temples. Until the next festival — next year or two years hence — little will happen there and the images gradually fall apart. The abandoned look so often mentioned in reference to village temples in South India, far from being a sign of neglect, is a testament to a conception of the sacred which recognizes a normal order, and, 'equally sacred,' in the words of Brubaker (1979: 152), 'its occasional destruction and recreation.'

Like pots, images are containers for only limited periods of time. The boundaries must be broken down as well as built up. The period when the deity is worshiped in the festival image is simply a phase, only possible periodically. The deity otherwise must continue the violent struggles by which evil is kept at bay and fertility, health, and prosperity are made possible. That the destruction that allows for rebirth and renewal can be violent is evident in the bloody sacrifice that is an integral part of the worship of local deities in earthen images. As proposed in Tamil mythology, it is a violent energy that gives new life to the universe (Shulman 1980: 26).

For Tamils, who the Vēḷār serve through the continual reshaping of images, the value of images, and thus their beauty and meaning, lies not only in their graceful shapes, brilliant colours, and fearful expressions, but also in their fragility. Embodied in these images is not only the promise of the approach of god but also the promise of his satisfied retreat, his return to that violent and uncontained state in which new creation occurs and in which the forces of evil and intrusion are encountered and vanquished.

For the Vēḷār, image making is a re-cycling and rejuvenation of materials. Each image includes, in the materials used to make it, the refuse of previous images that have broken down in order to provide new material. The Vēḷār, through his craft, symbolically stands astride a boundary, between human and divine but also between life and death. His involvement in the creative cycle means that impurity is inevitable.

**Monumental Images**

Another facet of Vēḷār work can serve to reveal some of the ongoing changes in the social organization of craft in South India. Additions to or renovations of temples occur periodically and are often scheduled to coincide with the celebration of a festival. The Vēḷār sometimes undertake this work, especially if the project involves a monumental image. Monumental images of local deities riding horses, often 10-20 ft. tall, stand in the courtyards or before the walls of many local temples in Tamil villages. Until about fifty years ago, these images were made mainly of fired clay by a process similar to that used to make the smaller cult images; now most are built of stone, brick, plaster, and cement (Inglis 1980).

The transition from monumental images of hollow clay (which were the exclusive work of the Vēḷār) to an image made of more permanent materials, for which the Vēḷār must compete with artisans of other castes, involves a transition in their thinking about craft and status. There is currently a hierarchy in material for new houses that ranks clay below plaster and plaster below cement. There similarly has come to be a hierarchy in work associated with these materials. The modeler who works in more permanent, more modern materials and moves from making festival images to large semi-permanent monumental images or temple towers and gates can now aspire to the title of *'sthapathi'* and can expect a certain demand for his services beyond his traditional lineage service area. Working on monumental images in such materials involves use of a wider range of tools than before and the brilliant enamel paints now used share in the popular aesthetic of calendar prints and the cinema.

The simple iconography of monumental clay images also is changing as more permanent forms are made to reflect new religious tastes and the growing cosmopolitanism of Tamil villagers. Once-simple monumental images now are made to include groups of subsidiary figures clustered along the sides of the main mounted deity linking the local god to the classical pantheon, to popular mythology, or even to recent political heroes such as Gandhi and N. S. C. Bose. Gaṇapati and Murugaṉ sometimes flank the ferocious local deity, not to imply any divine relationship but rather a human one; by this means, the villagers show their respect for all-India gods and goddesses and link their local temples to what they perceive as more all-important urban religious institutions.

The Vēḷār craftsman who can supply these changing needs becomes more independent, more flexible, and has more choice where and with whom he works than do his fellow craftsmen. The extent to which changes in fashion have challenged the Vēḷār community can be exemplified by the relatively well-travelled and independent Vēḷār modeler who recently renovated a monumental image at a temple near Ārappāḷaiyam and signed his name on the base. Other Vēḷār were astonished at such a gesture, as much for the religious irreverence as for the social irresponsibility to his lineage of the act.

A few members of the Vēḷār lineages we have discussed have left their traditional areas of service and moved to Madras, where they now model neo-classical statues for sale to wealthy urbanites and tourists. A few Vēḷār have even entered the world of the cinema, where they create sculptures for lavish sets that form the backdrop for movie song-and-dance numbers.

**Conclusion**

Both the process and products of craftsmanship in India are changing, yet not all recent innovations are counter to the tradition of replacement and cyclical time nor are they necessarily deviations from the deeply rooted social placement of craftsmanship.

An example from another phase of my research supports this. While the lithographed print has slowly grown in popularity and increased in production since the turn of the century and is now, in its calendar format, the most ubiquitous form of decoration and religious icon in India, far outnumbering the depiction of the deity in any other medium, the most successful artists in this medium, far from being simply commercially trained hacks, are the heirs to wood and ivory carving, metal casting, clay forming, as well as painting. The community of calendar artists in South India is loosely linked and their audience is vast and diverse, yet many of them continue to link certain phases of their work to the making of icons directed toward devotees. The fact that calendars are replaced annually may, in fact, help account for the astounding acceptance of this art form and its integration into the traditional Indian system of aesthetics and worship.

Some of these ideas of destruction and cyclical time which I have argued are a part of the living tradition of craftsmanship in India have even been maintained in the modern multicultural society in which I live and work in Canada. As an example, a group of Canadians of Bengali origin contacted me in Ottawa last summer. Their preparations for the annual celebration of Durgā *pūjā* were behind schedule because they were having difficulty raising funds to replace their image. Their clay festival image, which by Bengali tradition must be replaced each year, had already had its final trip to be immersed in a river delayed for three years because of the difficult logistics of bringing a new one from Calcutta. Three years is the absolute maximum that the cycle can be stretched, and then only under circumstances of crisis, for which life in Ottawa obviously would qualify. But finally the old image had to go and a new one had to come.

The Museum contributed to the purchase of a new image, which arrived just in time, and instead of consigning the old one to the river that runs through Ottawa the Bengali Association consigned it to another kind of oblivion — the museum on the bank of the river. Although that old clay will never make it back to Calcutta to be part of a new image, it was still important that it be ritually extinguished and a new version take its place. Even for urban professionals thousands of miles from their country of origin, the potter's special craft-knowledge of impermanence and renewal, of building up *and* breaking down, provides the proper medium for approaching the divine.

## Bibliography

Appadurai, A. and C. A. Breckenridge. 'The South Indian Temple: Authority, Honour and Redistribution.' *Contributions to Indian Sociology,* 10.2 (1976): 187-212.

Beck, B. E. F. 'The Right-Left Division of South Indian Society.' *Journal of Asian Studies* 29.4 (1970): 779-98.

Birdwood, G. *The Industrial Arts of India.* London, 1880.

Bougle, C. *Essays in the Caste System.* D. Pockock, trans. Cambridge, 1971.

Brubaker, R. L. 'Barbers, Washermen, and Other Priests: Servants of the South Indian Village and its Goddess.' *History of Religion* 19.2 (1979): 128-52.

Coomaraswamy, A. K. *The Arts and Crafts of India and Ceylon.* 1913, reprinted New York, 1964.

Fabian, J. and I. Szombati-Fabian. 'Folk Art from an Anthropological Perspective.' In *Perspectives on American Folk Art,* edited by I. M. Quimby and S. T. Swank, 247-92. New York, 1980.

Geertz, C. 'Art as a Cultural System.' *Modern Language Notes* 91 (1976): 1473-99.

Goldwater, R. 'Art and Anthropology: Some Comparisons of Methodology.' In *Primitive Art and Society,* edited by A. Forge, 1-10. London, 1973.

Hocart, A. M. *Caste, A Comparative Study.* London: Methuen and Co., 1950.

Inglis, S. 'Night Riders: Massive Temple Figures of Rural Tamilnadu.' In *Festschrift for Professor M. Shanmugam Pillai,* edited by V. Vijayavenugopal, 297-307. Madurai, 1980.

McGilvray, D. G. 'The Structural Position of Tamil Artisan Castes in South India and Sri Lanka.' A paper delivered at the XIth International Congress of Anthropological and Ethnological Sciences, Vancouver, August 20-25, 1983.

Pfaffenberger, Bryan. *Caste in Tamil Culture: The Religious Foundations of Sudra Domination in Tamil Sri Lanka.* Syracuse, 1982.

Shulman, D. D. *Tamil Temple Myths: Sacrifice and Divine Marriage in the South Indian Saiva Tradition.* Princeton, 1980.

Singer, Milton. 'Changing Craft Traditions in India.' In *Labor Commitment and Social Change in Developing Areas,* edited by Wilbert E. Moore and Arnold S. Feldman, 258-76. New York, 1960.

Stein, B. *Peasant State and Society in Medieval South India.* New Delhi, 1980.

Thurston, E. *Castes and Tribes of Southern India.* 7 vols. Madras, 1909.

Zvelebil, Kamil V. *The Poets of the Powers.* London, 1973.

# The Role of the Potter in South Asia

Louise Allison Cort
Freer Gallery of Art, Smithsonian Institution

My presentation consists of two parts. The first assembles some generalizations on the pan-Indian meanings of 'potter' and 'pot.' The second speaks from the point of view of the particular potter group with which I am most familiar, the community of potters serving Jagannāth Temple in Puri, Orissa. In the case of the Puri potters, my collaboration with the Oriya researcher Purna Chandra Mishra and my own halting grasp of Oriya meant that language (conversations with potters) shaped my understanding of what I saw. In the larger context I was without language skills, so my silent observation tended to focus not on the potter but on the pot. Each approach has its own validity, but the quality of comprehension in each is not comparable.

In relation to the two unequal parts of my presentation, let me comment that I see two goals for researchers studying crafts traditions in South Asia. First, we need more studies of local and regional traditions, such as are being done for ceramics by N. K. Behura in Orissa, Stephen Inglis in Tamil Nadu, Carol Kramer in Rajasthan, Daniel Miller in Maharashtra, Haku Shah in Gujarat, and Baidyanath Saraswati. It is from an eventual sharing of our specific insights that a truly rich overview of 'the role of the pot and potter' will emerge.

Second, we need more regional group studies after the model of the Orissa Research Project. Such efforts produce archives, and they create 'niches' for later researchers to fill without having to start over from scratch, and they produce experienced local colleagues. Because of the continued presence in Puri of my collaborator, Purna Chandra Mishra, we have been able to maintain valuable contact with the potters' community. Our eighteen months of field work in Puri (1979-81) were followed by one month in 1984 at the archive compiled by the Orissa Research Project team and now housed in the South Asia Department at Heidelberg University. (The major publication from the ORP is Eschmann, Kulke, and Tripathi 1978.)

In the second part of my talk, I wish to present a question that has occupied me in writing up my research: how to fill in the historical dimensions of the present-day potters' lives and work. This question emerged with particular clarity as we dealt with the documentary material in the archives that supported stories told us by potters, and I wish to take this opportunity to suggest the varieties of documentary materials available to researchers concerned with crafts communities in South Asia.

## I.

As a starting point for examining the role of the pot in South Asia, let me throw the question into relief by looking for a moment at another context for ceramics in Asia, the meaning of the pot in Japan. Some of the most important tea-ceremony ceramics in Japan are not Japanese but Korean; they have been used over centuries, as attested by their patina and gold lacquer repairs; they possess a personal history and lineage of ownership. Their history, moreover, is open-ended, for it extends indefinitely into the future. By contrast with these Japanese notions of the meaning of ceramics, the Indian tea *(chai)* cup (which, in Michael Meister's phrase, 'blooms like a flower' on the potter's wheel) is as short-lived as a flower. It possesses a brief, well-defined life cycle, with a decisive end. This clearly-defined life cycle is a central characteristic of the Indian pot and helps determine its role.

Before looking at 'the pot,' however, we must first consider the nature of 'the potter.' The countless Indian potters crouching at their wheels throwing thousands of *chai* cups in a single morning raise the issue of the 'creativity' of the potter. In the West, it is thought desirable for any ceramic of real importance to be 'unique' from its moment of making. In Japan, an ordinary object — one Korean tea bowl among hundreds like it — may gradually assume a 'unique' identity that intensifies its importance. In India, the potter, or any craftsman, 'creates' in the same sense that the gods 'create' humans: the same form is repeated over and over again, and the essence of its importance lies in the reliable sameness of the product. In India, the pot is always the *same,* but it is always *new.*

All South Asian craftspeople perform the same sort of work in that they 'create' in accordance with the specific sorts of objects expected by their clients. The potter, however, seems to have particular power as a metaphor for *creation.* This power is witnessed in the widespread worship of the potter's wheel at the time of marriage as an expression of the wish for the new couple's fertility. As compared with other sorts of craftspeople using more complex materials and technologies, the potter's work is easily and quickly understood. He works directly with his hands on a simple material, clay, the earth itself, analogous to the material that forms the human body. Compared to many other materials, the 'life cycle' of the object he makes is visibly brief.

The work of South Asian potters can be divided into two broad categories: images and vessels. My interest in India, and my presentation, centers not on the image but on the pot as vessel, container. After hearing Stephen Inglis' presentation, however, I have the feeling that the difference between the two sorts of clay objects is mainly formal; both are united by clay and its essential behavior. As Inglis explained, the clay image serves as momentary container for the deity and permits the deity's retreat as it decays. Inglis also noted that the more remote the village, the more abstracted the image. Whereas the clay image is made for one specific use, any sort of household clay vessel may suddenly be chosen, provided it is new, as a vehicle for ritual, especially when the ritual is simple, rural, or 'low.' It seems true to say that in the 'high' religious context the universal properties of the pot are given specific form as an image, not simply as a vessel.

Pots as vessels lie very close to Hindu ideas about food. The central meaning of the pot, both literally and metaphorically, lies in its nature as a container for substances to be injested by humans. Those substances may be either liquid, epitomized by water, or solid foods to be cooked in water, epitomized by rice. It is tempting from a Western viewpoint to divide the use of the pot as container for water and rice into 'everyday' and 'ritual' contexts, but Hindu attitudes toward food assume a continuum along which the ritual forms a 'special' or intense version of the everyday.

For brahmins, it might be said the *entire* continuum is more intense. In the case of a water jar, the continuum ranges from use for collecting and storing water to the role of *kalaśa* or *pūrṇa kumbha,* what might be called the 'archetypal pot,' with its brimming contents of water protected by mango leaves and a green coconut with stem. Similarly, a cooking pot for rice may serve either the family meal or a ritual feast.

The duration of use of a given 'everyday' vessel is related to events in the household of people who eat together. The life cycle of the household pots is determined by calendar events such as the New Year; by death and birth within the extended family; or even by their own fragility, if their destiny is to be used until broken accidentally in use. By contrast, the life cycle of a pot selected for ritual use is a short, clearly-predictable, moment.

It is fair to say that the 'everyday' situation intensifies as the context moves outside of one's own household into a public or unknown setting.

Thus clay pots seem to be more easily given up for aluminum or plastic in domestic 'everyday' situations and more reluctantly abandoned in more 'intense' public circumstances. Even the most ordinary *chai* stall will have a supply of earthenware cups on hand for customers who prefer not to drink from glazed white ceramic or from glass.

The locus of the pot's importance varies depending upon whether one is considering it in the abstract or in a specific context of use. In the abstract sense, *newness* and *purity* are the issues, not form. The pot as such is 'invisible,' an encasing for its contents, the form of which does not matter. The pot keeps the contents pure by acting as a sort of figurative sponge; any impurity that may threaten the contents is drawn away and discarded when the pot itself is discarded. In the specific sense, however, — that of a particular person in a particular place, thinking about pots — *form* is the issue. The pot (like all other material goods, including architecture) serves as a marker of boundaries — between caste or language groups, between regions or districts, between outside and inside. *Chai* cups collected at railway stations are not all alike in form: they vary from station to station along the Calcutta-Bolpur line as surely as they do between Calcutta and Jaipur.

The abstract issue of the pot's purity has a positive effect for the pot's user but a negative one for the pot itself and its maker. The pot, 'transparently' pure at the outset of use, is metaphorically if not literally 'black' by the end, having absorbed impurities. Similarly, the potter absorbs the pollution of making the pot (of digging the clay and burning it in a fire, of 'giving birth' and 'cremating') and passes on the pure vessel to the user. I would like to suggest an analogy in the roles of the three ritual 'cleansers' required in any village: the barber, who removes growths on the body (hair and nails); the washerman, who removes polluting substances from clothing; and the potter, who provides the means of removing the polluting aspects associated with ingesting.

The life cycle of the pot has specific analogies to the human life cycle. A human experiences a lifelong cycle alternating between states of being purified and being polluted. The pot endures only a single cycle, but it occurs in two phases. When the potter digs the earth, tramples it with his feet, and manipulates it with water by throwing, the pot is formed and exists in a polluted state. The potter then fires the pot, and it emerges from the kiln purified. Once the pot is put to use, it is polluted by that action, and it is finally discarded on a specially designated rubbish heap or, ideally, in the ritual context, washed away in flowing water. I see here an analogy between the two-stage life cycle of the pot and the life cycle of the 'twice-born.'

The manner in which the specific pot defines 'borders' or 'edges' is complex. In the case of the potters, this definition is reflected in technical aspects of their work from beginning to end, including the form of the wheel and the stance adopted for throwing on it, the tools for beating and the manner of using them, and the division of work between men and women. Clear boundaries exist between groups within a single region as well as from region to region. They may define the edges of language (as between Oriya- and Telugu-speaking potters in southern Orissa) or the borders of religion (as between Hindu and Catholic potters in Kerala). Glaze on pots is a clear indication of a Muslim clientele.

Among users, the forms of pots mark boundaries between *jātis.* This is partially an expression of group style or preference, but it also serves as a means of preventing mistaken use of another group's pot. In cases where a single potter serves various clientele, he varies his products to suit them, as does the potter in western Orissa making black water pots for Oriyas and red for Marwaris. (The deep reasons underlying differences between red and black pots still elude me.) Alternatively, two potter groups may sell their wares in the same market, each serving a particular clientele. An extreme instance of this pattern is the potters' quarter in the city of Ahmedabad, where the population is drawn from all parts of Gujarat and Rajasthan and has drawn after it potters to serve particular needs.

## II.

Jagannāth Temple, which dominates the religious and cultural life within most of Orissa, is staffed by over 100 categories of 'servants' *(sevakas)* drawn from both Brahman and Śudra groups. Among the Śudra servants, the potters' community consists of more than 300 men and their families, distributed in three villages. The men use the potter's wheel and the paddle and anvil to produce pots used for cooking the temple food-offerings, termed *mahāprasāda.* The women, using paddle and anvil on hand-formed shapes, make a variety of small containers and lamps used within the temple.

The pots sent to the temple from the potters' community fall into two groups. At the core is the assemblage used for offering and distributing the cooked food provided by the temple and for use within the temple, termed *kotha* ('public') *bhog.* The potters are obliged to provide the repertory of pots required daily for *kotha bhog* free of charge, in a continuation of their *jajmānī* relationship to the temple whereby, in return, they received land to live and work on and food to eat. Aside from the *kotha bhog,* the temple cooks also prepare extra food to be sold to pilgrims in the temple market. They purchase pots for this purpose from the potters in return for cash. Regardless of how the pots are to be used, however, all pots entering the temple must be red in color (a natural coloration resulting from the firing technique) and (with the exception of small lamps) must bear the beating marks from the paddle and anvil.

In course of our daily visits with the potters, we heard numerous stories about the potters' community, and we were challenged to understand how all of them fit together into a single 'history' of the community. I gradually learned, when asking about events in the past, not to take literally the phrases 'five or six years ago' and 'ten or twelve years ago' but instead to interpret them as meaning degrees of 'ago'; I realized that the potters' understanding of 'history' did not agree with mine. It was clear, nevertheless, from the cumulative sense of the stories we heard, that the 'history' of the potters as a group was long and rich. Our clues to its dimensions came from the stories the potters told us and our task was to relate their sense of the past in an understandable way, without distorting its character or amalgamating it to suit a different definition of history.

Upon consideration, it seems to me that the 'history' of the potters can be told in four distinct yet related and relatively sequential stages. For each stage, the documentary evidence supporting the potters' own sense is distinctive in nature.

The first stage can be termed the 'mythical past.' Its major text is the *Kurāla Purāṇa,* written about potters in a mixture of Oriya and corrupt Sanskrit by a scribe named Dina Krushna Das who seems to have lived in the seventeenth century. The entire tale is related to Gaṇēśa by Śiva, and it focuses in turn primarily on the dialogue between Rudrapāla, the first potter, and Viṣṇu, his creator.

The Purāṇa tells the story of Viṣṇu's creation of the potter after Brahmā had created fifty-six crores of human beings but had neglected to supply them with food. Brahmā subsequently created a farmer to produce grain, but the humans then complained about subsisting on only raw grains, peeled by hand, and cold water. From the sweat of his brow, the angry Viṣṇu created Rudrapāla and instructed him to prepare 'jewel pots' in which the grain could be cooked. A close connection between the potter and hulled and cooked rice is underscored by the fact that the same tree from Mount Meru was used to fashion both the wooden rice husker and the pivot for the potter's wheel. Viṣṇu's gifts to the potter included one of his eight wheels, Śurasena Cakra; a piece of his flag to wipe and polish the pots; his mace to use as a paddle; and his lotus to use as an anvil.

Once equipped to work, the potter was instructed to install and then worship his wheel over a period of twelve days, with the potter himself enacting the role of priest. On the first day he was to collect clay from a hole made by a wild boar (a reference to the Boar *avatar*) and to construct a dais for the deities. 'Formless' Viṣṇu was to be visualized, but the other deities — Śiva and Pārvatī, Brahmā and Savitrī, Lakṣmī, and Gaṇeśa — were to be installed on subsequent days in the form of lumps of clay. Particular *bhogs* were to be cooked and offered. The Purāṇa makes recurrent reference to Saleha Sūnī, the 'goddess who resides in the workshop.' Her worship centers around the kiln. On the twelfth day, the potter is to prepare seven *kalaśas* and one jar, to immerse the images, and to perform a final fire sacrifice.

Viṣṇu's instructions to Rudrapāla are reflected in the annual five-day worship cycle observed by the potters beginning on the fifth day of the dark fortnight of Mārgaśira month and known as Kurāla Pañcami.

Long sections follow on proper behavior in society, aspects of the human life cycle, and *guru* and meditation. Finally Rudrapāla begins work. He marries a daughter of Brahmā named Ratneśvarī, and they have four sons. One is sent to Orissa, one goes to Bengal, one works for demons in Lanka, and one takes up with a prostitute. The lineage of the 'Oriya Kumbhara,' descended from the son who went to Orissa, is traced through the four ages, culminating in Prajāpati, the potter who served King Indradyumna, legendary founder of Jagannāth Temple.

Nowadays the potters say that not the place-specific goddess Saleha Sūnī but Gaṇeśa presides over their workshop. The textual confirmation for this change is to be found in the *Sarala Mahābhārata,* composed in Oriya by the fifteenth-century devotee of Jagannāth, Sarala Das. In that retelling, the episode where the five Pāndavas hide in a potter's workshop is greatly expanded into the story of the potter and his devotion to Gaṇeśa, whose image he prepares.

The second stage of the potters' 'history' deals with the specific circumstances of the Puri potters. Its text is the daily record of temple events known as the *Mādalā Pāñji.* Purna Chandra Mishra and I were able to read the entire transcription prepared by the Orissa Research Project from one copy that is now in the State Museum, Bhubaneswar; unfortunately, however, the transcribing process had been stopped after only six bundles were read, and we feel certain that much other valuable information regarding the potter lies within the untranscribed sections. Thus, for example, only a separate (printed) version of the *Mādalā Pāñji* contains the story of the Puri potters' forebear, Nili Kumbharuni, who lived in a village far outside Puri and whose devotion in carrying the required pots to the temple each day was rewarded by Jagannāth through the king in the form of a land grant within the town where her nine sons were to live and work.

The dated leaves among those that we examined — dated by kings' regnal years — suggest that most of the document fell within the eighteenth and nineteenth centuries. One leaf gave a detailed 'history' of the potters' community from the temple's point of view, in terms of land grants, that seems to be unique among records of *sevaka* groups. Records of periodical expansion of the potters' community indicated that the increase of potter *sevakas* was tied to the growth of quantity and variety of *mahāprasāda,* with pots being calculated as an integral part of the cost of the dishes.

The *Mādalā Pāñji* entries also clarified the important connection in the past between the potters and the monasteries in Puri. Until the early 1970s, when the monasteries lost the great landholdings that had supported them, individual potters supplied pots to certain monasteries in a manner reminiscent of the traditional *jajmānī* relationship, the potters receiving grain and clothing, but no cash, in return for pots. Incidentally, the only wholly secular role that approximates the ordinary *jajmānī* pattern is the occasional provision, on a random and ad-hoc basis, so far as we could determine, of sets of pots required for use in non-brahmin wedding ceremonies.

The third stage of the potters' history is related, if only dimly, by the records kept by the British from 1803 until Independence, when they ruled Orissa and had responsibility for the Jagannāth Temple. The British correspondence and reports reveal an endearing obsession with practical questions of cleanliness and order. Precisely those concerns, however, contributed inadvertantly to an important clue to the iconography of the Puri pots with their conspicuous paddle marks. In Puri we had heard two interpretations of that iconography: the potters said that the paddle marks represented the lotus diagram that would otherwise have been inscribed beneath the pot when it was offered; the *rājguru* explained the marks as a *yantra* with Tantric significance. A British report, however, suggested a much more practical role — distinguishing authentic *mahāprasāda* from Jagannāth Temple from that being sold as *mahāprasāda* by dishonest priests from two other temples in Puri.

The fourth stage of the potters' community — one that is still continuing — represents the twentieth century, especially the post-Independence decades. This time span is documented, sadly, by a glut of court cases debating the nature of potters' obligations to the temple and the temple's obligations in return. This debate has become especially bitter in the years since temple management passed from the king to a government administrator, and since the temple lost the lands that had enabled it to support the huge *sevaka* community. The potters' community survives, but these documents raise the question of just how much longer it will continue to do so.

## Bibliography

Behura, N. *Peasant Potters of Orissa.* New Delhi, 1978.

Cort, Louise Allison. 'Temple Potters of Puri.' *Res* 7/8 (1984): 33-43.

Eschmann, Anncharlott, Hermann Kulke, and Gaya Charan Tripathi, eds. *The Cult of Jagannath and the Regional Tradition of Orissa.* New Delhi, 1978.

Fischer, Eberhard, and Haku Shah. *Rural Craftsmen and Their Work.* Ahmedabad, 1970.

Inglis, Stephen. *A Village Art of South India: The Work of the Velar.* Madurai, 1980.

__________. 'Creators and Consecrators: A Potter Community of South India.' Ph.D. thesis, University of British Columbia, 1984.

Miller, Daniel. 'Pottery as Ritual Paraphernalia: An Indian Example.' In *Earthenware in Asia and Africa,* edited by John Picton. London, 1985.

__________. *Artefacts as Categories: A Study of Ceramic Variability in Central India.* Cambridge and New York, 1985.

Saraswati, Baidyanath. *Pottery-Making Cultures and Indian Civilization.* New Delhi, 1978.

Saraswati, Baidyanath, and N. Behura. *Pottery Techniques in Peasant India.* Calcutta, 1966.

Shah, Haku. 'Forms and Many Forms of Mother Clay.' *Museum* 147.

__________. *Votive Terracottas of Gujarat.* New York, 1985.

# Spinning Independence

Susan S. Bean
Peabody Museum of Salem

A key element in Mohandas K. Gandhi's spectacular success as a nationalist leader was his uncanny knack for focusing public attention on actions that would be understood by the people of India as central to their life, yet subject to British control and exploitation. The act of spinning cotton yarn was perhaps the most important of these symbols and became the focus of Gandhi's national agenda to relieve poverty, create a united and egalitarian society, and win independence for India. Gandhi took a dying handicraft and transformed it into a program for Indian self-determination.

Spinning is an ancient craft in India. The earliest known spun cotton and spindle whorls in the world are from the Indus Valley civilization of the third millenium B.C. At least since the time of the Mauryan dynasty (*ca.* third century B.C.), cotton yarn has been an important commodity; until the early nineteenth century, women were its primary producers. Spinning was a respectable occupation by which women could augment their family income. In the Mauryan state there was a director of spinning; there were state-run depots for collecting cotton yarn; and there were regulations for the treatment of women spinners who brought their yarn for sale. A Jātaka tale of this period indicates that the accomplished spinner was respected for her skill, and for the autonomy this skill provided. In the story, a woman says to her dying husband, 'I know the art of spinning and by this means shall I bring up the children. Grievest thou not for me' (Government of India 1962: 3ff).

Cotton yarn, primarily spun by Indian women, was used to make textiles that became famous in the West beginning in Roman times: particularly fine muslins and colorful dyed cottons. By the early eighteenth century, oceanic trade had made Indian cloth so common in European countries that the governments of England and France passed laws prohibiting the importation of some kinds of Indian cloth in order to protect their own textile industries.

Daniel Defoe wrote in 1708, 'it crept into our houses, our closets, and bed-chambers; curtains, cushions, and at last the beds themselves, were nothing but calicoes or Indian stuffs; and in short, almost everything that used to be made of wool or silk, relating either to the dress of the women or the furniture of our houses, was supplied by the Indian trade. Above half of the woollen manufacture was entirely lost, half of the people scattered and ruined, and all this by the intercourse of the East India trade' (Defoe 1708).

In the early nineteenth century Francis Buchanan surveyed large portions of eastern and southern India and reported that everywhere spinning was an auxiliary occupation of women — with the exception of brahmin women in the south who did not spin (Buchanan 1807; Martin 1838). Although some authors (*e.g.* Baines 1835) have questioned the accuracy of Buchanan's estimates of the output and value of this domestic craft, it is clear that women were able to make a significant contribution to the household economy through their spinning, and that spinning (in contrast to field labor) was considered a respectable occupation for women. Cotton yarn produced by women was given out to weavers to be made into cloth for the family, or exchanged in the bazaar for other goods.

During the nineteenth century, the technology of cotton yarn manufacture, the organization of its production, and the patterns of trade were transformed. These changes were more radical in their effects than any in the preceding four millenia. The industrial revolution in Europe, which mechanized spinning, and British colonial domination, which controlled Indian exports and imports, transformed India from the technologically most advanced cotton producing and trading nation to a technological backwater and importer of cottons. By the 1820s India was importing an enormous amount of machine-spun cotton yarn produced in English mills. In 1853, Karl Marx published an article in the *New York Daily Tribune* in which he described the nineteenth-century British impact on India in terms which are the mirror image of Defoe's description of the eighteenth-century Indian impact on Britain: 'The hand-loom and the spinning-wheel, producing their regular myriads of spinners and weavers, were the pivots of the structure of [Indian] society. From immemorial times, Europe received the admirable textures of Indian labour . . . . It was the British intruder who broke up the Indian hand-loom and destroyed the spinning-wheel. England began with driving the Indian cottons from the European market; it then introduced twist [yarn] into Hindustan and in the end inundated the very mother country of cotton with cottons' (Marx 1853).

These passages from Defoe and Marx illustrate an evolving international discourse on Indian cloth. In this discourse, the artisans, the implements, and the cotton yarn and cloth transcend the realm of commodity production and trade. This complex of objects, activities, and actors come to stand for the international competition engendered by trans-oceanic trade, and to represent national dominance and subjugation.

R. C. Dutt, one of the architects of Indian economic nationalism, wrote in 1901: 'Spinning and weaving were the great national industry of India next after agriculture .... Weaving and spinning are [now] practically dead, as most of the thread and cloth ... are supplied by Lancashire' (Dutt 1901: 161-62). Because textiles were India's premier manufactured products and the first of European manufactures to be mechanized, cloth production came to represent the impact on India of the industrial revolution through the agency of colonial domination. Britain's 'fixed policy pursued during the last decades of the eighteenth century and the first decades of the nineteenth was to make India subservient to the industries of Great Britain and to make the Indian people grow raw produce only, in order to supply material for the looms and manufactories of Great Britain. This policy was pursued with unwavering resolution and with fatal success ....' (Dutt 1901: xxv).

Amidst the complex of activities associated with cloth production, Gandhi discovered spinning. In spinning Gandhi saw the way to alleviate poverty, achieve national economic self-sufficiency, create national unity, and nurture spiritual strength for the political and moral struggle. Gandhi said the Indian peasant 'cannot maintain himself from the produce of the land. He needs a supplementary industry. Spinning is the easiest, the cheapest and the best' (Jaju 1951: 16). Moreover, spinning alone 'can stop the drain of wealth which goes outside India in the purchase of foreign cloth' (Jaju 1951: 40). Everyone would have to spin in order to produce enough cloth to make imports unnecessary. This universal occupation, spinning, would create national unity. Gandhi maintained that the 'spinning wheel for us is the foundation for all public corporate life' and, more strongly still, 'it is impossible to build any permanent public life without it' (Jaju 1951: 79). Gandhi taught that spinning is a spiritual activity, that spinning would create the spiritual power needed to achieve national self-determination: 'those who know anything about the production of khadi know how patiently the spinners and the weavers have to toil at their trade, and even so must we have patience whilst we are spinning the thread of swaraj' (Jaju 1951: 79).

Gandhi had reinvented spinning. From a respectable women's

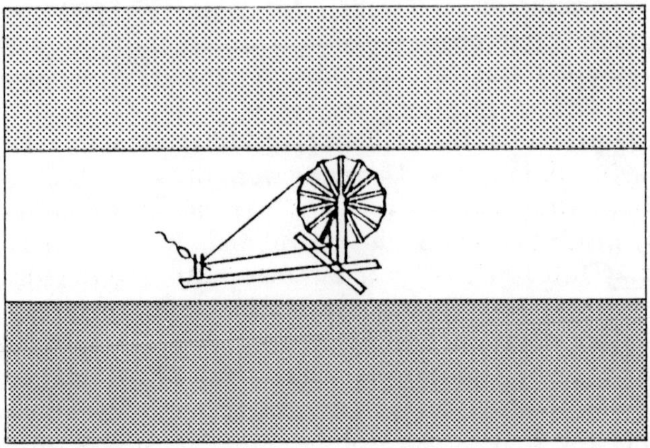

Fig. A.
Flag of the Indian National Congress.

domestic craft, spinning was transformed into the well-spring of *satyāgraha, svadeśi,* and *svarāj.*

Between 1920 and 1926, through Gandhi's influence, spinning became part of the program of the Indian National Congress. At the 1920 special session in Calcutta, a resolution was made to revive hand spinning in every house, linking hand spinning to self-descipline and self-sacrifice. In 1923 the All India Khaddar Board was formed to organize spinning, especially to facilitate the supply of carded cotton, and to aid in the marketing of the yarn produced. In 1924 it was resolved that all members of elected Congress organizations send 2,000 yards of even and well-twisted 'self-spun' yarn each month. In 1926 the wearing of clothing made of handspun cloth was made compulsory. And in 1929 the flag of the Indian National Congress was unfurled with the *charka* (spinning wheel) at the center (Fig. A) (see Chandra 1946).

This entire program was pushed through by Gandhi and with more than a little resistence from his colleagues, most of whom shared Gandhi's view that India's poverty was the result of British political and economic domination, but not his conclusions that machinery was the root of the problem and spinning the solution. Motilal Nehru laughed at Gandhi's pronouncement that one had to know spinning to participate in civil disobedience, yet he acquiesced to the wearing of *khādi*. Jawaharlal Nehru promoted industrialization, but also recognized the importance of spinning as a sign of identification with the masses and national unity. Like Gandhi, he worked at his spinning wheel in public. It was Nehru who dubbed *khādi* the 'livery of our freedom,' and Nehru who unfurled the Congress flag with the *charka* in the center.

Through the Congress program, spinning was to be reincarnated from a domestic occupation of women in their leisure time into a nationally organized, spare-time occupation for all, the alleviator of poverty and an easily comprehended symbol of national unity, economic self-sufficiency, self-discipline, and sacrifice. To succeed, handspun yarn had to compete with machine-spun yarn, which was cheaper, stronger, and of more consistent quality. The All India Khaddar Board and its successor organizations provided training and coordinated the supply of raw materials and the marketing of the finished product. These organizations also encouraged technological improvements to the spinning wheel, supported subsidies to the *khādi* industry, and encouraged middle-class participation.

Gandhi's program did not produce millions of new spinners, but it did transform the organization of production and distribution. As before, most of the spinners were rural women. New recruits, especially men, were usually part of the Indian National Congress or in the *āśrams* and schools organized by Gandhi's followers. However, the All India Khaddar Board and its successor from 1931, the All India Spinners' Association, helped revive a moribund handicraft by providing raw materials and markets for handspun yarn. (See All India Spinners' Association 1931.)

After Independence, hand spinning was again reinvented and its position in the Indian economy was redefined. In the second Five-Year Plan, *khādi* and village industries were considered as part of the process of industrialization. Rather than a means for rural domestic self-sufficiency — in concert with agriculture — spinning and other village industries were redefined as rural *industries* necessary for the development of a balanced industrialization. Under this and later plans, assistance was provided in the organization of cooperatives, in skills training, and in the procuring of equipment and credit. Efforts to increase production were so successful that in the late fifties and sixties production of handspun yarn doubled, but the market did not absorb the increase and an overstock was created. Production dropped back to early 1950s' levels. Despite government subsidies for the production and marketing of homespun yarn, mills continued to produce better-quality yarns at lower prices. Machine-spun yarn is preferred by weavers for its consistency and strength. Indian consumers for centuries have preferred fine cloth to coarse cloth and purchased the finest their means would allow. During the 1970s more attention was paid to this marketing problem by concentrating on the production of certain kinds of homespun cloths, such as coarse furnishing fabrics, which consumers accept (see Dagli 1976).

Since Gandhi's time, the distinction between industry and handicraft, then so clear, has become progressively blurred. Improvements in *charkas* encouraged by Congress programs have continued to be patronized by the Government of India. In the mid-fifties a four-spindle *charka* was developed and a decade later a twelve-spindle *charka.* In the early 1980s cotton fibers were blended with polyester to make slivers for hand spinning and *'poly-vastra' khādi* was produced (see Sreenivasan 1984: 145 ff). The distinction between handmade and machine-made which applied to India in the 1920s has now become obsolete. Machine-made goods (such as polyester fiber) and machinery that allows one person to do the work of four or six have penetrated the villages and transformed the technologies of village industries. The Government of India in fact now distinguishes centralized from decentralized industries rather than machine-made from handmade goods.

The significance of hand spinning has changed in other respects as well. Spinning has been abandoned as a symbol of national unity. (The flag of the Republic of India, in contrast to the Congress flag, has the wheel of Aśoka, not the *charka,* at its center.) The Gandhian goals of self-discipline and spiritual enrichment through spinning did not survive Gandhi's era. Instead, the government has promoted spinning as a monument to Gandhi and to the nationalist movement. In recognition of this symbolic importance, *khādi* has retained some autonomy among the village industries; it is distinguished in the name of the governing organization, the Khādi and Village Industries Commission, and by the interest-free loans available for *khādi* alone among village industries. Without Gandhi to direct the role of spinning in national life, the significance of spinning and homespun cloth has also changed. Ironically, through the activities of some Congress politicians (for whom homespun clothing had been *de rigeur* since 1926), spinning and *khādi,* which once represented the highest of spiritual and moral achievements, have come to connote graft and corruption.

As of the middle 1970s, cloth manufactured in India was 53% millmade and 47% from decentralized power and handlooms. Homespun cloth (produced in the decentralized sector) constituted only .7% of the cloth made in India.

## Bibliography

All India Spinners' Association. *Khadi Guide.* Delhi, 1931.

Baines, Edward. *History of the Cotton Manufacture.* London, 1835.

Bean, Susan S. 'Khadi: the Fabric of Indian Nationalism.' (In press.)

Buchanan, Francis. *A Journey through the Countries of Mysore, Canara and Malabar.* London, 1807.

Chandra, Prabodh. *Sixty Years of Congress.* Lahore, 1946.

Crawford, M.D.C. *Highlights in the Progress of Cotton Spinning.* Rocky Mount Mills, 1944.

Dagli, Vadilal. *Khadi and Village Industries in the Indian Economy.* Bombay, 1976.

Defoe, Daniel. *Weekly Review,* 31 January, 1708.

Dutt, R.C. *The Economic History of India.* Vol. 1 (1901). Reprinted New Delhi, 1976.

Government of India. *The Khadi Industry.* New Delhi, 1962.

Jaju, Shrikrishnadas. *The Ideology of the Charka.* Tirupur, 1951.

Martin, Montgomery. *Eastern India.* 3 vols. London, 1838.

Marx, Karl. 'The British Rule in India.' *New York Daily Tribune,* 10 June, 1853.

Sreenivasan, Kasthuri. *India's Textile Industry.* Coimbatore, 1984.

Fig. B.
'Past and Present Meet in India' (Crawford 1944).

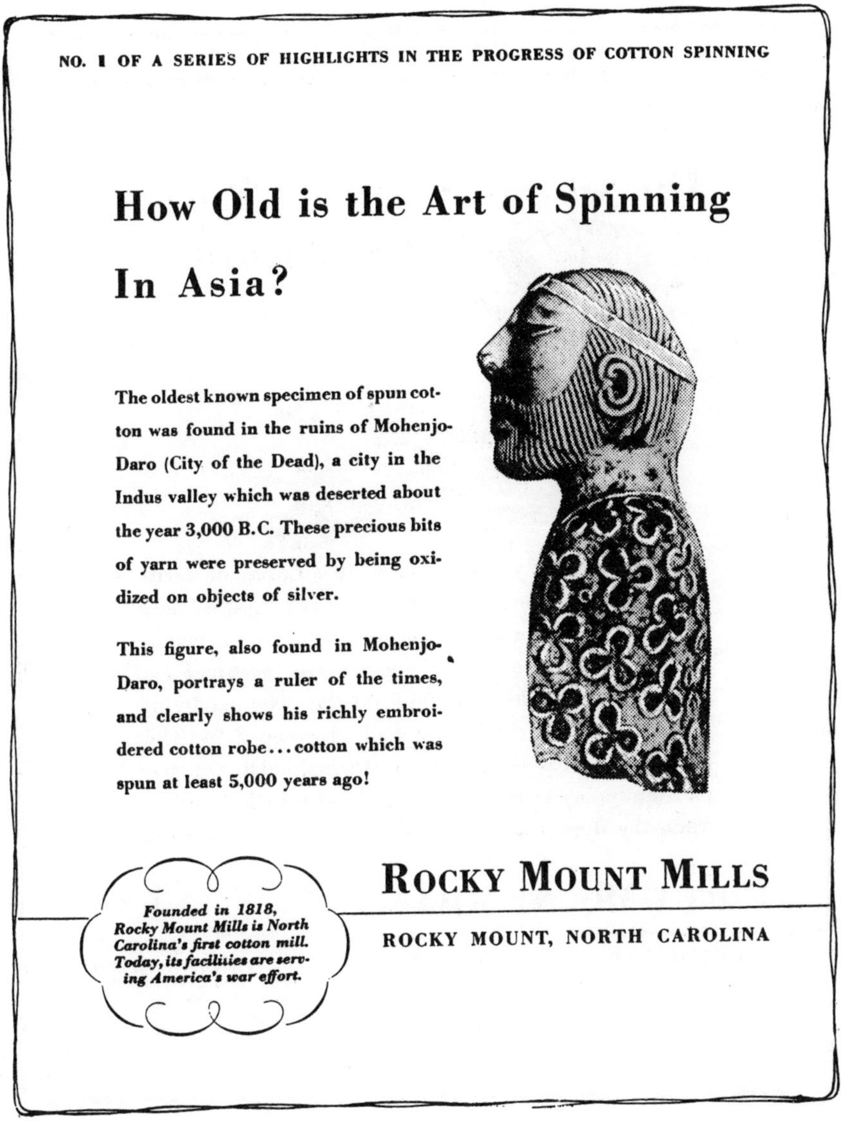


Fig. C.
'How Old is the Art of Spinning in Asia?' (Crawford 1944).

Fig. D.
'The Oldest Spinning Wheel on Record' (Crawford 1944).

# Living Institutions: The Social and Cultural Organization of Craft in Modern India

Joan L. Erdman
Columbia College, Chicago

The intertwining of performing and visual arts in India has been demonstrated to me as I have conducted research on arts patronage and performance in Rajasthan and elsewhere in India. Some institutions combine painting, puppet-making, papier-mache, and woodcarving with set design, puppet shows, singing, and dance. Costume design incorporates craft skills, and museum exhibits illustrate the range and quality of craftsmanship. The performance of Rajasthani *paḍ,* for example, presents one singer/story-teller, or two, illuminating a huge painted scroll while describing the adventures of a legendary hero or demigod. Even the most abstract of performers — the classical musicians — use the subtlety of Lucknow *kurtās,* chikanwork embroidery, fine *khādi* silk, and elegant durries or carpets to give performances a visual attraction on a par with the quality of music produced.

A few notable institutions in India have promoted the interface of plastic and performing arts, based on the revival and rediscovery of India's cultural traditions and the urge to create dialogues between them. My present research on Uday Shankar has led me to such a center, the Uday Shankar India Culture Center, founded at Almora in 1938-39, which lasted only five years. Shankar, who studied painting at J. J. School of Arts in Bombay and at the Royal Academy of Art in London with Sir William Rothenstein before turning to dance with prima ballerina Anna Pavlova in 1923, used his skills as a painter to mount productions and block dances, and his knowledge of India's arts to explore (with art historian Alice Boner's designs and guidance) authentic Indian costumes for his dance productions.

When Shankar founded his culture center at Almora, he had hoped to have painting and sculpture as subjects of teaching and study as well as classical and modern dance traditions and music; drawing was encouraged, and Shankar thought a complete course should include art history as well as practical training. While a few lectures during the center's brief duration addressed these subjects, it was not until decades later when Shankar's students founded their own institutions that the goal of integrating plastic and performing arts actually was achieved.

The late Devilal Samar's Bharatiya Lok Kala Mandal at Udaipur and Sundari Shridharan's Triveni Kala Sangam in New Delhi are among the better-known institutions that promote this integration, as do the new arts complex at Bhopal — Bharat Bhavan — and in a less structured way, the Bhule Bisre settlement of Rajasthani folk artists and performers near Pusa Institute in Delhi as well as Kalakshetra at Madras where dance takes precedence (but dance of course is a visual as well as a performing art).

One of the most important structural components of India's present crafts organization is descended from an exhibition held nearly a hundred years before Uday Shankar founded his Almora Center — the 1851 Crystal Palace Exhibition of the British Empire. In a paper on 'Jaipur Patronage and the Exhibition of 1883' (1981), I pointed out that that exhibit of art treasures — industrial, mythological, and decorative — was intended, in its own words, to:

> instruct and amuse the common people, to present to the craftsman selected examples of the best art work of India, in the hope that they would profit thereby; to bring together specimens of local manufactures, in order that strangers might see what could be obtained in the neighbourhood; and to form a collection of raw products in the State and surrounding districts, regarding which full information could be obtained . . . . (Hendley 1883)

The purpose of the 1883 exhibition in Jaipur, initiated and planned by an Englishman with the patronage of Jaipur's enlightened ruler, Maharaja Ram Singh II, differed but slightly from that of the Crystal Palace Exhibition. In fact dozens and perhaps hundreds of exhibitions were modelled on the 1851 extravaganza, representing the empire's cultural models, if not the contents, again and again in European and Asian settings. Thus craft as art became part of the commercial empire of India's rulers. In Jaipur, the museum became a permanent part of the complex of zoo, garden, and park that tamed the wilds outside the city wall and created an urban environment for civilized recreation. Crafts were people's arts, which could be bought and sold for aesthetic and symbolic as well as functional purposes.

Just as the conjunction of liberal and vocational arts — or performance study and the study of performance — causes some discomfort among educational planners and elite universities, so also the British in India made an attempt to separate the appreciation of artifacts from the production of crafts objects. Certain pieces were 'museum pieces,' while others were 'just functional.' Modern Indian handicrafts promoters and institutions have attempted to modify this distinction, introducing crafts villages that produce quality items, museums where craftsmen work, and exhibits with living craftsmen demonstrating their special skills and expertise. While the latter have been criticized for putting people on display as exhibits, their intention is as blameless as other methods of integrating production and product.

For Indians, the artist is in the work — whether as performance or product. Just as each *rāga-tāla* performance develops uniquely with its particular combination of context, audience, artist, and patron, so also each crafted object is unique, and while patterns or structures or subtle underlying characteristics remain the same, the process of making the music or object is the creative act. A craftsman at work is more admired in traditional India than even the ultimate result, which is mundane when segregated from the artist.

This investment in the artist as the font of craft is inimicable to a commercial policy of object-value. Only in alienated objects can commercial value — buying and selling — obtain. Modern India has recognized this necessity for alienation — in the rediscovery and placement within museums of ancient art objects as in the development of markets for handloom cloth and (more recently) other handmade objects of leather, wool, ivory, or metal. The personal, private connection between artist, object, and patron or owner has been severed, and while a nostalgia remains for the artist/craftsman's process as the highest value, it is the objects themselves that support the enterprise of craftsmanship, in the functional sense. This new relationship is, like much in India, also old, since village potters and metalworkers have long existed primarily by the functionality of their crafts, which are now threatened by plastics and machine-manufactured goods. Yet the labor-intensive village economy still can provide, as Ashoke Chatterjee, Director of the National Institute of Design in Ahmedabad, has clearly shown, a locus for the commercially viable development of crafts.

For the artist/craftsman — the ideal, integrated, creator of aesthetically wonderful objects the functionality of which does not detract from commercial viability — there remains a paradox, which can be illustrated by a story. A well-known cultural organizer in Jaipur had several near-careers before turning to performing arts administration. Among them was apprenticeship to a renowned ivory-carver in Delhi, who, it was said, could carve a hundred roses without ever duplicating one. Eventually his expertise came to the attention of a buyer for a major department store, who came to the ivory-carver to place an order. What was wanted was 500 ivory roses, which were to be all the same and all of perfect quality. The craftsman/artist refused that order with disdain — who would want such an uninteresting and unartistic [un-craftsmanlike?] order, and one so irrelevant to the artist's creativity?

Duplication or replication is merely mundane; the subject and object of the artist/craftsman is divine. Without the support of an understanding patron, craft is merely work, not creative work; but in modern India, as in the rest of the modern world, mere work (employment) can be the harbinger of creative artistic activity.

## Crafts Institutions

Whether arising from indigenous social structures and cultural habits, or created as campuses for guild-like activity, or developed as an adjunct to educational ahistorical exhibit and display, crafts institutions in India today in their multiplicity reflect the paradoxical historical development of values and symbols in art and artworks. Some institutions celebrate the extremes of vulgarity of an excessively indulgent patronage, such as the collection of the Raja Kelkar Museum in Pune, with its hundreds of brass lamps and betelnut crackers. Others reveal the varieties of simplicity evidenced in agricultural and rural utensils and storage vessels, such as the Vechaar Foundation at the Vishalla Environmental Center for Heritage of Art, Architecture and Research, on the Sarkhej Road outside Ahmedabad.

This latter collection focuses on the utensils of everyday life rather than 'precious art.' Utensils, according to their brochure:

> belong to that class of cultural objects which have, for ages, been an integral part of everyday life, and which have displayed in their conception and making a remarkable degree of aesthetic awareness and a tremendous sense of usability combined with practicality and beauty.

Rarely collected, these objects, like costumes and other everyday items, have been neglected even as they are being replaced by stainless steel and plastics. Their forms are sculpturesque and often symbolically readable, their utility compressed into their design.

Vishalla also has an outdoor, leaf-plate and-earthenware restaurant as well as performances by folk artists in its rural compound. Created by the interior designer Surendra Patel as 'an oasis of peace and tranquility in the chaos of urban life,' it has become fashionable among Ahmedabad's numerous 'yuppies' as an experience of the rural life which these city-born Indians lack without their own village *'deś.'* The era of Raja Kelkar's craftsmen and their indulgent royal patrons may have ended, but the time for Vishalla's crafts is both past and present, as a museum and in its efforts to reclaim a functional past for a commercial present.

A somewhat different establishment is the Cholamandalam at Kanchipuram near Madras, where a colony of batik-makers and other artists have founded a cooperative institution designed to provide workspace, marketing, and other facilities. Like the new studios for artists founded by Shankho Choudhuri in New Delhi, Cholamandalam is the creation of the artists and craftsmakers themselves. It has been designed not as a collection of past achievements nor as a program for the future, but rather as a presentist solution to the difficulties and problems of being an artist/craftsmaker in modern India.

There are also modern patrons other than the government (a patron too extensive for me to discuss in detail here) worthy of study and consideration. The Sarabhai family was the major patron for the magnificent Calico Museum in Ahmedabad and its publications (Irwin and Hall, 1971 and 1973). This private collection and museum served as inspiration for new designs and modern production while preserving past heritage in an elegant setting. Living craftsworkers were not involved in the museum, which has recently been shifted to the Sarabhai family compound.

Naika, a small crafts workshop in a former caravanserai in Mahrauli on the outskirts of New Delhi, is purely for the production of crafts by local and rural artists, brought to the center by its director, Inder Raz Dan. Naika was one of the chief craft centers for the original *Aditi* exhibition in New Delhi in 1978, and has become a model for village crafts centers, bringing together the intensive labor, market skills, and quality control necessary for commercializing domestic industry.

Other patron-sponsored crafts institutions are the outcome of unique artistic situations, not models for crafts patronage so much as illustration of the multiple ways of modernizing India's crafts. On the Paldi Road in Ahmedabad, near Vishalla, is the rural compound of the artist Piraji Sagara, painter, collage-maker, sponsor of traditional woodcarving, and middleman for embroidered and other handicrafts from the Rajasthan/Gujarat border area that was his family's *deś.* He and his brothers had lived in a joint household in one of the old parts of Ahmedabad, but Sagara moved his extended family to this farming area about two decades ago, when land was inexpensive and its rural setting not yet a suburb. Sagara has forged his pragmatic idiosyncrasy into a small business with complex family ties. A philosopher who reads Sartre, successful as an artist, supportive of indigenous handicrafts, a local 'character' with patrons stylish, artistic, and humble, his personality dominates the entire enterprise.

So also does the expertise and personal knowledge of another studio and its patron-entrepreneur, Kunwar Sangram Singh of Nawalgarh in Rajasthan. In Sangram Singh's family *haveli* in Jaipur you can see, hold, and photograph artworks of a quality that most museums store away from public eyes. Sangram Singh's Rajput heritage and membership in a patron family (with their *jagir* at Nawalgarh, in the Shekhawat District of Rajasthan) have inspired him to develop a modern patronage, beyond collecting older miniatures, giving to current artists/craftsmen who paint miniatures a chance to use their skills and perhaps move on to regenerate miniature painting in India. Motivated by economic as well as heritage goals, this patron-entrepreneur has opened a studio in his huge mansion, where master craftsmen copy paintings from his collection for sale *as copies* abroad. Since the export of the originals is forbidden, and since the artists who paint the copies are not only under the tutelage of a master craftsman, but also the highly educated and sophisticated eye of their patron, the production of copies for export fills the needs of the artist for work, the patron for earnings, and the nation for artistic export.

The Bharatiya Lok Kala Mandal at Udaipur is an extensively developed museum and performance center, founded by one committed man, the late Devilal Samar, and supported by both private and government funding for its activities. Samar, son of a modestly well-to-do businessman, was inspired during a summer at Uday Shankar's India Culture Center to return to local surroundings to search for traditions unknown to anglicized urban elites. Creative in developing his own expertise in local folk traditions and handicrafts, and in designing an institution alive with activity and educational in its displays, Samar gave Udaipur a museum visited by thousands of tourists each year, a center for crafts and performing groups who have toured abroad and won prizes for their puppetry and folkdance programs, and a research institute for study of local indigenous crafts and artworks. His institution has survived the demise of its founder, though not without difficulties. One of its successor-leaders is Komal Kothari, another patron-entrepreneur whose researches in Rajasthan's folk traditions have brought worldwide attention to Rajasthan's folk and professional performance traditions.

With the writer Vijay Dan Detha, Kothari has founded a folklore institute in the prosperous village of Borunda, near Jodhpur, named Rupayan Sansthan. Developing expertise in grantsmanship and fund-finding, they have been able to support research activities begun by Kothari when he was with the Rajasthan Sangeet Natak Akademi at Jodhpur. A huge institute building has been built on a hilltop overlooking Borunda, with a museum and concert hall, library, administrative offices, hostel accomodations, recording studio, and other facilities. A central breezeway channels currents of wind providing a relief from the often oppresive heat; the rooftop offers quiet access to star-filled desert nights. Scholars, dignitaries, and touring groups visit the institute, sometimes staying several days. Collection of instruments, puppets, and other traditional folk crafts related to performance and costume continues, and craftsworkers bring special items to the institute and to the attention of its researchers.

Unlike Borunda — an institution purposely created as a center for traditional craft and performance — the small village of Nathadwara north of Udaipur has been a center for a specialized artwork for centuries. *Pichwais,* the curtains which hang behind the deity in temples of Śrī Nāthji, are painted at Nathadwara by families who, patronized by pilgrims and devotees, have for generations transmitted their skills from father to son. *Pichwais* of highest quality are still painted on commission; lesser *pichwais* are painted for sale in Nathadwara, or elsewhere in India to urbanites who appreciate their artistic value. Some sons of *pichwai* families have become modern artists. Mohan Sharma, for example, has completed a doctorate in London on color symbolism in Rajasthani painting and teaches painting at the School of Art in Jaipur. Sharma still also paints miniatures on ivory and has been successful in finding purchasers for his traditional as well as modern works (the former, mainly to Rajasthanis, the latter to Delhi elites).

Another source of the past for artists in Jaipur is the museum of the City Palace, where, in addition to displays of a small percentage of the extensive Jaipur family holdings, there are exhibits of royal clothing, instruments, weapons, and other accouterments of past power and riches. The museum retains only one small living institution, the daily noontime concerts of *śehnāi* and *naqqārā* now held near the armoury (previously it was in the *naubatkhānā*) marking past periods when Jaipur used its own astronomical instruments as a guide to the passage of time.

The finality of Jaipur's royal collections is the reverse of new crafts developments in Jawaja, a village south of Ajmer selected by the

National Institute of Design in Ahmedabad for a joint project with Ahmedabad's Indian Institute of Management (IIM) and other organizations. Determining what kind of activities would be appropriate to local resources, skills, and facilities, developing designs and products that could circumvent traditional routes to markets, trying to get more of the final cost to the producer-craftsworker, and gaining a reputation for quality (as The Jawaja Collection), design and other experts sent to Jawaja had as their goals the activation of local involvement and the gradual irrelevance of their own expertise. As Ashoke Chatterjee, Director of NID, has pointed out, institutionalization of village crafts today is the key to their continuity and self-motivation. But there are subtleties, as Ray Owens may have mentioned in this forum in his discussion of Mithilā painting cooperatives. The Jawaja Weavers Association and Leather Association avoid the word 'cooperative,' which has a negative connotation in the area. Crafts and art have been part of numerous rural development projects in India — Worli paintings, Sankheda work, block-printing, etc. — but no single model has, as yet, proven to be nationally or even regionally feasible. The necessity for local initiative and appropriateness of projects to local conditions if crafts development is to survive beyond the departure of experts and advisors, suggests that while there are lessons to be learned from both successes and failures, each project has its own history, integrity, and particularity.

Crafts centers are often dependent on short-term, intense marketing events, primarily 'exhibitions' in urban centers. Sponsored by middlemen, cooperating crafts groups, a particular patron-entrepreneur, or a generous patron, these events are widely advertised but brief, offering urban dwellers artifacts at low overhead prices. While quality control varies for such exhibits, the opportunity for bargains usually outweighs a consumer's need to search for better items. In New Delhi, where there is a rich market of diplomatic, business, and government consumers, exhibits are nearly daily events in hotels, homes, or neighborhood markets. Unlike Kashmiri crafts, which are sold both in modern emporia and by private sale to households, such handloom, embroidered, leather, and other crafts appear periodically and lack regularized marketing infrastructure. The flexibility of irregular exhibits, however, gives new craft organizations the potential to search for new and wider markets. Not every craft organization can manage to get its products in a major government-sponsored emporium.

With the *Aditī* exhibition (subtitled 'the Living Arts of India') and the Festival of India, the cultural model provided by the Crystal Palace

Exhibition of 1851 has been redifined. Added to it are the traditional Sanskritic model of divinely-inspired craftswork and Perso-Arabic traditions of patronage and *kārkhānās.* This reclamation of the 'living arts' of Indian tradition returns to a craftsworker who is also an artist, to symbolically significant productions (imbued with both pan-Indian and regional characteristics), and to an international formula melding work and worker, art and artisan, creativity and creator into a single seamless process, while not denying the alienation necessary to accomodate modern economic realities. The craftsman/artist has become a performer, and the process of making itself again marks India's crafts as singular, ingenious, and intriguingly universal in their significance.

It is possible to develop analytical categories and continua for the institutional development of India's crafts and artists and their roles in Indian society, but it is also important to remember that the indigenous (and autochthonous) paths are many, and while comparison and categorization are possible, they do not represent the ways India's craftsmen and artists perceive their development as a process. From self-initiated modernization of craft production to carefully structured foundations and museums, from persistent production of traditional items to adaptive forms and functions for traditional skills, from a dichotomization of craft and art to the integration of skill and aesthetic, the particular institutions which are centers for inspiration, production, and creativity in India's crafts fall on all points of the continua, and approaching any of the multiple streams of development must be done through respect for its peculiarities and particularities as well as its place in a schema or categorization of types.

Anthropologists are often criticized for their unwillingness to make generalizations about things; in fact it is the combination of universals with specificity rather than generalization which attracted me to the discipline. Only by taking into account the cultural and human factors in crafts production can the things made, the makers, and the art of each be understood. For a culture which relates more easily in anecdote, archetype, and aesthetic *(rasa),* and in process, duration, and the temporal as symbolic, than in boundaries, definitions, units, or categories, the research and findings — if not the process of analysis itself — should reflect the values of its producers, bearers, and participants as well as those of the observer and buyer.

## Bibliography

Bharat Bhavan. Pamphlet. (Bharat Bhavan, Shamla Hills, Bhopal, M.P.)

Erdman, Joan L. 'Jaipur Patronage and the Exhibition of 1883.' Presented at the College Art Association Annual Meeting, San Francisco, Feb. 1981. (Unpublished).

_________. 'Painting and Art History as Bases for Uday Shankar's Choreography.' Presented at American Dance Guild Conference, Durham, N.C., June 1986. (Unpublished).

Hendley, Thomas H. *Memorials of the Jeypore Exhibition 1883.* London, 1883.

*India A Festival of Science.* Catalogue of exhibit. Chicago: Museum of Science and Industry, 1985.

Irwin, John and Margaret Hall. *Indian Painted and Printed Fabrics. Volume I, Historic Textiles of India at the Calico Museum.* Ahmedabad, 1971.

_________. *Indian Embroideries. Volume II, Historic Textiles of India at the Calico Museum.* Ahmedabad, 1973.

Jain, Jyotindra. *Utensils.* Exhibition conceived, collected and designed by Surendra C. Patel (Sharad Gandharva). Ahmedabad, 1980 (?).

*Kalakshetra. Art and Education.* Quarterly Journal of Kalakshetra, an International Centre for the Arts, Madras.

Kelkar, D. G. *Lamps of India.* New Delhi, 1961.

Khokar, Mohan. *His Dance, His Life. A Portrait of Uday Shankar.* New Delhi, 1983.

National Institute of Design. Pamphlets. Ahmedabad.

Shreyas. Pamphlet. Ahmedabad.

*Treasures of Everyday Art. Raja Dinkar Kelkar Museum.* Bombay, 1978.

*Uday Shankar: A Picto-Biography.* Commemorative Volume, Uday-Utsav, New Delhi, 8-11 December 1983. Edited by Sunil Kothari and Mohan Khokar. New Delhi, 1983.

Vishalla Environmental Centre for Heritage of Art Architecture and Research. Pamphlets. Ahmedabad.

# Making Exhibitions Indian: 'Aditi' and 'Mela' at the Smithsonian Institution

Richard Kurin
Deputy Director, Office of Folklife Programs
Smithsonian Institution, Washington, D.C.

Presentations by other scholars in this seminar series have dealt with the relationships which obtain between South Asian artisans and the objects they create. But what of the higher order products of such artisans? To what extent and how do such people artistically shape and craft the contexts, situations, and social structures within and through which their creativity is expressed and presented? Here I consider two extraordinary exhibitions — 'Aditi: A Celebration of Life' and 'Mela! An Indian Fair' — which took place in the summer of 1985 on the National Mall in Washington, D.C., as part of the Festival of India program mounted by the Smithsonian Institution. I do so in order to explore how Indian participants crafted these exhibitions as products, albeit not usual ones, within which traditional attitudes, skills, and creative expressions came to the fore, making the exhibitions quite different from those typically found at the Smithsonian or other similar museums. Exploration of these differences not only reveals Indian aesthetic and organizational notions, but also is revealing of our own.

In the *generic* American Museum exhibit, objects find their way into cases, purportedly for insurance and security reasons, and are hence removed from makers, users, and viewers. If the object is considered an art object, it gets a pedestal or a nice place on the wall with a spotlight (Chandra 1985). If it is a craft object, it often is displayed in some arbitrary artistic grouping of like items. The people who make or use the object are not usually included in exhibits. They may be included vicariously, as through photographs — which remind the viewer of what he is not seeing — or through manikins, which are frozen representations of people as objects. When authentic practitioners *are* included in a living exhibition, their participation usually takes a demonstration format. They sit at standard tables, or on standard floors next to standard signs, or perform on procenium stages, occupying a space in either an indoor or outdoor museum neither designed for them, nor suggestive of the usual context (home, workshop, community center) of their artistic practice. An alternative mode of presentation, the living history exhibition as exemplified by Colonial Williamsburg, may replicate such physical settings, but by substituting actors or revivalists for authentic practitioners this tends to disarticulate demonstrated traditions from biographical, historical, and social contexts.

Museums and museum exhibitions may be considered meta-analytically as forms of presentation, with their own cultural roots and richness of meanings. In a museum, we expect to see exhibitions: exhibition halls or spaces tend to be separated from people-function spaces. Restrooms, cafeterias, information desks, and stores are kept distinct from exhibition areas — enforcing divisions between education on one hand and commerce, provisioning, and maintenance on the other. Whether offering a presentation or reconstruction, we understand an exhibition to be just that, removed from the reality of those represented as from our own. Exhibitions are bounded spacially by entrances, exits, and walls; temporally by grand and daily openings and closings. Exhibitions have their own routinized organization and processes of formation involving institutional structures, curatorial and support staffs, funding arrangements and sponsors, building management, loan agreements, and so on.

If exhibitions are a nineteenth and twentieth century mode for the presentation of culture, one may ask whether the format and aesthetics of that form are appropriate to that which is represented. If folk art is distinguished from elite and commercial art in its unification of object and context, pleasure and utility, meaning and audience in everyday contexts, does it then make sense to have exhibitions which generically present the objects of folk art as if they were paintings in the National Gallery? In short, folk arts and folklife — in particular that of India — suggest aesthetic and organizational notions somewhat at odds with generic museum exhibitions. It would make sense if folk arts and folklife were to be presented in a format consistent with the features of those arts and cultural activities.

The Smithsonian's Office of Folklore Program, with curatorial responsibility for the Aditi and Mela exhibitions, and two decades of experience in the presentation of living cultural traditions through the annual Festival of American Folklife, was able to achieve such a format. This was accomplished partially through design — as a result of Indo-U.S. scholarly, bureaucratic, and technical collaboration — and largely by providing an appropriate context for Indian craftspeople and performing artists to be themselves and to structure their own environment.

**Aditi and Mela: Background**

While organized in America under the aegis of the Festival of India, both Aditi and Mela had been discussed and were in the making prior to the Festival, Aditi since 1979 and Mela since 1981.

The Aditi exhibition was mounted in the National Museum of Natural History from June 4 to July 28, 1985. The exhibit hall was completely remodeled to simulate a rural Indian environment and to house some two-to-three thousand objects ranging from pieces loaned by the Queen's collection, in London, and by more than fifty Indian museums, to contemporary handicraft items. The exhibit was arranged thematically in terms of the life cycle — inspired by but only approximating the Hindu *saṃsāra.* The exhibition began with signals of fertility and continued through marriage, birth, growing up, and moving out (Fig. A). Rather than a linear representation of biography, the switch from parents having children to children becoming parents illustrated the cyclical nature of life evoked by the goddess, Aditi, who, in the Vedas, is both the mother and daughter of Dakṣa. The thousands of objects were arranged in appropriate sections of the exhibit associated with their use — fertility objects in the first section, wall paintings in the nuptial chambers, cradles with birth, toys in growing up, and so on. As an alternative to a chronological or spacial ordering, objects — royal and rustic, contemporary and ancient, Hindu and Muslim, southern and northern — were arranged according to theme in an effort favoring cultural holism over atomistic particularism. Only a small portion of the objects were in cases. Most were set in mud-wall niches, apportioned on platforms, displayed in stalls, and otherwise directly available to visitors.

Complementing the objects and their setting were forty craftspeople and performers who worked in designed spaces to illustrate their creative role in the life cycle. A Warli wall painter depicted tribal courtship dances, women applied *mehndi* as in preparation of marriage, Muslim Langa musicians sang songs to welcome the newborn, and story tellers initiated children to India's history, myth, and wisdom. Ten of the artists were themselves children. A family with two sons, aged nine and four, were included in the forty people drawn from thirteen different Indian states.

In addition to objects, people, and setting, the exhibit included considerable descriptive, interpretive, and expressive commentary as signs and also translators who interpreted between folk artists and visitors.

'Mela! An Indian Fair' was part of the 19th annual Festival of American Folklife held outdoors on the National Mall between the U.S. Capitol and the Washington Monument from June 24 to July 6, 1985. Mela served as a much expanded form of the last section of the Aditi exhibition.

Mela was a composite fair-within-a-fair presenting ritual, craft, performance, food, and commercial traditions from a variety of Indian regions. More than 100 tons of terracotta tile, bamboo, cocoanut leaves, *śāmiyānā,* and *kanāth* were sent from India to construct the temporary *mela* site. Some 45 structures were built, including a masonry facsimile of a shrine, stalls for craft sales and demonstrations, and a tandoor kitchen.

Mela was conceptually organized on the basis of indigenous Indian models. Hindu action orientations *(mokṣa, dharma, artha, kāma)* informed the selection of ritual, educational, commercial, and entertaining activities to be included in the *mela.* Naturalistic notions of the elements *(pañca mahābhūta)* and their associated sensations (*i.e.,* sound, touch, sight, taste, smell) provided a model for the exhibition's spacial organization. Animated by thirty-five artisans from India and thirty Indian-Americans, ritual activities included daily Gaṇeśa *pūjā,* the making of a Durgā icon and a *tāziā,* and the construction and burning of Rāvaṇa effigies. Educational exhibits included an elaborate photo-text exhibit. Sound sections were animated by drummers from different parts of India, performances of Punjabi *giddha,* Gujarati *garbā,* and Bengali Bauls, and featured stalls selling musical instruments. The touch section (associated with the element air) included cloth, mobile, and fan stalls, a kite maker, acrobats, and a juggler. The sight section (associated with fire and form) was replete with magicians, trick photographer, potter, toy maker, impersonators, and shops of varying descriptions. Some forty cooks demonstrated their skills — cooking in tandoors, making *jalebis,* and serving in *deghchis* more than 5,000 meals per day. The smell section included incense, essence, and cosmetics stalls as well as a flower-garland maker (see Fig. B). In sum, the exhibit offered to visitors an event within which, as in a *mela* in India, ritual practice, education, commerce, and pleasure are interwoven (and arguably more completely and appropriately understood in this context than when considered in isolation).

The Aditi and Mela exhibitions were quite successful from the perspectives of the public, the local Indian-American community, educators and staff, sponsoring organizations, the Smithsonian, and the

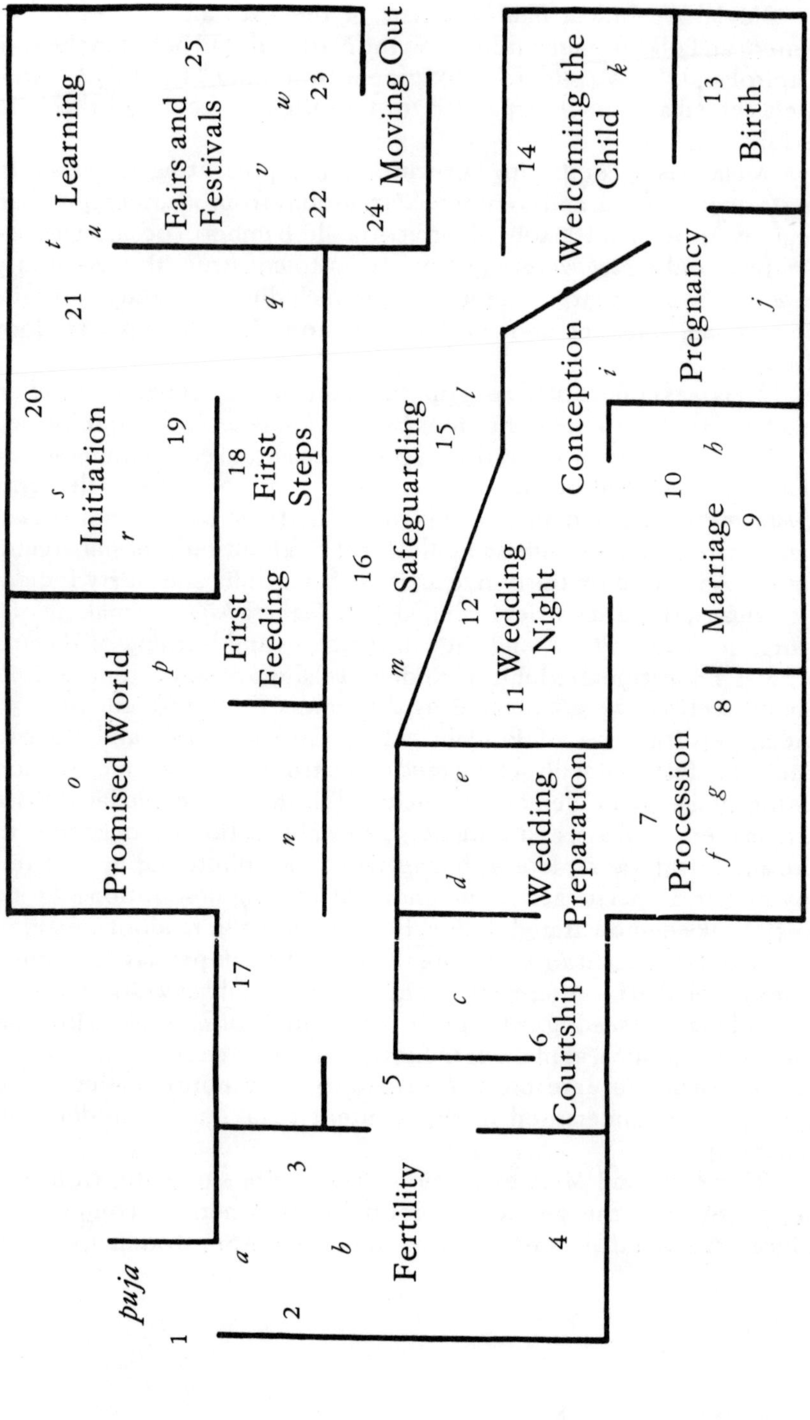
Learning
Fairs and Festivals
Moving Out
Welcoming the Child
Birth
Initiation
First Steps
Safeguarding
Conception
Pregnancy
Promised World
First Feeding
Wedding Night
Marriage
Wedding Preparation
Procession
Courtship
Fertility
puja
1
2
3
4
5
6
7
8
9
10
11
12
13
14
15
16
17
18
19
20
21
22
23
24
25
a
b
c
d
e
f
g
h
i
j
k
l
m
n
o
p
q
r
s
t
u
v
w

**Fig. A.**
**Aditi: A Celebration of Life, exhibition plan.**

**The Life Cycle**

**I Signals of Fertility**
1 Mother goddess
2 Female icons
3 Male icons
4 Aniconic Symbols
*a Baul singer*
*b Bahrupiya m/f impersonator*

**II Courtship and Betrothal**
5 Kanyakumari tableau
6 Combs, pipes, presents
*c Warli wall painter*

**III Wedding Preparations**
*d Mithila wall painter*
*e Mehndi hand painter*

**IV Wedding Procession**
7 Rural courtyard
8 Wedding dress and ornaments
*f Kacchi ghori dancers*
*g Kalbelia snake dancers*

**V Marriage**
9 Dowry items
10 Wedding tableaux
*h Mithila sculptress*

**VI Wedding Night**
11 Nawab's nuptial chamber
12 Mithila chamber

**VII Conception**
*i Veil maker*

**VIII Pregnancy**
*j Glass painters*

**IX Birth**
13 Parent-child depictions

**X Welcoming the Child**
14 Cradles
*k Langa musicians*

**XI Safeguarding**
15 Votive pottery
16 Aiyanaar horses
*l Bastar potter*
*m Aiyanaar potter*

**XII Promised World**
17 Toys
*n Sikki grass weaver*
*o Kathputli puppeteers*
*p Magicians*

**XIII First Feeding**

**XIV First Steps**
18 Walkers, shoes, bells

**XV Initiation to Learning**
19 Goddess of learning
20 Models and toys
*q Juggler*
*r Bhopa story singers*
*s Chitrakar scroll maker*

**XVI Learning to Be and Do**
21 Village tableaux
*t Potwa painter*
*u Krishnagar toy maker*

**XVII Fairs and Festivals**
22 God and goddess icons
23 Temple stall
24 Masks
*v Acrobats*
*w Bahrupiya*

**XVIII Moving Out**
25 Village, city, fair tableau

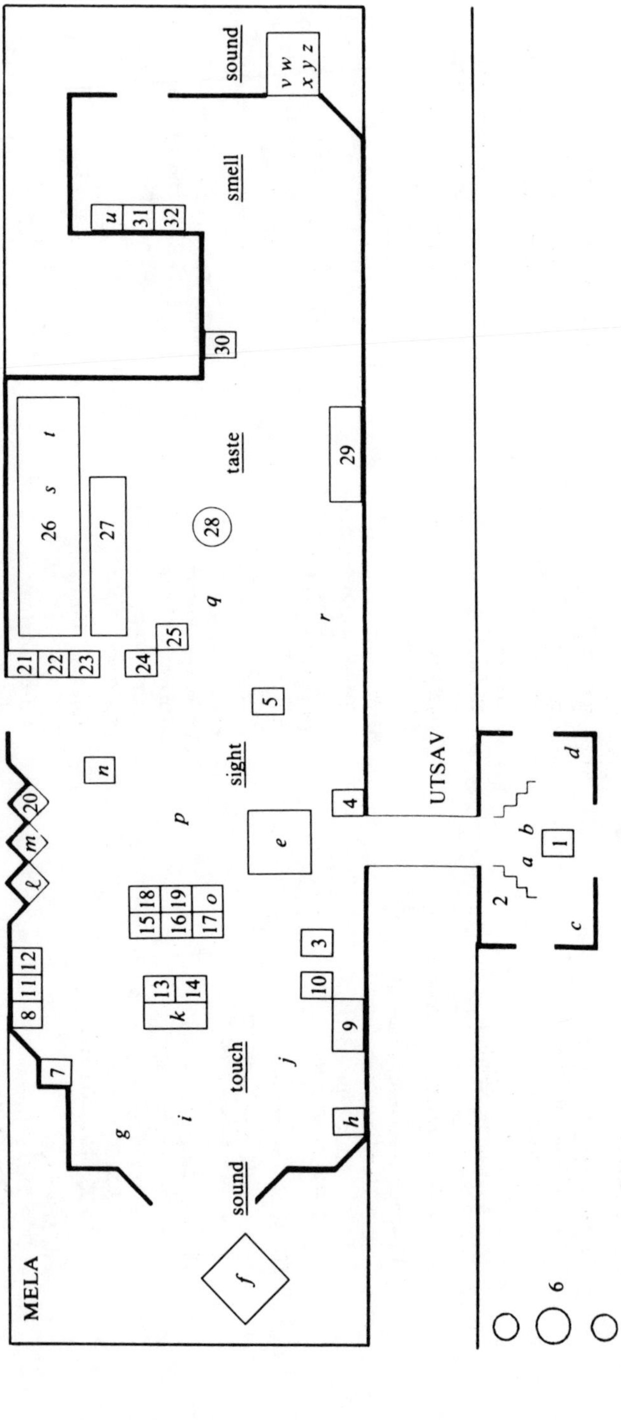
MELA
UTSAV
sound
touch
sight
taste
smell
sound

**Fig. B.**
**Mela! An Indian Fair, site map.**

**UTSAV (ritual festivities)**

1 Ganesha puja (worship)
2 Fairs and festivals photo-text panels
3 Puja items stall
4 Icons stall
5 Shiva temple
6 Ravana effigies
*a Brahman priest*
*b Kolam floor painter*
*c Ravana makers*
*d Taziya builders*
*e Durga statue makers*

**MELA (fair sensations)**

**Sound/ether:**

7 Musical instrument shop
*f Percussionists*
*g Folk dramatists*
*h Kathputli puppeteers*

**Touch/air:**

8 Pan shop
9 Clothing shop
10 Mobile shop
*i Nat acrobats*
*j Lagam juggler*
*k Kitemaker*

**Sight/fire:**

11 Animal goods shop
12 Footwear shop
13-14 Basket shops
15-16 Household goods shops
17 Floor covering shop
18 Pottery shop
19 Pipe shop
20 Bangle and trinket shop
21-23 Toy shops
24 Fireworks stall
25 Oil lamp shop
*l Mehndi hand painter*
*m Bangle maker*
*n Potter*
*o Pith toy maker*
*p Bahrupiya impersonators*
*q Magicians*
*r Trick photographer*

**Taste/water:**

26 Food preparation
27 Food service (degh)
28 Sweet shop
29 Beverage stand
30 Spice stall
*s Tanduri cooks*
*t Jalebi maker*

**Smell/earth:**

31 Cosmetics stall
32 Incense stall
*u Flower garland maker*

**Sound/ether:**

*v Baul singers*
*w Giddha singers/dancers*
*x Garba/ras dancers*
*y Bengali folk singers*
*z Qavvali singers*

participants themselves. Mela attracted 1.2 million visitors, Aditi a museum-limited maximum capacity of 130,000 (with two-hour lines on weekends). Both exhibitions were hailed by the popular media in the U.S. and India. Hosts of VIPs including Prime Minister Rajiv Gandhi and Nancy Reagan visited the exhibitions. Local Indian community groups were mobilized and strengthened — planning events around the exhibits, furthering their own programs, institutionalizing their relationship to the Smithsonian. Even local Indian restaurants and groceries benefited, gaining customers and attention. Ancillary to the exhibitions, the Smithsonian produced a catalog, *Aditi: The Living Arts of India,* with essays by leading Indian scholars which sold more than 25,000 copies and has won both scholarly and popular acclaim; an award winning documentary film on the Aditi exhibition; an educational packet on Indian culture distributed to South Asia outreach centers and museums for primary and secondary schools; an ethnographic film series; workshops for teachers using the exhibits as a pedagogical tool; and workshops for visiting children wherein the Indian folk artists initiated and instructed hundreds in their artistic practice.

In India, the success of the exhibits contributed to the Prime Minister's decision to institute various regional centers for the study and presentation of the folk arts as well as a national cultural festival. Record sales of Indian handicrafts through the Smithsonian prompted government corporations like the Handicrafts and Handlooms Export Corporation, which co-sponsored Aditi and Mela, to further support and strengthen folk-artistic activity. Organizations such as the Birla Academy and the India Tourism Development Corporation (another co-sponsor) have taken up plans for developing permanent on-going structures for presenting the folk arts. The expectations of individual artists who participated in Aditi and Mela have been raised. Some have directly benefited from their celebrity upon returning to India. Others have faired less well. Overall, the publicity, attention, and acclaim received by the Aditi and Mela participants should extend to their brethren in legitimating their role in Indian society and insuring their rights to practice their art and, in some cases, to own the land which they have been promised. Government support of regional centers, plans for festivals in Japan, France, and the U.S.S.R., promises to ammend the beggary laws and to grant land to dislocated itinerant performers, as well as initiatives by Government corporations speak to this possibility.

**Making Aditi and Mela Indian**

Importantly, for Indian folk artists, Aditi and Mela were not merely exhibitions. The core group of participants were members of a co-operative, Bhūle Bisre Kalākār (Forgotton and Neglected Artists), living as squatters in a makeshift tent and shanty village in Shadipur on the outskirts of Delhi. Forced there as a result of government slum-clearance policies a decade ago (Sandal 1984, Rushdie 1980), they have since been working to secure a legitimate place in Indian society. Bolstered by the talent of designer Rajeev Sethi and the patronage of scholar and government advisor, Pupul Jayakar, members of this community have sought, through political action, cottage industry, and artistic exhibitions, recognition and rights to their land and livelihood. The exhibitions in Washington, as well as Aditi's previous incarnations in Delhi (1979) and London (1982), were conceived of as means to this end. The exhibitions were not diversions from reality but tools for its reconstruction.

Both exhibits were real for the folk artists in ways different from those of Smithsonian staff and general public: they simply did not share the Smithsonian's notion of an exhibition as a rationally planned, statically ordered, and predictable set of activities. Despite initial and continuing efforts from a variety of quarters to 'control' them, they continued to obfuscate the boundaries that define exhibitions as such. For these participants, the exhibitions were part of life, organic events calling for creativity and improvisation as a means of dealing with life's contingencies. 'What do you mean an exhibition?,' asked one of the participants on the opening day of Mela in response to my context-setting speech. 'I perform at fairs in Rajasthan, in Gujarat, in Harayana. This is just another *mela* only it's in Washington.' This participant came prepared to perform his magic and to sell his rings and gemstones as he bantered with the crowd.

In another paper (Kurin 1985b), I have described the culture of collaboration that characterized the relationship between Indian and American scholars, designers, bureaucrats, and staff in mounting these exhibitions. Here, I would like to offer several very brief ethnographic vignettes which illustrate the way in which folk artists defined and modified the exhibition's context in terms of their own aesthetic and organizational notions, while at the same time forcing Smithsonian staff-assumptions into relief.

**Aditi pūjā.** The Aditi exhibition filled the Evans Gallery in the Museum of Natural History, much as any exhibit would have a designated hall. On arrival in Washington, Aditi participants found this would not do as they needed a place to perform appropriate *pūjā* prior to the exhibit's daily openings. It was decided that the site of such a *pūjā* would be at the entry, which meant, much to the chagrin of Museum security and staff, placing it in the foyer. For a shrine, the older women in the group searched for stones and boulders, eventually finding in the Museum's collection several meteorites which in their pattern of cleavages and gouges bore construed likenesses to appropriate divine figures. The shrine was elaborated by several women who then embellished the marble floor of the foyer with *alpanā, kolam,* and *raṇgolī* designs making the space receptive to divine presence. Visitors to the Museum and its staff were daily confronted with the group's *pūjā,* singing of *bhajans,* and distribution of *prasād* in the reconstituted foyer. The *pūjās* were done solely for the group and not intended as part of the exhibition. It was a real *pūjā* for a real event, which transformed the nature of the Museum's public space, appropriating it as Indian sacred space in control of the participants rather than Museum personnel.

**Mela temple.** Since *mela* sites in India usually host a shrine or temple marking its association with divine figures or saints, it was appropriate to construct such a structure on the Mall grounds. After consulting architects, brahmin priests, and scholars, Smithsonian staff constructed a small masonry temple-structure. In keeping with our attempt to produce an exhibit and to avoid overt sectarian displays, it was decided to cordon off the structure and to place signs around it indicating that it was a facsimile illustrating architectural form, and that such temples are associated with *mela* sites. The notion of a facsimile did not sit well with *mela* participants. On the first day, signs came down. In ensuing days, the Aditi potter made a *yoni* to serve as a receptacle for one of the exhibited polished stone *liṅgams.* The priest painted appropriate symbols on the structure to indicate a Śiva temple. Once the *liṅgam* and *yoni* were installed, the flower-garland maker made appropriate decorations and dressings. A sculpted Nandi also emerged. By the end of the first week, daily *pūjā* was performed in the no-longer-facsimile temple. Gujarati dancers performed in its previously undefined courtyard and *bhajans* were sung there. A space and a structure intended for one use by Smithsonian staff were appropriated for other uses by participants. This was achieved in an organic and creative way, as participants contributed their various talents to bring to life not only the temple but also their status as a community.

**Building Mela.** Smithsonian staff, including construction personnel, were inexperienced in working with bamboo, terracotta tile, cocoanut leaves, *śāmiyānā, kanāth,* and other building materials sent from India. Production plans called for an Indian crew of carpenters and craftspeople who could work with the Smithsonian crew to build the *mela* structures. The tool kits, techniques, flexibility, and improvisation of the Indian carpenters confounded the Smithsonian labor crew, engineers, and carpenters who valued mechanization, precision of measurement, standardization, and notions of sound construction. After some days of mutual denial of each other's abilities, American and Indian crews developed an appreciation of each other's craft: Indian carpenters experimented with power drills and augers and Americans discovered the need for flexibility when dealing with bamboo and came to understand the rationale of interlocking terracotta tiles. Indian carpenters, communicating through their work, demonstrated the contingent nature of construction at an Indian *mela,* building around trees, making use of materials at hand, etc. Smithsonian personnel, who have historically viewed the construction of the Festival of American Folklife as a closed system, actualizing measured plans, gained from these carpenters a new perspective on their own work. In the end, while Smithsonian engineers reworked stress equations on their calculators and puzzled as to why the structures stood, scores of American volunteers, including builders and roofers, came to the Mall to help and to learn from the Indians.

**Presentation.** While the Smithsonian planned the exhibitions to be living ones, the Indian folk artists meant it. The registrar of the Aditi exhibition did not expect to see new objects come into the exhibit every day. Participants would hang new items on the walls or place them on stands or platforms. The Warli wall painter ran out of room to paint in his designated area, so he continued down the hallway. A Mithilā painter was moved to embellish a blank wall in the fertility section. Performing artists throughout the exhibitions expanded beyond their designated boundaries. The Aditi *bahūrūpiyās* would often leave the exhibit hall to wander through the Museum and inflict their impersonations on the unknowing, much as they do in India. Acrobats would accost the Internal Revenue Service across the street with their loud drumming to stir up a larger crowd. The monkey men of Mela, langūr *bahūrūpiyās,* would hide in trees, throw branches onto the crowds, scamper and yell as befitted their role. My daily exhortations to them — 'Get down from there. The trees on the Mall are national monuments. You will be arrested by the National Park Service Police' — were taken not as warnings by a supervisor but as banter to be incorporated into the performance routine for the enjoyment of the audience. Similarly, standard Festival operations, tightly scheduled as presentations on stages, were routinely disregarded — as at times were the stages themselves. For the Indian folk artists, the exhibitions were living events that had their own dynamic rhythm and flow different from our preset and prescribed order.

**Aesthetic and Social Order.** The Aditi and Mela participants lived in accomodations with Indianists who spoke their languages. They had Indian cuisine for meals, redesigned squat toilets, and various other appropriate ammenities. Over the years, the Office of Folklife Programs has evolved a means for dealing with participants' culture shock. One standard procedure is to have various cultural liaisons live with and serve as counselors to participants, aiding their adaptation to a different environment. The model is generally one of individual counseling. For the Indian artists, particularly those of Aditi who spent two months in Washington, this model was of limited value. The housing, working, and general living situation more closely stimulated a small community or village than it did a collection of individuals. The Indians themselves recognized this quite quickly and constituted a group *pañcāyat* to discuss and regulate behavior among each other. The group would meet when needed, squeezing into one of the apartments to talk about someone's drinking, another person's verbal abuse, and so on. Problems were openly discussed. Some of the older and wiser artists would be asked to give their opinion. Yelling matches might erupt. Distractions were continual. The group often proposed restitutive actions and levied fines. Operating much as it might have in India, the group exerted a measure of social control over activities in a way not anticipated, but nonetheless appreciated, by Smithsonian staff.

Control aesthetically was also exerted by individuals over their own experience. The teenaged Krishnagar toy-maker, having visited the National Gallery of Art, reduced its sculptures to his own scale by making clay models. The Indian street performers, not satisfied at being mere curiosities, learned enough English to banter effectively and engage American audiences much as they do Indian ones. And Banku Patua, the Bengali *citrakār,* approached his American experience as an artist and story teller. Painting a scroll and composing lyrics in the traditional style, Banku Patua took back with him the story of Washington D.C., replete with pictures of the Washington Monument, the Potomac River, of people in wheelchairs coming to Aditi, of Rāvaṇa burning on the Mall, and his accompanying song: 'Come and listen all the friends gathered here, all the people present. I will give you a description of America . . . .'

## Conclusion

In planning for the Aditi and Mela exhibitions, organizers attempted to conceptually order and physically construct contexts appropriate for the presentation of Indian folk arts. An aspect of these exhibitions only partially anticipated and envisioned was the role participating folk artists would play in adapting and recasting those efforts in their own terms, for their own purposes. This they did in a number of ways, the more dramatic of which I have briefly summarized here.

Museums and their exhibitions engender questions of control. Museums and exhibitions define and legitimate not only certain types of culture, knowledge, and aesthetics but also our understandings of these as generic forms. During the past 100 years, museums have played a leading role in democratizing *access* to culture, knowledge, and aesthetics. That the Smithsonian, for example, annually receives more than 25 million visitors to its museums is an ample illustration of this democratization. Museums have generally played less of a role in democratizing their *presentation* of culture, knowledge, and aesthetics. While museums may be willing to let anyone in to look around, they are less likely to surrender curatorial control to those not sharing in museum culture and the select European and American conceptual bases from which it is derived and by which it is maintained.

Aditi and Mela provided a fairly rare occasion during which a great measure of control over presentation was given over — to Indian scholars, designers, and technical staff on the one hand and to Indian folk artists on the other. In doing so, the Smithsonian was able to host, be a part of, and even substantially contribute to two extraordinary exhibitions. Sometimes we at the Smithsonian were easily moved, other times control was relinquished only partially, or not at all, and sometimes events and the creativity of the Indian participants simply overtook everyone. Yet by taking control, those participants were able to present their culture and themselves in a way that made sense to them, and at the same time to teach us much about ourselves.

## Bibliography

Chandra, Pramod. *The Sculpture of India, 300 B.C.–1300 A.D.* Washington, D.C., 1985.

Kurin, Richard. 'Aditi: A Celebration of Life.' *Festival of American Folklife Program Book,* 95-96. Washington, D.C., 1985.

_________. 'The Culture of Collaboration: Smithsonian Festival of Indian Exhibits.' Museum Educators Roundtable. Washington, D.C., November, 1985.

_________. 'Mela! An Indian Fair.' *Festival of American Folklife Program Book,* 66-71. Washington, D.C., 1985.

Rushdie, Salman. *Midnight's Children.* New York, 1980.

Sandal, Venu. 'India's Traditional Folk Artists Fight for a Place in the Future.' *Smithsonian* 16.3 (1985): 44-53.

Smithsonian Institution. *Aditi: The Living Arts of India.* Washington, D.C., 1985.

# Index


Abd as-Samad, 79-80
Abu'l Hasan, 78
*ācārya,* 20, 61-62
adaptability to environment, 146-47
Aditi Exhibition, Washington, D.C., 192, 196-209, *200-01 (Fig. A);* context, 205; *pūjā,* 205-06
aesthetics, 14, 16, 56, 62, 150, 160-61, 192
Ahmedabad: Calico Museum, 189; National Institute of Design, 6-7, 187, 191-92; textile center, 115; Vechaar Foundation, Vishalla Environmental Center for Heritage of Art, Architecture and Research, 188-89
Ajanta, xii, 34-44; change, 40-42; iconography, 40-41; painting, 39-40; patrons, 34-35, 39; plans, 35, *36-37 (Figs. A, B),* 38; prototypes, 35, 38, 42; stylistic plurality, 40; tools, 35; working methods, 35, 38-39
All-India Handicrafts Board, 6, 136-37
All-India Handlooms Board, 6
All-India Khaddar Board, 178-79
Almora: Uday Shankar India Cultural Center, 185, 190
analogies with the body and life cycle: architecture, 96-100; pottery, 156, 159, 166-68
Archer, Mildred, 140
Archer, William, 135
architects: inscriptions, Calukya, 61-62. See also *sthāpati*
architecture: commissions, 64; Kerala, xii, 96-97, 101; measurements, 97-98; plans, 35-38; plots, 99-100; prototypes, 22, 26; rock-cut, 34-44; *śilpaśāstras,* ix, 14-15; symbolism, 96, 98-99; temple, 15, 64, 100-01; texts on, 14-15, 22, 26, 96, 99, 101; traditional, 38, 96-99, 147; wood technology, 96
*aripans. See* floor designs
*Arthaśāstra,* 12-13, 21
artists: caste system, 19; definition, xiii, 10; identity, 10, 13-14, 52, 153, 161; individual, by name, xii, 13, 53, 55-56, 59-60, 64, 70; individuality, xii, 52-53, 59-60, 64, 103, 139-40, 150, 161; inscriptions, xii, 53-54; itinerant, xii, 52, 55, 87; location of, 12, 104-12; migration, 34, 86-87; participation in exhibitions, 140, 207-09; portraits of, 53; specialization, 11; status, 11, 19, 21, 153, 207; training, 20. *See also* craftspeople, *śilpin*
ateliers, 137
Bauā Devī (Mithilā painter), 139
Bengal: Santiniketan, 4; textiles, 105, 107-08
Bharat Bhavan, Bhopal, 186
Bharatiya Lok Kala Mandal, Udaipur, 186, 190
Bhopal: Bharat Bhavan, 186
Bhūle Bisre Kalākār, Shadipur, 205
Birdwood, G., 153
Borunda: Rupayan Sansthan, 191
boundaries: architecture, 96-100; exhibitions, 205, 207; pottery vessels, 168-69
*Bṛhatsaṃhitā,* 22, 26
calendar artists, 161
Calico Museum, Ahmedabad, 189
carpets, xiii, 127-33; authenticity, 130-132; design, 128; dyes, 129-30; economics, 130-33; factory production, 131; imitation, 130-32; materials, 127-29; symbolism, 129; technology, 127-29; trade, international, 130-32; tribal, 128-29
change, x-xiii; Ajanta, 41-43; crafts products, xiii, 7, 146; forms, 15; markets, 7; materials, 168; Mithilā painting, 140; pottery, xiii-xiv, 160-61; rituals, 150; social organization of crafts, 160; spinning, 170; textiles, 67-69, 119
Chatterjee, Ashoke, 187, 192
Cholamandalam, Kanchipuram, 187
Colonial influences, 4
commercialization: of crafts, 103-12
commodities, 10
connoisseurship, 78-85, 130-31, 133; Akbar, 79, 83-84; Humāyūn, 79-80, 82; Jahāngīr, 78-79, 81-85